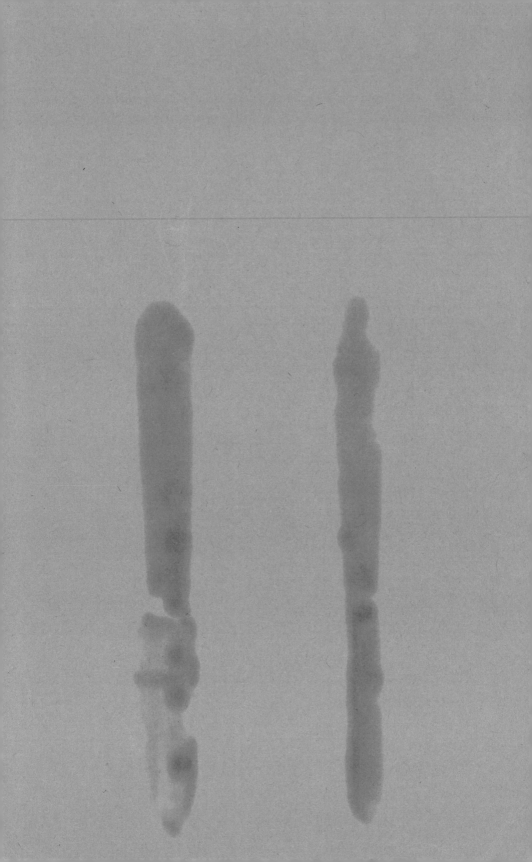

Selected Prose

Northwestern University

STUDIES IN *Phenomenology &*

Existential Philosophy

The Writings of
Jean-Paul Sartre

Edited by

Translated by

Volume 2
Selected Prose

MICHEL CONTAT
and MICHEL RYBALKA

RICHARD McCLEARY

NORTHWESTERN UNIVERSITY PRESS

EVANSTON   1974

Originally published in French as a section of *Les Ecrits de Sartre: Chronologie, bibliographie commentée* (copyright © 1970 by Editions Gallimard). This is volume 2 of a two-volume edition of that work.

Contents

[vii]

Translator's Preface

THE WRITINGS PUBLISHED HERE are not so much an epitome as episodes. But most do not digress. They mark the turns and turning points of a human style, the tropes of an expressive life embodying the changing tempos of an age. Until we fall silent, all of us are trying to say. These fragmentary efforts to speak to, rejoin, and help create a new community of liberated human beings constitute the epigraphs of Sartre's historical inscription.

"We Write for Our Own Time," one of them snaps out at those who dream of ancient absolutes. The passionate loves that you choose and live out from day to day until you die are your absolute, and all these loves together constitute the absolute we call an age. Books express a life and times. In their own time, in their concrete situation constituted by the specific changes they seek to effect, their truth is absolute. The times, and the writing which helps constitute them and the writer himself in his relation to them, are a product of the understandings, choices and commitments which make sense of human situations. So there is no banality in saying that the writings published here are varying expressions of Sartre's attempts to shape the meaning of his life and times.

Sartre himself has told us in *The Words* that the sense of time which ruled his life when he wrote the early works in this volume was the timeless one in which he viewed such literary efforts from beyond the tomb as they had reached fulfillment in the undying and immortal *Writings of Jean-Paul Sartre*. Michel Contat and Michel Rybalka think that this "neurosis," as Sartre

[ix]

calls it, this "assurance that he was one of the *elect,* had been granted a mandate to save the world through literature," [1] attains its most complete expression in "The Legend of Truth." Yet Sartre's "individual myth," as Lacan terms neurosis, still seems evident a decade later in the timeless time of obsession ("Foods"), phenomenological intuition of essence ("Official Portraits," "Faces"), and increasingly successful pursuit of the bourgeois career of "famous writer."

With the war journal, "Sick at Heart," it is quite evident however that history has invaded Sartre's writing along with his times; and in this piece and the writings immediately following we recognize the Sartre we first heard of at war's end. "Sick at Heart" turns toward *The Roads to Freedom.* Bariona, the prison-camp play which first gave Sartre a sense of the theater's power to move men, toward *The Flies.* "A More Precise Characterization of Existentialism" toward *Existentialism Is a Humanism* and the postwar polemics. "The Liberation of Paris" is recognizably the work of the journalist who wrote so observantly about life in America. "We Write for Our Own Time" and "For a Theater of Situations" are complements of *What is Literature?*

The writings which complete this volume are primarily the work of a Cold Warrior living through a public time of manifestos, movements, and polemics—raging as in "Mad Beasts" or mocking as in *Nekrassov*—yet struggling in a private time of shattered ideology and existential doubt. The two times interfere with and reinforce each other in a dialectic of complementarity capable at times of desperate sublimity. We get glimpses here of what we know more fully from Sartre's own revelations concerning his private break with Merleau-Ponty and his public battle with Camus.

There is one piece from this period, however, which hints at something different. "Julius Fucik" gives new meaning to the interest Sartre has had for thirty years in man's ability to withstand torture, marking a transition from the earlier conception of time as generated by the choice of the isolated individual to the later one of its creation through the individual choosing as a part of a collective and historical action. Without abandoning his claim that freedom to say no is basic both to human dignity and to the commitments through which time and the world's prose are generated, Sartre relates it to the solidarity of class

1. Vol. 1, 31/6.

struggle for a new history. This development is evident if we compare the academic thesis *Being and Nothingness,* with its promise of an ethics, and the beginnings of fulfillment of that promise in "Determinism and Freedom," [2] excerpts from Sartre's remarks before the Roman Gramsci Institute, in which he analyzes the meaning of time in relation to the positivist ideologies of the bourgeois era and to the choices and responsibilities of individual members of the rising classes for the era which their choice and their responsibility will create.

During the past decade, Sartre has been developing a concept of the "singular universal," which he said was first suggested by Kierkegaard, and which he described in this way in reference to his friend Carlo Levi:

> For Levi, being himself means making himself a singular universal; writing means communicating the incommunicable, singular universality. What this means is that in his writing he has bound himself into the selfsame knot of contradictions which his life expresses and which Merleau-Ponty once described in these terms: "Our bodies are enmeshed in the fabric of the world but the world is made from the stuff of my body. . . ." [3]

What we see embodied in these writings is the singularity of Sartre, a writer in our time.[4]

2. See Vol. 1, 66/436.
3. Vol. 1, 67/482.
4. There have been previous translations of some of the texts which follow, but the translations published here have been done especially for this volume.

Selected Prose

The Angel of Morbidity

A PLATEAU IN THE VOSGES with shaggy slopes. The mountains round about rose up or fell away like roller coasters, darkened by their mop of pines, at times mussed up by buffeting winds, at times combed out with care, trimmed on the sides, and to the tranquil gaze disclosing the oasis of a green field or red house. These distant roofs, built out of bricks, owed to the surrounding forest their contrasting calm: people set out to walk to them for the sheer pleasure of meeting men again after having crossed through a lonely place. They stood for human life, poor representatives which nevertheless implied a host of worldly and luxurious ideas mysteriously attached to them, no doubt because of their distance. On the plateau a village, Altweier, had grown up, carefully divided, like all those in the Upper Rhine, into two parts: the Catholic hamlet and the Protestant hamlet. Each had its own church, and the houses bunched obediently around the two bell towers. The Catholic faction had laid hold of the summit. More modest, or more lately arrived, the Protestant faction had set itself up a little lower down, tied fast by a loop in the road. The cobbler, a freethinker, had taken up a dwelling even lower down to show he was an independent party. Hermaphroditic hotels served as go-betweens, as hyphens.

It was in one of these (which had been called Hôtel de Sedan from 1870 to 1918, and which took the name of Hôtel de la Marne after the Armistice—without, however, changing hotel-

This story was published as "L'Ange du morbide" in *La Revue sans titre*, January 15, 1923. See also Vol. 1, 23/1.

[3]

keepers) that Louis Gaillard went to stay during the three-months' vacation that the university grants its professors. He arrived carrying a valise and clothed in the indispensable gabardine—and in the glum look that habitually goes with it. He was hot and thirsty, had quarreled (without having had the last word) with the bus driver; and the nausea, the disgust, of journey's end, which is so upsetting to our poor little sedentary bodies, weighed heavily upon him. He was a mediocre man, scared silly by bad company. Just as it is harmful to a poor boy to live in the shadow of rich ones, so having to do with those more intelligent than oneself can be harmful. Stupidly corrupted by the friendship of social climbers or mischievous jokers who had no belief in the theories they set forth, Louis had turned the whole force of his youth toward the morbid, out of snobbery, and also because his mind was now no more than a poor misguided thing, a worn-out piece of whirling clockwork. He looked for unconventional ideas with that patient application of the little-minded, like a child who bites his tongue when he begins to write. Customarily, and in all innocence, he borrowed the ideas of others, whittling them down, however, to his own size.

He had passed his different exams, and he made use of the leisure he enjoyed as sham pervert, as wayward intellectual who remains chaste in his wildest mental orgies, to compose verses in the style of

O you, the catachresis and syringe of chestnuts . . .

or pessimistic, blasé novels packed with glimpses of illicit love affairs. But he himself had stuck to the common path, not having known a woman till he was twenty-two, and then by chance at a wild party with no sequel. His buddies, the freethinkers, having fallen into their own trap, had become his disciples: they took for a genius the odd monster they had made by grafting their own unsuccessful "superman" maxims onto his mediocrity. He was even beginning to make a name for himself in avant-garde magazines when he was named junior high school teacher at Mulhouse. Personally, he had the greatest admiration for himself. Unfortunately, he read some of his poems to his students, real Alsatian hell-raisers: he was hooted at and hit on the head by several inkwells, became bitter, then sad, and during the long vacations came to coddle his melancholy in the calm, fresh silence of the towering Vosges.

He immediately conquered his hostess, who was much taken with "city gentlemen" and much too used to wagonmen. She was a chatterbox with an ugly goiter. "'Ve used to haf many more guests!" she said. "But dat stinking pastor got together vit da doctor to bilk us! He iss turning all da hotels into 'senatoriums' for consumptives of da veaker sex. Dey efen made me rent my annex. Da guests don't come no more: imachine, alvays rubbing elbows mit infected people. My business iss ruined."

And sure enough, all that was left in the hotel were a blind priest and three hopelessly sedentary old maids. Louis did not complain; he thought he enjoyed this pitiful company. The setting for the meals, which he ate beside the old man with the dead eyes, had a certain etched hardness which appealed to his morbidity. He would only have liked the three old maids to be less clean and more gruesome. They irritated him, these three pink old maids who laughed like children; he was sorry they weren't yellow, angular, and frozen in uncompromising bigotry.

He had banished all concern for others from his modus vivendi. Furthermore, the sentimentality inherent in his twenty-five years had found another means of expression: he loved himself with all the tenderness, the goodness, and the endless acts of kindness which in mediocre people take the place of intellectual worth. From morning till night he went on long walks through the deep dark woods. There he nursed his melancholy and did exercises, climbing up and down the slopes while abandoning himself to ethereal daydreams. What excited him most of all was being near consumptives. He hoped for a romance with one of these poor creatures, and in his reverie, a bizarre mixture of morbidity and naïveté, he saw himself putting his arm around the waist of a skinny tubercular.

His desire for this strange love was so overpowering that he got what he wanted. One afternoon while he was prowling around the sanatoriums, vast ramshackle buildings in the woods, he saw a young woman sitting on the grass beside the trail. She was in mourning. Her sweet and horsy face was wrinkled like a rumpled collar. She coughed repeatedly as he went by. At first he paid no attention, but shortly afterward that face and cough pursued him. They simultaneously attracted and irritated him. Gradually, however, he became aroused, because she was a woman and because he suspected she was consumptive. After an hour of desperate indecision, he ended up desiring her, imagining her snuggled up against him, tiny, no more than a bit of warmth with (for reasons he was unaware of) arthritic bones that cracked. For he was one of those ignoble beings who become attached to the little particularities, the trivial inferiorities, of the women they love. In the last analysis, he had no really clear image of her; he was simply fascinated by a sort of label he stuck on her: "Consumptive." All evening long he dreamed of his consumptive and talked about tuberculosis to the blind priest in the hope (unfulfilled, as it happened) of finding out something about the woman he had caught a glimpse of.

The next day he saw her again, and the day after that, and one day he got up enough courage to speak to her. Still out of breath after a few minutes of walking, she was seated on the moss beside a path, staring vacantly. After having racked his brain for a more raffish turn to his opening line, he clumsily said, "It certainly is hot!" suffering from his lack of originality as if it had been a wound. She raised astonished eyes to him and answered softly, "Oh, I don't mind. I love the sun so much." This sentimentality made him scowl a bit. "How can you prefer the cacophony of that caterwauler to the silence of misty skies?" Then he joyfully constructed a whole theory about the comparative value of July and November skies. She listened to him, scarcely convinced but happy in her solitude to find a chatterbox. He sat down beside her on the moss and kept on pouring out his pedantic rhetoric in a lukewarm stream. He found out, in one of those rare moments when, while he was catching his breath, she had a chance to answer him, that her name was Jeanne Hongre and that she was here "to rest up from a great weariness." She did not live in the sanatorium at all but in a nearby village. He went there with her, left her at the door, and went away full of little shivers of joy.

During the days that followed, their romance evolved with each new meeting. Louis felt his timidity disappear before this poor little sagging being; he risked bold gestures, spoke in a loud voice, and experienced a sort of sadistic joy in saying to himself, when he took Jeanne's hand, "I love a consumptive, it's a consumptive I love, the one I love is a consumptive." Above all he exulted in feeling healthy and masculine. He had already written a dozen letters to his buddies the freethinkers to tell them about his adventure. Jeanne went along without really understanding, too sick to care about modesty or have a second thought. She did not care much for this phrasemaker, but he warmed her at the fireside of his words, restored her with that healthy mediocrity of his which sometimes, unbeknown to him, showed through his established morbidity. She tried above all not to cough in front of him; it was her only bit of coquetry. Nevertheless, their love remained wholly Platonic. Each time he tried to make a slightly insistent move she said, without repugnance but wearily, "You're making me tired, dear."

One morning while he was tying his tie he made up his mind to bring things to a head. He liked to make such resolutions, which he usually did not keep. But this time he was more persistent. As soon as he caught sight of her, he put on the pout of a punished child; and when she feebly asked him why, he answered heatedly, "Because you are reducing me to the role of a comic character." Then he set forth his ideas on love while craftily trying his hand at gestures aimed at softening up things for the attack. Abruptly, as one pushes a creaking old rusty door, he threw her down wailing. She was suffocating, tried to speak, and suddenly began to cough. He let go of her then, vexed with himself at his brutality. She coughed at his side, a fruity cough which began with an unbearable rasping in her throat and ended with a phlegmy lapping like the sound of a wave of spattered vaseline or of a jellyfish slapped down on a sea wall. Her face, from its usual decent dullness, had grown dark. It took on a look of abject misery, its skin stretched tight on its cheekbones, the lower lip disagreeably twisted and all puckered up. She spit blood into her handkerchief. Then her cough became dry and painful; at each spasm a shudder ran through her body. Finally, too tired to respond, she gave in to her illness, and the violence of its onslaught pushed out her bust with the regularity of a clock pendulum. At last she closed her eyes, exhausted, and stretched out like a corpse on the grass, perhaps with a bit of affectation.

Louis looked at her with a child's horror at the toy he has torn apart. His quaint and wholly intellectual image of consumption had not prepared him for this spectacle, his mediocrity was not made to bear it, his fake morbidity provided far too weak an armor against his horror of this nightmarish lover. He forgot all about this woman's real sweetness, her true character; it seemed to him that another being, mysterious and terrifying, had slipped into her, something like the Angel of Morbidity, that morbidity which he had looked so hard for. Then he thought with horror that he might well be infected; gripped with a fear like that one has after having made love to a prostitute, he briefly regretted all the kisses received and given, and like a coward, while she was still stretched out on the grass with her eyes closed, he fled down the path.

That evening he left the hotel and the blind priest who now horrified him and the three old maids who now seemed too old, seeking above all to escape the horrible specter of Disease. Shortly afterward he had his chest examined by a specialist who proved conclusively that he had not in any way been affected, broke with all his old friends, and married a pink, blonde, dumb, and healthy Alsatian girl. He never wrote a thing again and at the age of fifty-five was awarded the Legion of Honor, the indisputable mark of "Bourgeoisie". . . .

Jesus the Owl,
Small-Town Schoolteacher

IN 1917, AFTER A SERIES OF EVENTS which I need not relate here, my parents decided to send me to the *lycée* at La Rochelle. I was fifteen then and was going into second form. My parents did not live in La Rochelle itself, but in Aigrefeuille, a place nearby. They had to make up their minds to part company completely with me and put me in the *lycée* as a boarding student. My extreme fragility as a child long nourished on a special diet, and on the other hand, my absolute innocence and total incompetence in practical matters (consequences of a rather permissive yet scrupulous and conscientious education) very much perturbed my mother. "He's going to be thrown together with vicious, coarse, much older children," she said. "He'll have to eat unhealthy food; no one will look after him and keep him from drinking his wine without water or taking dishes he is forbidden to eat. Boarding school will be the death of him; it will undermine his physical and moral well-being." She was looking for a way out when she learned from a superintendent who was a friend of the family's that M. Lautreck, "a first-rate pedagogue" and no other than my future second-form teacher, took in some of the *lycée* students as boarders. There was a brief correspondence between them, and she even went to see him at La Rochelle and came back enchanted, declaring that, to tell the truth, M. Lautreck was not at all the calm and sweet old man

This fragment of a novel was published as "Jésus la Chouette, professeur de province" in four issues of *La Revue sans titre* in early 1923 under the pen name of Jacques Guillemin. See also Vol. I, 23/2.

she had pictured him as, since he was barely fifty-five years old, but that, notwithstanding his extreme nervousness and a certain high-flown preciosity, he seemed to her to be a man of great intellectual worth and impeccable morals. So I set out on October 2, 1917, for La Rochelle.

Personally, I would have preferred to board at school; the schoolboy novels I had been allowed to read had led me to think of the life of a boarding school student as an uninterrupted sequence of ever-changing joys, and above all as a free and capricious life which would completely transform my slavish and methodical existence. But the fundamental reason for my preference was my excessive timidity, or more precisely the bizarre direction my frailty had taken, a direction evident in almost every child at the "awkward" age: to the extreme audacity my mother admired I joined a strange timidity when it came to getting involved in other people's private lives. Going into a store horrified me, above all when I saw the saleslady was talking to someone. Then it seemed to me I was about to stray into some forbidden intimacy. When I did go on in, it seemed to me the whole time I was in the shop that I could feel indignant, scornful glances being cast at me. In order to avoid this shame, which reddened my face and made my cheeks burn, I used to go walk around in some isolated spot until the store was empty, and then go in. This is why I have sometimes stood for an hour in front of the barbershop before I dared to cross the threshold. It is this timidity which had, for example, kept me from coming back twice in one day to the same merchant because I was afraid I would bother him. In short, such expeditions were so obviously unbearable for me that my mother herself, although she considered them completely natural, had scruples about sending me out on them.

Furthermore, the thought of living intimately with people I did not know made me ashamed and (when I thought about it) neurotically ill. There was only one consideration which made this prospect bearable and even desirable: my mother, when she had come back from her meeting with M. Lautreck, had said to me, "Your professor for the coming year, M. Lautreck, has a tall and beautiful twenty-five-year-old daughter who has promised me to look out for you. You be sure to be nice to her." And on this basis I had built a whole little novel.

My knowledge of sexual matters was rather extensive but

scarcely precise. It was accidental knowledge stolen from a bookmarked page, deduced by patient labor from a snatch of overheard conversation, and above all breathed into me by many of my more knowing playmates who delighted in such perverse proselytizing. I disregarded it anyhow and dreamed of pure, chaste loves with intellectual women. I had taken as my dream girls (because they secretly attracted me, or because I was so innocent) the four or five repulsive *filles de joie* who, spurned by the entire population of Aigrefeuille, skimmed tearfully along the walls at six o'clock each winter evening as if they had been stricken by a fear of open spaces. I transformed them alternately into Russian princesses beguiled by my good looks, or young French girls attracted by the fame of my intelligence. Then they got to know me (I imagined) and we took monotonous and sentimental walks through Aigrefeuille together.

It was their image which was replaced by that of Marguerite Lautreck, my teacher's daughter. I was not at all conscious of the difference in our ages. I had arbitrarily given her a blue blouse, a black skirt, and hair like Joan of Arc's, and in my mind she took on the air of a roguish adolescent, all the more easily so because I had never seen the Lautrecks. I could picture her clearly, alone with me in the moonlight, in a rather conventional landscape. Then the images tumbled after one another with kaleidoscopic rapidity: I saw myself raising my arm skyward and pointing out the moon. My lips pronounced lyric and definitive words which I had dreamed up in my idleness, sensing clearly that they would fall short of the heights of my desire. At first Marguerite looked at me wonderingly; then, won over by my eloquence, she fell into my arms.

After that my visions got fuzzy. But the ones that did come were all I needed, and I could go over them again for an hour at a time (with slight modifications such as introducing a rival at my heroic moments) without ever tiring of them. That is how I spent my last days at Aigrefeuille, sometimes reddening with shame at my position as an interloper at the Lautrecks', sometimes swelling with a joyous languor at the image of my Oaristysnaï with their daughter. Finally, the day before school began, I was sent to La Rochelle on the four-o'clock train. I had insisted out of *amour-propre* on traveling alone. I reached La Rochelle at five-thirty on October 1, a Sunday.

My mother had thoughtfully exempted me from bringing

along the suitcase and the little boxes which are the obligatory accouterments of the bourgeois family's shortest move. At first I had not been very conscious of my mother's considerateness, because I had believed that my self-esteem required me to take along heavy suitcases which would, in my estimation, give me considerable dignity in the eyes of my traveling companions. But before long I saw the advantage of it: the Lautrecks were not at the station, I was going to get to stroll along toward the Villa Remember where they lived, and there would be no suitcase riveted to my arm to weigh upon or spoil my wandering.

Towns could be classified, in a more inconvenient but less arbitrary way than they are classified administratively, according to the hour at which their type and beauty are the most pronounced. A town is like a woman: it has to have a special lighting and a definite surrounding if it is to reach its peak of elegance. And like beauties, towns can be day or night ones, morning ones or evening ones. La Rochelle is a five-to-six-o'clock town, an autumn twilight town. The old port at sunset is softened by the livid evening grayness of the final rays, like an old Vernet print touched up by a hazy modern colorist. The lighting is distributed in slightly overlapping planes like a Monet. The sky's pale colors encroach on the old guard towers on the Anse and give a blue tinge to their harsh forms which makes them a little less rigid. In the port, dense water, coated white, lies drowsing like the black swamps of oil that automobiles drop on the pavement. The sailboats float silently, supernaturally, back. Pianos play wildly in the dives around the port, and the mixture of these café tunes brings forth one single vague and monophonic melody which takes the place of the sea's missing song.

I was only slightly moved by this sight: young boys' eyes are blind to the infinite and unbroken variety of landscapes. They do not yet have the tact required to perceive the innumerable modifications which can be introduced by a tree, a roadmarker, a simple play of light and shadow; and above all the changes, the nuances which are the result of the real but indefinable personality of a landscape. For them this sweep is broken into eight or ten panoramas, frames into which they instinctively put the landscapes that they see. For me the colors that the setting sun's pomade had coated on these ancient towers or on this viscous water or these ships were nothing more than undistinguished aspects of a twilight. I was responsive solely and dumbly to the vague charm of the semidarkness. So I focused my attention on the route I had to take and on the characters who typify a Sunday afternoon.

I soon began walking on the mall and stopped having any clear idea, feeling only heavily oppressed by my apprehension for the immediate future. This wholly physical pain which slowed down my breathing and sped up my heartbeat no longer involved, as my fears in Aigrefeuille had, the image of my future humiliations: I was simply petrified by a white and always-growing silhouette on the horizon, which I took to be the Villa Remember. I came up to it anxiously. It was not the one, but immediately much of my emotion vanished, as if, like those old folks who have cried too much to have any tears left, I had been too moved to be able to maintain for long my perturbation.

The Laubrés'[1] villa was a little farther on. I reached the front gate and was struck by the unexpected appearance of my new dwelling. A long acquaintance with the university circles I had lived in had accustomed me to a certain stamp—bright, spare, but not inelegant—the prerogative of earnest Latinists and Hellenists, which they set upon their immediate entourage—furniture, house, and even friends. Furthermore, I had been picturing the Villa Remember as a white building in the classical Greek style, white as the terraces of Ithaca or Mycenae must be. Instead, the exception to an almost universal rule, it had both the heaviness of a Jewish casbah and the gimcrack inconsistency of a Swiss chalet. Serried plantings of exotic shrubs—heavy cactuses and graceless yuccas—gave the air of an over-stuffed hothouse to the front-court garden. Two unruffled lion cubs, a masterpiece of bad taste, symmetrically framed the three gray stone steps leading up to the entryway. The red brick façade, the blue door, the brown wood shutters and balconies, and the green stucco rose windows stuck on to the rest—everything, in short, was as graceless, gross, and ostentatious as a paste jewel. This dwelling shadowed gloomily by the mall's overarching chestnuts and buried underneath its own garden's wildly flourishing verdure had all the malsain dankness and distressing dreariness of bad romanticism. This disagreeable

1. From here on the name *Lautreck* for some reason becomes *Laubré*.—ED.

impression was, however, very fleeting, for my youth forbade extended melancholy, and the sadness of the Villa Remember was no more than a dark spot in a joyfully colored whole.

I rang the blue door, my heart pounding. Yet I was beginning to acquire a taste for this sort of bourgeois adventure, which left a little room for the unknown. A maid came to open the door. She was very young, redheaded, and vigorous; but with a weary grimace she assumed the pose of dawdling resignation, and everything she did breathed negligence.

"Is it the young gentleman, the young gentleman they are expecting?" she asked me with a twang.

I scarcely had the nerve to answer yes; but a door was already opening in the dark hallway and a masculine voice cried out, "Here he is! Come in, my young friend, come in!"

I came in hurriedly, bumping into the maid in my confusion, and found myself in the living room.

There were a man and a woman there whom I could only vaguely make out because they were against the light. A woman's voice, dry and precise, asked me, "Are you our new boarder?"

But the man had already taken my arm with a nervous exuberance and was saying, "I am very happy to know you. Your mother has given me the responsibility of caring for you, my young friend; I promised her to make a man of you. But you must promise me to always take the path of honor. I hope that you will always follow my example!"

The grandiloquence of this beginning, with its lack of all relation to the mediocre circumstances, deeply displeased me. But far from seeing it at first as a bit of rhetorical vanity, the self-promoting bravura of a timid soul, I thought that it revealed in my teacher an austerity of manner and of taste which augured very badly. There is nothing I have ever prized more than gaiety, and I saw immediately that in the Villa Remember the tedium of virtue ruled unrestrained.

But Mme Laubré was already rising up in majesty:

"Would you like something to eat before dinner?" she asked; and as I was about to accept she briskly added, "If you are not too hungry, I should appreciate your waiting till mealtime because we are having trouble with our maid and the slightest complication in the serving will make her leave us."

And, as I was insisting that I was not hungry, M. Laubré turned toward the door and said with a threatening gesture,

"Vile breed!"

"It is so hard to find a maid," his wife sighed; then, turning toward me, she added with interest, "Does your mother also have trouble with her servants?"

I answered that we had never had anyone but an old cook who was very fond of the household. She murmured with a disappointed air, "You are truly fortunate; my dream would be a maid devoted to her masters. I must say I have never found one."

Then she started to recite the litany of her troubles with her maids: they were all insolent liars and thieves, vagabonds who never stayed put more than a month, and who ate and cost too much when they did.

"You are boring my young friend with this nonsense," her husband interrupted softly. Without the least intention to please, his voice was naturally honeyed. First he took his words apart by clearly articulating each syllable and making stops between them; then he put them together again by prolonging the final vowel sound of each syllable in a tremolo which set up the next sound. He seemed to be lifting each term up in order to stress it, like an elocution instructor giving his students their very first lessons in correct pronunciation. It was extremely unpleasant.

He took a few slightly limping steps with an affectation which reminded me of the rhythmic majesty of opera kings and then came to sit near me, arching his back.

He was tall and rather well proportioned. He held his head high and did not lack hair. To be more exact, his skull was rather bare, but the abundant locks curling slightly on his neck mildly compensated for this semibaldness. He wore a beard cut like a truncated pyramid. His naturally red brown hair was disagreeably tinged in his beard with a thousand adventitious nuances: white, dirty gray, even black or blond. With his big hooked nose, sharp as an eagle's beak, his blood-red mouth, his yellow orange color, and his nearsighted eyes hidden behind a gold-circled *lorgnon*, he looked quite a bit like a seventeenth-century tragedian—one of those Herods of the highways who roamed about in little carts and had, beneath their noble air of bearded tyrants, a meek and peaceful nature. He wore a beige suit of English wool, which I thought was now quite worn and never very elegant. The frayed buttonholes of the coat looked like the caked edges of an old woman's eyes. The pants, which had lost all their crease, stuck to his skinny pipe-stem legs and fell on button shoes whose style was even more old-fashioned than their own. And yet a certain natural elegance slightly compensated for the unfortunate state of his clothes.

Mme Laubré, even though she was dressed in black, seemed more elegantly attired. She had the peculiarity—which I have never found in any other person—of bearing a gaunt, bony, and horselike head on the fat, heavy-jowled, bloated, and elephantine body of an ailing woman, as if the evil jinni of Arabian tales had amused himself by topping a fat German *Hausfrau* body with the head of a tall skinny Englishwoman. The effect was startling. Disproportioned as she was, with her brownish gray locks as thick as horsehair, she reminded me very much of some Alecto or Tisiphone; and it was always according to her features that I imagined the Furies when we were making critical analyses of Aeschylus.

"Come along, my young friend," M. Laubré said, taking me by the arm, "we must take the owner's tour." "It is your due," he added in response to my polite protest; "it would be a fine thing if you were not fully informed about your new dwelling. Besides, you know," he said laughing, "we observe Scotch hospitality." And he dragged me through a number of rather poorly furnished rooms in which I found that same odd extravagance that had first struck me in the garden. The dining room, which he told me he was proud of, looked to me like the back room of an antique shop: every style was represented there by some undisguised horror. There was everything, from the cut-rate Norman wardrobe closet to the medieval bishop's chair, including five or six fluted chairs of the most recent make. Above, on the second floor, I looked at my room and was astonished to find that odor of wild herbs and piety one detects in ancient country rooms. As much as the lower rooms showed gaudy, agitated bad taste, my room was simple and quiet. M. Laubré explained to me that the year before this room had belonged to his old mother. She had arranged it carefully according to the tastes she had as an old bourgeois woman accustomed to little sleepy villages whose narrow streets all converge on the church.

"Personally," he told me, "I don't like this room. It is depressingly barren; not like our dining room, I'll tell you! But I think you'll be comfortable here: the room faces on a quiet street and the bed is good."

Next we went by other rooms without entering them. I learned that M. and Mme Laubré had a son who was going to be in the same class I was. So I felt obliged to ask him about his children.

"They're fine," he answered laughing; "bad seeds grow well. My youngster is going to be your classmate. You'll see how much he likes to have fun! Too much, maybe . . . As for my daughter, she's a tall young lady of twenty-five: she'll soon find a husband," he added sighing. At first I thought his sigh meant that he was sad at having to lose his daughter soon. Not at all, for he added with a musing melancholy, "It's hard to find good husbands nowadays." But, he added sharply, "It's not that there haven't been enough offers; it's just that I have a certain ideal which today's young men are far from measuring up to. Don't follow their example, my young friend; the paths of virtue are steep, but how satisfying it is to reach the summit. When one is getting near the age at which the devil in the flesh loses his spirit, as I am, how rewarding it is to be able to look back on a spotless past . . . It makes up for many things," he added in a toneless voice heavy with implication. "May I please wash my hands?" I asked him.

"Go ahead my young friend; go ahead."

And he pushed me toward my room. I heard his heavy and uneven tread go down the stair.

II

As I CAME OUT OF MY ROOM, I heard down in the living room a feminine voice whose tone was new to me. My discomfort, which had vanished, suddenly reappeared: I sensed that I would soon find myself in the presence of Marguerite Laubré. It was indeed she; and once the introduction had been made I felt all of my beautiful dreams of tender intimacy crumbling, as my hopes of love always crumble. I saw clearly that in her eyes I was only an insignificant little boy. She had the disagreeable beauty that long-faced skinny women have, and the excessively pronounced bone structure of her face impaired the real attractiveness of her two beautiful eyes and full lips.

She questioned me with polite and charming condescension: she just missed talking to me in that lisping prattle guests put on to talk to their hostess's little children. I sensed this and was really upset. But since I was too timid to dare to get mad about it, even inwardly, I gave no sign of it. Timidity is not only expressed by outward signs of disturbance; it is also manifested in the absolute impossibility of making an unfavorable judgment about the people who are intimidating you. That is probably why timid people are generally meek.

M. Laubré took out his watch as he would have unsheathed a sword: "It's seven o'clock. Isn't Adolphe here yet?" he asked.

"No he isn't," the mother answered; "where can he be?"

"Maybe the rascal is playing with his friends?"

"It doesn't matter," Mme Laubré continued; "how that child torments me!"

Then bursting into cries of pain she alternately deplored modern education and her own failing as a mother, her son Adolphe's willfulness, and the bad example the young people in La Rochelle set for him. "He has never given me anything but trouble. I told him to come in early. That boy will be the death of me yet." And her eyes upraised toward the ceiling called upon heaven to witness her disappointments as a mother.

"This is the last straw, Elisa," M. Laubré said; "it is high time we got tough with that boy!"

But at that moment the door opened and admitted a boy my age, a puny boy with shaggy red hair whose prematurely long pants and weird little bright eyes with circles under them made him seem older than he was. The Laubrés' wrath seemed entirely soothed by his arrival. His mother hardly asked him where he had been. He answered evasively that he had been having a great time, and, when they still wanted to know, he looked stubbornly at the floor.

"Listen; are you going to tell us?" his father said firmly.

Mme Laubré interrupted: "Leave him alone now; you see he doesn't want to tell us. You're wasting your time; you won't get anything out of him!" I could see by the look in M. Laubré's eyes that all his beautiful theories, all his fine principles concerning education and virtue, were being trampled in the dust. He shook his head dejectedly and shut up.

Adolphe, however, looked at me with curiosity: he bent his head to one side and examined me with a studied and mistrustful look. Finally, he held out toward me two wet fingers he had first stuck in his nose, and snuffled at me under his breath:

"If you're a good buddy, we'll have a ball. I know this crazy sailor who can really break you up; you'll see, he'll let us come aboard his ship. But I don't like stool pigeons."

Then Mme Laubré rose and we went in to dinner.

After the soup course, while the stewed pork was being served, Mr. Laubré explained to us—minutely and with the same oratorical precautions he would have taken to tell us about some witticism—the etymology of "pork" and its relation to the Latin "porcillana."

"The assistant teacher didn't say hello to me this afternoon," Marguerite suddenly broke in.

"M. Colrat?"

"That's right! I ran into him in front of the palace and he avoided my glance . . ."

"It's outrageous," Mme Laubré cried in a cutting voice.

M. Laubré, who had become very pale, raised his eyes heavenward and said, "What a town, what times, what manners!"

Mme Laubré's anger was more coarse: "There's a little old man who ought to have some politeness slapped into him," she exclaimed.

"Ah," Marguerite said resignedly, "if he were the only one! But unfortunately, the number of people who no longer say hello to us is growing."

"Your father is too weak," Mme Laubré said harshly; "he ought not to let us be insulted."

The conversation went along on this tone for a while. At first I had thought that the Laubrés were being spurned by the whole town, but I learned from the rest of the conversation that they were simply complaining, in their thirst for recognition, about the way in which some ill-mannered big wigs had slighted them. "We're worth as much as all those people," Marguerite said sharply. Mme Laubré spouted out tales about their wives in a steady stream: "Everybody knows," she said, "that Mme Colrat would have been only too happy to have us say hello to her last year, when everybody was avoiding her after her involvement with Commander Hurepoix." One sensed in Mme Laubré the bitterness of the woman who has to pay court to the headmistress, the mayor's wife, and the school inspectress and drag her dirty skirts in winter into all those stony, hostile drawing rooms and speak in platitudes where she would love to rule instead. Her daughter seemed to have gotten this same crazy urge to be recognized from her. One could see, moreover, that time, by thinning her lips, yellowing and baring her teeth, and wrinkling her cheeks, would turn her into a shrew just like her mother.

But M. Laubré was preaching in a throbbing voice "what the Galilean called forgiving our debtors."

"Words, words!" his wife interrupted. And I did in fact begin to realize that this display of inopportune virtue was only empty rhetoric.

Then they deigned to consider me. Mme Laubré gave me some advice about the *lycée* I was going to go to. She depicted it to me as a sumptuous and patriarchal place in which her husband (whom her glances and her tone of voice, by the way, relegated to the bottom rank) played—by the mere fact of being her husband—the dominant role. Listening to her, I saw the teachers she was telling me about in pure white columns, dressed in snow-white robes and wheeling like archangels, powers, and seraphim around a lordly and impassive M. Laubré.

M. Laubré drank some more of his tisane; then we got up from the dinner table. It was already dark. "Marguerite and Adolphe," Mme Laubré said, "come go out a while with M. Paul. While you're out I'll take a last look at his room." I accepted with joy; for one instant I was going to have this Marguerite I had so often dreamed of back in Aigrefeuille all to myself. The sea was only a few steps away. We went and sat down on the jetty at the spot where a gray stone breakwater, dribbling sea slugs, slowly plunges into the sea. The harsh light of the moon was yellowing some big clouds framing it. Beneath, it was like the hideous swarming of a bed of black turtles, whose shells had the dark and glaucous transparency of the ocean at night. The waves were singing the rhapsody towns sing when you look down on them from a hillside. And the waves' healthy monotone, wedded to the cold, salty odor of the ocean night, produced a sense of piercing calm.

Adolphe, who was sitting on the guardrail with his legs hanging over, asked me under his breath, "Do you like to have fun? If you do, I warn you, you can't have fun at my old man and old lady's house! It's not that they're mean, but they take everything for the gospel truth. But you'll have fun with me." Filled with repugnance for this expansive gnome, I did not reply. "Which do you like better," he went on, "drinking or chicks? There's everything at La Rochelle. Me, I like chicks better and I know some lulus." In spite of myself, I caught myself hoping that Victor would help me get to know some women. I have already said that, always hoped for and always missing, they were the sole desire of my awakening puberty. So I questioned him with interest, and all my repugnance disappeared.

"Who are these chicks you know?"

"A whole bunch; you'll see!"

He threw a circumspect glance at his sister. She was swooning over the sea with that stupid sensibility women have, and no doubt constructing some novel ending in marriage. Erect, arched taut with affectation, and protecting her hat from the sea breeze with one hand, she was casting her eyes over the ocean. Adolphe went on in a whisper: "They're really great; they buy me drinks at the Café Français, because I give them a good time." Then, lost in some erotic dream, he fell silent too. He seemed to me the very incarnation of vice, and he filled me with a sort of fright. But I wasn't able to imagine his conquests as little girls or prostitutes, which they obviously were. Thanks to him, I hoped to find the Princess Charming who would make up for Marguerite's scorn. The latter shook herself as if she had come back from her dream and declared, "It's too cold. Let's go back, young ones. Anyhow, Paul, you won't mind going to bed too much after a whole day of traveling . . ."

And we started back along the road to the house.

The Theory of the State
in Modern French Thought

I
THE STARTING POINT

IN THIS SHORT STUDY we can scarcely talk about state sovereignty without pointing out the position that philosophers and jurists have taken in respect to the natural rights of the individual. Duguit has in fact shown quite clearly the parallelism of these two polar concepts.

State sovereignty, disguised as divine right, actually existed under the *ancien régime*. Natural right, which dates back to ancient times, had since its original formulation by Grotius been developed into the finished form it had for the men of 1789. American and French revolutionaries gave natural right an actual existence and state sovereignty an ideal sanction. The two concepts went hand in hand, and Esmein and the classical school in France still argue that these two concepts are inseparable.

Nevertheless, a strong current of realism had spread through France from Germany prior to 1914. There was a clash between realism and idealism, terms which speak for themselves. After the war, the problems of natural right and state sovereignty became particularly acute.

This essay was published as "La Théorie de l'état dans la pensée française d'aujourd'hui" in the *Revue universitaire internationale,* January, 1927. See also Vol. 1, 27/3.

[22]

To begin with, the basic problem still remained. Davy has stated it very clearly:

All civilized men have or tend to have a sense of their liberty and to demand that liberty in the face of the governmental authorities of their nation. On the other hand, all nations constituted as states assert their sovereignty both in respect to their neighbors and to those who fall under their jurisdiction. And hence come, within each state, perpetual conflicts between individual and collective rights, between the state and the individuals or collective bodies which compose it; and between states, conflicts of national sovereignty.[1]

But no more is involved here, after all, than a problem of limitations. It is in no way a problem for the classical theory, whose rather opportunistic idealism pushed back the boundaries which separated the realm of the individual from that of the state, to the benefit sometimes of one and sometimes of the other, depending on temperaments and circumstances. Experiences during and since the war, however, have made the problem more significant.

Let us take the war first. Davy writes in another work that the war "seems to have posed the problem in this way: is right only a force or is it, on the contrary, an idea? The war's answer was expressed by the spontaneous uprising of all forms of idealism against the slavery of realism."[2]

Putting the problem in this way—and on this emotional level—means settling it in idealism's favor at the outset. It means, furthermore, making a mistake; for if there was any one theory which justified the war, it was instead the idealist theory of the self-limitation of the state. But like all of his contemporaries, Davy felt the prewar influence of Ihering and Savigny. He is flirting with realism. And it is exactly the same with almost all his contemporaries. Realism is born of reason, idealism of a legitimate development of feelings which we owe to the war; and it is in their efforts to resolve this antinomy in their theories of right that the French philosophers and jurists have encountered insurmountable difficulties.

But the postwar period has raised two practical questions on

1. G. Davy, *Eléments de sociologie* (Paris: Delgrave, 1924).
2. G. Davy, *L'Idéalisme et les conceptions réalistes du droit* (Paris: F. Alcan, 1922).

the two parallel levels of individual right and state sovereignty. The first is: "Is it possible to retain the old natural right *without endangering the state?*" The problems come from labor legislation.

The assertion of natural right has as its consequence the assertion of the individual's right to work—whence comes the Chapelier Law of June 14–17, 1891. Now the Waldeck–Rousseau Law of March 21, 1884, recognizes and regulates trade unions. But it leaves the individual's right to work, a necessary consequence of his natural right, untouched. It simply adds to it the right to associate.

Now these two rights, although they seem complementary, are really incompatible. Scelle writes:

> However we examine the matter, we see that the trade union does not embody the trade. What is more, trade-union legislation is still not sufficient to produce social peace. It is this defect which lies behind the combative attitude trade unionism adopts when it tries to win *de facto* possession of the juridical powers refused it *de jure*—that is, when it tries to become the *representative* and *sovereign* of an organized and unified trade, to move from the realm of private law into the realm of public law, from an associative to an administrative formula, to take on the obligation to defend the interests of the trade and by means of compulsory trade unions to eliminate the fundamental and irreducible antinomy between the individual right to work and the representation of the corporate interests of the trade.[3]

Mario Gianturco says in the same vein: "It is really a dilemma which presents itself as follows: either the absorption of the unorganized or the impotence of the organized. The principle of trade-union solidarity is much more important than that of the right to work." The absurdities and incongruities of French labor laws would therefore seem to tend to constitute a critical point for the natural right of the individual. The individualistic viewpoint of the Revolution would seem to have to be abandoned or reformed. And what is more important, the interest of the individual as such and his inalienable rights would seem to contradict each other.

But with a fearful symmetry, exactly the same problem arises with respect to state sovereignty. It really seems as if the

3. *Droit ouvrier.*

League of Nations, an association of states, is being reduced to impotence by just this principle of sovereignty. In the first place, the obligations imposed by articles 10, 12, 13, 15, 16, and 17 of the Treaty of Versailles were reduced to the barest minimum just to avoid interference with this principle. In spite of this reduction, we know the difficulties which these articles have encountered, particularly the American Senate's attitude toward article 10. Furthermore, the work of the Assembly at Geneva is always being hampered by the same principle. I need only recall the position too many states took when the establishment of the Hague Court and arms reductions were being discussed in 1920.

In other words, to sum up what has just been said, since 1789 serious dangers have arisen to threaten nations as well as individuals. Men have sought to guard against them through associations. But the association must no longer be considered a contract whose cocontractors are only trying to protect their respective rights. Although the words, and even the tendencies, of many preserve this ancient aspect of the association, it seems that an urgent necessity is compelling the associates not just to give up their rights temporarily but to abandon definitively the very concept of rights. Thus, the philosopher's task will be to reconstruct the concepts of natural right and state sovereignty on a factual basis.

But, on the other hand, there's no denying that a war has taken place. Now if we consider a dispute among a number of individuals, we notice that it leads each of them to think first of all of his own just right. In this sense every belligerent country, Germany as much as France, has seen the war bring about the revival of the concept of a just right which is wholly ideal and superior to the facts.

We therefore have to determine the value of the efforts French philosophers and jurists have made to reconcile natural right and state sovereignty, and if indeed reconciliation is really possible or even desirable.

We shall examine the doctrines of Hauriou, Davy, and Duguit. The nature of this essay will not permit us to do more. But to mention other equally well-known names, let us say that Emmanuel Lévy should be classed with the movement represented by Davy, and—not without some reservations—Michaud with Duguit. As for Gény, he comes midway between Hauriou and Duguit.

II
THE ATTEMPTS AT RECONCILIATION

THERE IS A PHILOSOPHICAL WORK called *Vers le positivisme absolu par l'idéalisme* [Toward Absolute Positivism by Way of Idealism]. I believe that in setting forth Hauriou's doctrine we may invert the terms: "Toward Absolute Idealism by Way of Realism." This is the general title we could give his works.

It is time to define these two words. Idealism in respect to rights is the intellectual attitude which regards fact and idea together, with idea supporting fact. Realism in respect to rights regards fact only; hence arises the German notion of force, since force is a fact.

But it is also possible to set out from fact—since we have felt the effect of prewar realism—and then seek the idea. The result will be, if you like, an experiential idealism. This is the position which Hauriou tried to take.

He does set out from fact: the primary datum will be the fact alone, that is to say, the interest that the objective institution is based on. At this stage there is neither sovereignty nor individual right, since—as Hauriou points out—these are ideas. There is only a body, although it is a body which is waiting for a soul, whose objective validity tends to find fulfillment in subjective validity. There is fact, but this fact tends toward right. There is, for example, a state born of a complex of interests, and this state tends to become a sovereign person. You can see that the ticklish point here is the transition from one term of the antinomy to the other. Hauriou says:

> Although we identify political and juridical centralization with the body and moral personality with the spirit, we are not taking the position of explaining body by spirit but, on the contrary, spirit by body. We are making the spirit, as in the Aristotelian and Thomistic formula, "the act of the organic body" and explaining how the body itself, which potentially contains the corporate soul, works in such a way as to actualize it. Our view of public law is not subjectivist, for we do not explain the organization of the state by the decrees of the subjective will of a preexisting moral person. Our view of public law is objectivist; for we admit that the body politic organizes itself as an order of things through its own basic activities. although we do add that

through a need for liberty the body politic tends toward personifi-
cation.⁴

But this is only a metaphor. How this transition from *de
facto* to *de jure* occurs is precisely what has to be shown. According to Hauriou, it takes place as soon as consciousness
thinks about fact. Objective individuality is a center of interests.
Subjective individuality is the subject representing his interest
to himself. The state, insofar as it is an objective institution, is
born of circumstance. But the various individuals grouped in
this state *think about* the state, and through this consciousness,
the *fact*, state, is transformed into the *idea*, sovereignty. Hauriou pushes his analysis still further. A number of individuals
come together to found an institution, to create a social work.
This work is thus, if you like, no more than the group's conception of it. But the group is unified by this conception of a common goal it is trying to attain. It is this idea which gives it its
"moral personality." In Hauriou's system, Davy says, "the subject he is seeking is in the last analysis the interested parties
thinking about the interest involved in their collective undertaking."

At this stage, the subject still lacks the free will it needs in
order to be a *moral person.* You will note that Hauriou considers
it of secondary importance. Among all these writers, who have
learned from events, we see a rather strong distrust of unconditional will. The result is that the social goal to be attained moves
into the foreground of their thinking. Hauriou, for instance, regards the will as an executive, and therefore dependent, organ.
And he has so many reservations about incorporating it into this
system that he begins by saying that it has a tendency to turn
against the *de jure* subjects who are using it—and so we have
absolute monarchy. The *de jure* subjects parry by absorbing and
assimilating it—and so we have national sovereignty.

What then is the state for Hauriou?

An institution born of necessity—this is what a government
is. Some men take part in this government, others represent it,
and so the state becomes their common idea. As such it is sovereign.

But we see quite clearly that Hauriou cannot stop at this
point. To think about a fact is not after all to transform it into

4. Maurice Hauriou, *Principes de droit public*, 2d ed. (Paris:
Société du Recueil Sirey, 1916).

a right. My thinking about this table, which is a *fact,* does not make it exist by right. That is why Hauriou is going to take another step and say, "The moral subject, the state, is the social idea thinking about itself through the common will." But here he is clearly abandoning his premises. A sentence like this and many others in the same vein show that the social idea no longer arises from fact, that it is no longer fact thought about, but has an independent existence of its own. Here Hauriou is clearly an idealist and must admit that he has failed. He wanted to set out from the "is" to construct the "ought," and not being able to do so, he has had to postulate the "ought" not as issuing by a natural process from the "is" but as existing independently. And at this stage his theory becomes confused: the *de facto* and the *de jure* coexist without any comprehensible relationship to each other. This is best shown by the fact that in his latest work he feels the need to go back and base the *de facto* on the *de jure.* Thus he writes:

> We shall shortly show that the founding of all social institutions presupposes the intervention of an objective idea realized by the founder in some work or undertaking. The founding of the state presupposes, therefore, the idea of the state; and subjective wills coordinate their actions only in relation to this idea, which transcends them just as all objective ideas transcend individual consciousnesses. It is thanks to the element of objective idea that the founder, who acts with a prestate power, can give rise to a state power.

This is Hauriou's most recent thinking, and indeed he can hardly go any further. First he assumed that the *de facto* objective institution is prior to subjective individuality, the *de jure* subject. Then he presented idealism developing out of realism as its natural upshot. In this light, the realists and Duguit seemed to have stopped short, for pure and simple lack of perspicacity, just when they were heading in the right direction.

But Hauriou thought that the fact that the state was represented to consciousness did not suffice to make it a *de jure* subject. He therefore posited the idea as an independent reality which was alone capable of conferring legitimacy. At this second stage of his thinking, idealism and realism coexist, with each one serving a dual purpose.

And lastly, trying to clear up this confusion, and becoming more clearly aware of his own intentions, Hauriou reverses himself and gives priority, with respect to the objective institution, to a free will serving a pure idea. And in so doing he admits his failure: he has had to give up realism completely, since he proclaims that the idea and freedom are the bases of sovereignty. The concept of just right regains its place with honor, but the practical problems we mentioned remain unsolved.

DAVY TAKES A POSITION familiar to the sociologists of the Durkheim school: he sets out to show that a scientific explanation of social facts does not, so long as it is sociological, rob them of any of their ideal value. Durkheim thought, naïvely enough, that he could show how religion was the product of a social reality external to the individual and still leave its bearing wholly untouched.

Davy treated the problem of sovereignty from the same point of view.

A few preliminary explanations are necessary. The fundamental postulate, not of sociology but of French sociology, is the existence of collective consciousness. Durkheim writes:

> Here, then, is a category of facts with very distinctive characteristics: it consists of ways of acting, thinking, and feeling, external to the individual, and endowed with a power of coercion, by reason of which they control him. These ways of thinking should not be confused with biological phenomena, since they consist of representations and of action; nor with psychological phenomena, which exist only in the individual consciousness and through it. They constitute, thus, a new variety of phenomena; it is to them exclusively that the term "social" ought to be applied. And this term fits them quite well, for it is clear that, since their source is not in the individual, their substratum can be no other than society, either the political society as a whole or some one of the partial groups it includes, such as religious denominations, political, literary, and occupational associations, etc.[5]

These uniquely patterned facts constitute *collective consciousness*. Collective consciousness is conceived of as acting in exactly the same way that individual consciousness does. Consequently, there will be said to be collective value judgments just as there are individual value judgments. Bouglé writes:

5. Emile Durkheim, *Rules of Sociological Method*, 8th ed., trans. Sarah A. Solokay and John H. Mueller, ed. by George E. G. Catlin (Glencoe: Ill.: The Free Press, 1938), p. 3.

I base my judgment on a certain number of habits, on a certain complex of rules, and on certain types of ideals which I have not personally created. I observe them existing in the society I live in: they are facts. Values stand before me as given realities, as things. Value judgments embody kinds of realities which impose themselves in the society I live in. But isn't the reason why they impose themselves in this way that in a sense they are the creation of this same society whose life they are safeguarding? . . . Society creates ideals. . . . Values are *objective* because *imperative,* and *imperative* because *collective.*[6]

We can see the skill with which the sociologists set forth their theory: value is a fact; consequently it should be studied scientifically. But in the process it does not cease to be value. Consequently, there is room in sociology for the scientific study of values.

We can also see how these principles apply directly to the problem we're concerned with. Davy writes:

In studying these facts, and from a purely realistic point of view, we note the existence of rights. Each of these rights denotes a value which has been recognized and consecrated as an ideal to be respected and not tampered with under pain of sanctions.

Thus right is not based upon "the ideal essence of man as an end in himself." It is a value the collectivity gives to certain facts and persons, and the sovereignty of the state is nothing but a value given to that institution.

But Davy does not limit himself to these general considerations; he goes on to show from this point of view how society evolves.[7] In the beginning, that imperative, coercive value, sovereignty, is distributed throughout the whole tribe. Every man is bathed in sovereignty; the state does not exist. There is a coercive imperative with no individualized power. But little by little this diffuse force, the effect of collective consciousness, is going to be concentrated in a few individuals. It is the same force as before, only now someone has absorbed it all. This is the way we have evolved from tribes to empires. The founding of republics simply marks a further change: this force, which heretofore was concentrated in a single man, belongs hence-

6. Célestin Bouglé, *Evolution of Values* (New York: Kelley, 1926).

7. A. Moret et G. Davy, *Des clans aux empires* (Paris: Renaissance du Livre, 1923).

forth to the nation. Thus political history is allegedly the study of the various vicissitudes this force has undergone, never changing but having more or less extensive consequences and belonging sometimes to a single individual and sometimes to the whole community.

Thus state sovereignty exists both as a fact and as a value. *For the time being,* the state is indeed a moral person making use of a single, all-powerful will. Similarly, the individual does indeed have a personality which gives him rights, and these rights have an ideal value. But this sovereignty and natural right do not come to the individual or state from their own essential nature but from a value attributed to them by a collective power whose decrees are binding on the individual. In this way realism and idealism go reconciled hand in hand. In this way too we can catch a glimpse of a solution to the practical problem of the postwar period. As entities in their own right, the state and the individual could not respectively accommodate themselves to the League of Nations and a compulsory trade union. But here it is a question of values which the collective consciousness can learn to transfer. All we need to do is pave the way for a transfer which will take the moral person and his juridical attributes away from the isolated individual and the single state and hand it over to the group.

This theory represents a real advance over those we have previously discussed. Yet it is not completely satisfactory. In the first place, it calls itself realist in method without even dreaming that at bottom it involves a metaphysical hypothesis. For the sociologists are as a matter of fact implicitly presupposing, as the condition and foundation of the scientific postulate of a "collective consciousness," the concept of creative synthesis. In other words, the reason why society, according to them, has an independent life of its own and is greater than the individuals composing it is that the latter are governed by the principle that "the whole is greater than the sum of its parts." But let us point out briefly here the metaphysical problems raised by such a principle. The reason why I say the whole is greater than the sum of its parts is that I can compare this sum and this whole. But this presupposes that the sum of the parts can be given to me without the whole being given, which by hypothesis is impossible. In the world there are wholes and parts. That is all there is. Consequently, I cannot know whether something completely new may spring from an addition of parts. It is true that the whole is greater than the parts, but this truism does not suffice to justify the postulate of a "creative synthesis."

In French sociology, then, there is recourse—at the outset or the conclusion, as you wish—to a very dubious metaphysical concept. It follows that, wherever French sociologists have held sway, the transition from factual observation to theory is always debatable. Take Durkheim's brilliant study of the elementary forms of the religious life, for example. His very exhaustive study of Australian religions leads us to the concept of "mana." At this point in his investigations, Durkheim tries to explain mana in terms of the idea of symbolic group self-representation. But *that's just it:* this explanation is based on the weakest argument in the book. It seems superimposed rather than developed from the facts. We can understand when we are told that there were fundamentally and originally two poles to the investigation— the facts and the general theory of society—and that Durkheim was seeking common ground on which to bring the two together. In the same way Davy's investigations of "La Foi jurée" ["The Oath"] [8] do not support his conclusions, which remain unattached and suspended above the facts. But let us for an instant accept this theory. It is explanatory but not normative. It does indeed, in my view, explain the origin of this innate belief in right which I find in individuals. But it is simply boasting if it thinks that after it has given such an explanation it can still allow us to keep the same attitude toward rights as before. No matter how he may have tried to preserve idealism, Davy eliminates the concept of "value" from the facts that he has studied. All that's left is facts. In other words, Davy has not—in spite of this metaphysical postulate which mars his idealism—been able to provide the slightest place for idealism in his theory.

III
DUGUIT AND THE REALIST THEORY OF RIGHTS

IT WOULD SEEM THEN that coherence, and thus the greatest likelihood of truth, will be with those who make up their minds to renounce one or the other of the two contrasting tendencies which we have pointed out and to declare themselves frankly realist or frankly idealist. Nowadays, the classical

8. G. Davy, *La Foi jurée* (Paris, F. Alcan, 1922).

idealism represented by Esmein, that is, the only rational form of idealism which is presently possible, attracts only a few disciples. For, among other things, it cannot adapt itself to the new facts of the postwar years. We can justifiably consider it a relic. And so we have to turn to Duguit and realism. "I claim," Duguit writes,

> that the concept of the state as public power which can impose its will in sovereign fashion because its nature is superior to that of its subjects is imaginary and has no basis in reality, and that the alleged sovereignty of the state is to be explained neither by divine right, which implies a belief in the supernatural, nor by the will of the people, which is a gratuitous, unproven, undemonstrable hypothesis. The state is simply the product of a natural differentiation.

The state is not a person and can take no sovereign action: it is a *social function.* This social function pursues an end which is of common interest, and therefore has certain powers needed to attain this end. But these powers tend increasingly to be more narrowly restricted to the end pursued. Idealism's mistake was to lose sight of the end and to postulate an independent existence for the power of the state. But our legislative evolution is in just the opposite direction and tends to determine what powers shall be granted in the light of the ends pursued. The state has therefore gradually been recognized to be only "a group of individuals with a force they ought to use to create and manage public services." What becomes of internal sovereignty then, that is, of the power to make laws? It becomes simply the power to issue edicts which are compulsory because they conform to social need. And where does this need come from? From solidarity considered as primordial fact.

Thus at bottom there is but a single fact—solidarity. This solidarity conditions the differentiations or divisions of social labor. From it arise diverse functions, some of which, such as the *function* of the capitalist or the *function* of the wage earner, are fulfilled by individuals, and others by groups of individuals, such as the state. The concept of *de jure* subject is thus replaced by that of function. But these functions are not arbitrarily established. There is no question here of force, but of necessity, and necessity presides at their birth. Society is an organism whose different organs carry out their functions as the different organs of the human body do, but "with consciousness besides."

The value of this theory is plain. I have no right, and my neighbor no more than I, any more than the hands of a watch have a right to turn. I simply have—simultaneously or successively—a certain number of functions to fulfill. If anyone interferes with me he violates no mysterious virtue—human dignity, let's say—which I allegedly possess. There's merely something wrong with the social organism. My functions are impeded, and it is precisely to assure their unimpeded functioning that a set of steps to take have been established to protect me. My liberty is thus no right; it is a duty.

Here the idealists will answer that to do away with right in order to preserve duty is after all to grant them more than they are asking for. But Duguit is careful to reply to them:

> Why does a certain pattern of behavior impose itself upon a man? Because if he did not act in this way, the very principle of social life would be destroyed. Society would fall apart, and the individual himself would disappear. . . . It is no more a "duty" in the ethical sense of the term than it is a "duty" for the cells of the living body to contribute to the life of the living body.[9]

What conclusions can we draw from this line of argument? Let us reconsider for a moment the preceding arguments. In all of them it is maintained that the individual does not have simply an organic individuality, and that organic individuality, furthermore, does not suffice to constitute the individual. What is essential is a certain trenchant quality of freedom and intangibility which makes man something like a sort of spiritual force that is impossible to take apart. Respect is addressed to a noumenal self, which is supposed to float above the organic self. The state, on the other hand, is analogous to the individual. Thus it too is recognized to have a spiritual force and a noumenal self.

It is precisely this noumenal self which Duguit does away with. Thus nothing is left but organisms. If Peter differs from Paul, it is not by right but because each of them is the effect of a determinate causal sequence. And, indeed, Duguit, no more than Hauriou or Esmein, considers numerical individuality sufficient to establish *personality*. The real source of personality is *function*. I am a person only to the extent that I play a unique

9. Duguit, *Souveraineté et liberté* (Paris: F. Alcan, 1922).

role in society. But it is quite possible that a number of men may have to fulfill the same function. And they will in that case derive a collective individuality from their function. Thus the ideal of realism will be to do away with the fiction of the autonomous individual and make him only the tenant of a function, and to replace the autonomous state with the functional state. The individual then becomes a cog, and this lets the trade union become compulsory without infringing on any of his rights; and the state becomes a function with respect to the governed, on the one hand, and to other states on the other. Will the day ever come when social need will require the creation of a superior function, a superstate? The different states would lose their separate and spiritual personality, retaining only their national individuality, that is, the one they derive from the natural differences of their nationals. So there can no longer be any question of robbing the state of sovereignty: there is no state sovereignty.

What then is Duguit's ideal? That Europe become an immense organism made up of interlocking functions which owe their individuality to the end assigned to each. At the top would be the superstate, which is itself only the function of functions. It would unite states deprived of the aggressive personality which constitutes their sovereignty. Within these states, groups or trade unions would function as wheels within wheels, and it is only as members of these unions that we would find—instead of the irreducible personalities we are acquainted with—numerically distinct organisms called men whose liberty is but their duty to fulfill their functions.

I may be accused of exaggerating Duguit's ideas, and there is no doubt that he has nowhere given a clear formulation of his ideal; but my own statement of it is plainly recognizable as the tendency of all his works. We can see that he offers a clear and simple solution to the practical problem of the state, and that he gives a new formula for international accord which may be expressed in this way: different states' pursuit of interrelated ends requires a harmonious action on their part which will only be realized when we cease to believe in their noumenal personality and think of them as merely the representatives of natural differences (of territory, race, and language) between nations.

It seems that this must be the necessary upshot of Europe's political evolution.

To CONCLUDE, it seems that in France they have more or less universally decided to deal with questions such as that of state sovereignty by the realist method. But the national feelings aroused by the Great War have led certain authors to use this method to reach an idealist conclusion which will safeguard the idea (or rather feeling) of just right. In doing so they are neglecting pressing problems. But the complexity and fragility of their systems are losing them the support of a new generation enamored of simplicity and solidity. And so it seems that the future lies with those who will resign themselves in these matters to expecting only realistic consequences from realist methods, and who will recognize that he who sets out from *facts* will never end up with anything but facts.

The Legend of Truth

To START WITH, truth was still unborn. The warlike nomads did not need it; they needed lofty beliefs. Who can say what truth there is in a battle?

Later, the plowman's vegetable tasks required no more than an over-all dependability, a reliable faith in the immutable nature of those vast and boundless realms, the seasons. I imagine that he welcomed the wandering gods and listened to their wondrous tales without emotion or suspicion, leaving truth and falsehood in limbo, while outside the wheat's green tufts imperceptibly yellowed. Familiarity with the grains' uninterrupted growth imparted supple power to his mind. He did not demand that the objects which fell beneath his gaze be contained within the limits of an uncapricious nature, and he calmly accepted their sudden changes, leaving it to their inmost powers to give them a unity still too protean for our reason to grasp. The clamor of the common herd did not pursue him into the silent chambers of his thoughts; among his thoughts he was assured of an absolute solitude. They were gnarled and deeply rooted forces stubbornly resisting discourse, and adapted, so it seemed, to him alone. His attention strayed from one to the other as a traveler who has come back to his hearth looks by turns at his kinsmen's faces, some full of smiles, others bathed in tears. These faces bent toward him in the shadow as plants

"Légende de la vérité" is a portion of a larger work of the same title which was never published; the portion included here was published in *Bifur*, June, 1931. See also Vol. 1, 31/6.

turn toward the sun; and feeling so many living things within him, he sometimes took fright.

Truth comes from Commerce. It went to market with the first manufactured objects. It had been waiting for their birth to spring full-blown from the head of men.

Conceived in order to answer to rustic needs, it retained all their primitive simplicity. The pots, quite round with a crude handle, were no more than an outline of the movement of drinking. The scraping tools, the harrows, the millstones seemed to be no more than the other side of the most commonplace concerted actions. It was from these actions that a unitary thought had to be worked free, a thought at rest, immobile, mute, ageless, and depending more on objects than on minds, the first impersonal thought of those remote times, a thought that, when the men themselves were absent, still hovered about the works of their hands.

The reason why skepticism came up from the fields—bringing with it the arguments of the bald and hard to grasp, the horned wild things, and the bushel with its hidden truth—was that no definitive view could be adequate to growing crops. But the first implements, which were born dead, were to have deathless words spoken over them. What could be said of them held true until they were destroyed, and even then there was no imperceptible change to disturb judgment: when vessels fell they smashed to bits. Their eponymous thought, suddenly set free, leaped to the winds and then returned to settle on other vessels.

The artisans had in fact been quite conscious, in fashioning their flint or clay, of the growing concern for form. But their abrupt effort, exhausted en route, had stopped far short of beauty in that ambiguous domain whose angles, lines, and planes are indiscriminately elements of Art and Truth.

The first specifically human products were to clash absolutely with the products of nature; and once they had been perfected, the stupor into which they threw their craftsmen can be compared only to that of certain scientists confronted with mathematical essences. It put them within a hairbreadth of discovering the famous myth of true thoughts.

The economy did the rest. In the market place the naïve hosts of the gods had their first taste of deception. People lied before they told the truth, because it simply was a matter of obscuring the exact nature of a few novel and singular things whose nature they did not in fact exactly know. A spontaneous riposte to this experience of deception immediately brought the first truths to light. They did not yet bear the name of Truth, destined to such future glory; they were simply specific precautions against tricksters. Each man examining and reexamining the merchant's vessel took care to embody the specific idea of this vessel in his precept and to relate all his discoveries to it. It was agreed that a vessel should not be simultaneously intact and cracked. Who would have dared to set similar limits to the spontaneous fruits of the earth? But in this case it was simply the hidden intention of the potter himself that was being disinterred from the clay. And in no case was this precaution, and a hundred others like it, deduced from some general principle: these regulations governing the policing of the market were established in relation to the singular occasion, to specific reflections, and to the very nature of the goods themselves. Thus these young truths were at first only so many principles governing barter, having to do with human relations, and applying to industrial products. They were born of man's reflection on his own works, not on natural existents.

A speech market was easily established on the public auction block. It was there that the prudent calculations and displays of merchants, their tricks and dodges, were traded. The products of discourse were rationalized there well before other products were. A single model was established. It was as if this standardization had taken the needs and purchasing power of the poorest into account. Simple, clear, and durable entities were put into circulation.

The power of the market freed men from the great forces within them. In the image of their wooden implements, they introduced a lathe and workbench into their innermost councils. They laid hold of inimitable natures in the depth of their being and laid them by on their shelves. They went at it with a will: curving, shaping, knocking out knots, and making the chips fly. Then they took their handiwork—well planed, truly squared, and nevertheless closer to their original depth than our own—to the truth fair. Of course people were deceived, bought worthless oaths or spoiled words, but when they found in practice that they could not pass them on to others they became aware of the deception. Suddenly these painted thoughts, like made-up animals whose blemishes begin to show, stood forth in all their inexplicable nakedness. Then, terrified of being the only one who held them stored in his memory, the frustrated man slung them furiously on the scrap heap. After similar mishaps, people got used to handling words, like those money-changers who bite coins or ring them on marble: each one, from his full height, let them fall to the depths of himself, listening for the sound they gave off. Thus evidence was born, the precaution against these precautions.

But no one believed that in doing these things he was engaged in trade, or that there was a truth economy. This was because each man, when he balanced his books at home and found his own goods underneath his recent purchases in his memory, thought that he had gotten something new for nothing.

Thought thus slowly worked its transformation from fixed to movable capital.

But in the process man experienced a mysterious inner turmoil which he tried to explain in chiefly mythological ways. He thereby produced, in two stages, the legend of Truth. I feel somewhat abashed at the prospect of retracing a myth which took so many different forms. In order to approach the problem correctly, we should look at the myth as a transposition of the inner disarray experienced by men of that time; and we must therefore begin by making clear the nature of this inner turmoil.

Man had long produced his thoughts as he produced his life; they stuck to his body like those half-born Egyptian animals, sun-shaped in the silt of the Nile, with paws that melt into the mud. They had no tie with things beyond a universal sympathy, no action on them other than a magic one. They did not resemble them as a portrait resembles its model, but as a sister resembles her brother, through a family resemblance. They no more expressed plants than plants express the sea. Instead, just like the plants, the winds, the sea, with their seasons, equinoxes, ebbs and flows, precocious or retarded growths, retreats, advances, and first halting blossomings, these thoughts lived as a process that developed and disclosed—in short, an absolutely natural sequence of events.

Then, suddenly, by an irresistible movement, these thoughts were thrust into another world, among the products of industry. Their life was carefully extracted from them. All their ties with nature were severed. Technical regulations were imposed on their production. In short, they were transformed into a valuable but lifeless triumph of human artifice and at the same time granted the redoubtable title of "representations" (a new honor, a new duty), and an anonymous herd thronged relentlessly into each man's mind in an effort to control the use of the representative function. Man was no longer alone with himself. When he had dealt with his thoughts according to the industrial methods dictated to him, he no longer recognized them as his. They stood beneath his gaze distinct, independent, decisive, so different from his life and heart he could not believe they came from him and imagined he had brought them in from outside. With the best of him mutilated in this way, all that was left to him were the body's organic movements, passions, and blind spasms. Above this flesh in torment, tortured by its shame at itself, soared Homunculus the mind, which was already being called "impersonal." Here we see the first glimmer of Christian humility. In short, respect, shame, and the need to know gave birth at first to four gods who had little in common but were nonetheless homonymous, like the countless Phoebuses in Greece.

The common herd of men, who are generally more inclined to value material things than the labor that produced them, endowed our ideas with a precious and subtle substance. They called it Truth, and thought that even if wear and tear of flames were to rid it of every trace of our own labors, it would still regain its natural place without losing one whit of its inestimable value.

On the other hand, the men of refinement, who were inclined to be struck by the variety of technical devices, paid homage to Form. It swooped down out of the sun onto its prey like a falcon and immediately took the heavenly path again, leaving the wondrous mark of its talons to dwell forever among us. This goddess also took the name of Truth.

Magic said its say: the idea's relation to its object was conceived in the image of the living and irreversible link which bound pin-stuck wax dolls to men. The fabrication of ideas became a sort of magic rite. It seemed that man imitated things in his heart in order to entice them living into it. This voodoo was also called Truth. Its power to charm was imperceptibly extended to the object itself. Now the object of true thoughts was at that time no more than the totality of art works, pottery, knives, and carvings—of everything which could not possibly exist without an abstract justness of proportion. Thus a divine power of Measure, a vital force that drew beings from nothingness (and which is still evident in the closing pages of Plato's

Philebus), was conceived. Through natural assimilation, this force (which was a mythical projection of human industry) took on the name of Truth, so much so that henceforth men could say that "it is not true because it exists; it exists because it is true."

Form, Matter, Relation, Measure: no one of these four gods was strong enough to subdue the three others. They became accustomed to living together as best they could, looking beyond for their definitive unification.

Some merchant chief settled the matter. Up until then, Commerce and Truth had required that men reach an agreement about certain principles, which were at first as numerous and special as the contracts. The merchant chief took it into his head to reduce their number. He was undoubtedly a brilliant, abstract man, like those who replaced our old provincial measures with the meter. Throughout the hall where the merchants had grouped themselves according to the interests of their trade and in the grossest ignorance of the customs governing the neighboring interest groups, a herald stirred confusion and emotion by announcing that all special principles were to be abandoned in favor of the following general maxim: "A thing cannot be itself and something other than itself at the same time and in the same respect."

By the time the merchants had become familiar with this new law, all the roads which could have led reflection toward the past and a historical explanation had been blocked. But at the same time the four rival gods, who were nonetheless tied closely to one another, lost their clear outlines and melted into one. This new idol did not, however, eliminate the internal conflicts among them. (It was still held that in order to be true a thought had to concern an existing object, whereas in order to exist an object had to be true, that is, be matter for a true thought. It was assumed both that the Truth of a thought could be discovered by simply examining the thought and that this Truth dwelt in the relation of idea to object.) What gave the new idol its unity was less its inner harmony than the strong will of its faithful, coupled with a heedless unconcern for contradictions. Thus the major gods were born, and gobbled up alive, from head to foot, the local gods. A subtle wind breathed through the world and through its souls: Truth in minds, Truth in things, Truth in the close union of minds and things—a flawless universal force which soon would slip into the place of that faceless god whom first the savages and then the sociologists called Mana.

What was essential to these imaginary projections, and what had so many sequels in so many other realms, was the idol's crowning adornment, eternity. It was accepted without question, since man's timidity barred his road to understanding: what he had actually invented he believed he was only discovering. Thus these beautiful offspring had to have existed prior to him in some secret place, and to have been concerned only with their own proper ordering. The term *contemplation,* which had great success, removed the final doubts. Now thinking was only a matter of contemplating an impassive world of overlapping links, embroidered trimmings, knots tied and untied, vestibules and passageways, figures merging into other figures, forms which a slight warping changed into different forms, like those geometrical designs which change from hexagon to triangle according to the movements of the eye. The sacrifice of Truth was consummated (as it was to be again in times of Christian quibbling) by the following reasoning:

"I am free to think what I want. But I can only think of what is true, because what is not true does not exist. No doubt what is true already exists, prefabricated, fitted out, and imposing itself on my view; and I feel within myself, like an uneasiness, the reproach of my frustrated freedom. No doubt. But that is the wrong way to look at it, and furthermore I am free to think what I want, because I only want to think of what is true, and my freedom is only my power to liberate myself from false appearances and from myself. What is troubling me at present is only weakness, childish egotism. Right reason will put things back in their proper places, put my body among the other bodies, and will reveal the skeleton of impersonal relationships which keep my poor flesh from crumbling into nothingness. I shall be only too happy if I succeed in elevating the truths that constitute my essence to the bosom of the Mother Truth, and in uniting these truths once more with the pure spirit that breathes through these flawless forms."

So there we have men bare and unaccommodated, alone with their bodies and mistrusting their bodies, their minds racked thin upon these manufactured essences. Nature and its secrets, the winds, the meteors which suddenly fall across the sky as fingers trace a sign upon the sand, the trees which stretch unequal arms toward the sun, the valleys and the countrysides composing from the light and color of the hour harmonious ensembles filled with vague insistent meaning—all these have vanished. In the same way, a flashlight lit at night suddenly shrinks the universe to the torchbearer's face. No man raised his eyes, no man dreamed of plunging Truth like a sword into the heart of things: between the advent of this Truth and the reign of Science there is a missing link.

What I am saying is that Truth, the mythical daughter of Commerce, in turn engenders a very real democracy, the original constitution, the only constitution, of which different kinds of government are only passing forms.

It is in vain that certain philosophers have pushed their precious inequality back into the Golden Age; there is no place for it there. If these people want to gather up a weakened leaven of it, let them look for it among those backward peoples where the women are denied the right to speak among themselves the language of the men, which has a different syntax, different principles, a different way of thinking. The man makes himself understood just enough to command. His orders, furthermore, come hurtling down like meteors from unknown spheres beyond the true and false to populate these lesser souls with great hard solitary blocks. Heaven-sent commands, the common feeling that the ways of the master are inscrutable, the impossibility as a matter of principle of reaching any agreement with him or (if it were possible) of arriving at some common course of action on the basis of it—in short, everything that confines us to the use of either naked force or face-to-face and quasi-magic power —this is what inequality among men can produce.

But in the presence of their new idol, cold Truth, the lowliest felt that they were the equal of the mighty. The slave could understand the master's orders or, if not, could understand that the master had obeyed the promptings of his stomach. Every command, no matter how imperious, presupposed a prior agreement. It mattered little that the leaders were rich old men, conquering generals, hereditary kings. Rich young men whom the Sophists had taken in hand easily cornered the word market. Thereby at fairs and public places they imposed their own opinions. But it can be seen from the preceding that this accumulated capital was only an item of barter, precisely because men had put all of their effort into detaching their thoughts from themselves, and because this transitory master entrenched in his arsenal of political ideas did not command assent in virtue of his own uniqueness but in virtue of a consensus with the common herd which he had sought for and been granted, and in virtue of the large number of particular contracts he had in his pocket.

This is how the matter appears in our eyes. In the eyes of the time, Truth was there making all things equal. No doubt the schemers were more quick to see it. But each citizen told himself in his heart that if a Sophist showed him the true idea, he would be able as the Sophists were to retain it without fail in his own memory. Furthermore, when Alcibiades has offered an idea in the Agora, it is no longer his; and he must ceaselessly restock his store if he is going to keep up his reputation.

And when Socrates stopped to discuss mathematical diagrams with a slave, it was as if he had said, "This slave can be a member of the Prytany as much as I can."

The essence of the democratic constitution, which is older than history, is that each man may always take another's place because a Socratic dialogue based on agreement and reason may always take place between them. It is the democratic spirit which, under the most absolute of monarchies, inspired the man who wrote: "Good sense is the commonest thing in the world."

The pharaohs' rise to power, the Roman cult of emperors, and divine right are only playthings, tricks, or baubles; I want to see my subject clear and I shall pass them by. From now on the city I am considering is the Democratic City, inhabited by Equals.

Towering ramparts protect its men from every natural onslaught. The forests are far off and mute. Only the sky rests upon these walls, and some people are already drawing triangles on it. The houses are aligned according to the rules of Measure, and all enclose behind their shutters one true thought. Each citizen feels this artificial universe around him like a carapace. He turns toward other intelligent and expressionless faces and nimbly makes countless logical pacts. Truth is a cruel and adored tyrant; in its name the happiest of men can be persuaded to commit suicide. Drive around in these straight and regular streets; all you see there is commerce, quibbles, and inventions by the rule. Only the bird, drawing his light shadow across the swarm of speechifiers, flies high enough to find the vague power of vast natural voices in that clamorous concert.

Men have learned to be mistrustful of the solitary man.

Their forefathers still recalled with fright the unforeseeable and awesome arbitrariness of tyrants. These immense and secret men—born in the seed time of the Republic like a race of giants in the world's seed time, and butchered in the end because they were inherently powerful—suddenly produced surprising cataclysms so completely out of proportion with even their own stature that the disaster, once it had occurred, could no longer be related to them. On the gates of the city it was written that the only strength is unity, and that the man who unaided does the work of many is aided by the power of evil.

This resulted in a fruitful period. The wonder workers had been banished but found family within the woods, and it was thus that there appeared an awesome line of autochthonous men who traveled alone bent over their staffs. The waters of Greece reflected and revealed to them their towering, dark, and suntanned faces; and those who thereby came to know themselves in the wave's mirror and became the captive of their own appearance set up a strange housekeeping with their thoughts. At times they toyed with them cynically without a care for that Truth which weighed heavily on the distant cities. At times, if they remembered their own hot and furrowed faces, they were frightened at the sight of the indistinct transformations and ungeometric forms they bore within them, and fled away wildly to live without Measure, deceivers of their fellows or themselves. Nature loved them and lavished her secrets upon them. Fear provided them with wonderful sights. They awakened from their all-consuming terrors, elated and full of bad faith.

Out of need, maliciousness, or prophetic calling, these marvelous scoundrels went from town to town with their terrible knowledge on leash like a bear, and let it tug the rope a bit in order to scare people into giving them alms.

They spoke of those inhuman powers surrounding man which the citizens did not want to see, they told about their nocturnal terrors and their sunlit joys, and vague echoes awoke in the troubled minds of the Equals, as if behind their conventional wisdom there were still something monstrous that they had not been able to confront and that had condemned them to solitude.

It goes without saying that each time the people managed to take these charlatans from the rear, they put them to death. But when their entire race had finally been exterminated, a widespread uneasiness still remained: behind these bald, familiar hills, behind these flint quarries, what terrible sight lay in store for men, what unheard-of danger threatened the Republic? A fearless Senate sent an expedition out to wage war against nature.

The first people who, feeling they had the support of an entire nation of Equals, cast a democratic look at things were shocked by the great inequality of effects. A seed small enough to be held under a fingernail gave birth to the tallest of trees, the vibration of a slightly raised human voice sometimes caused landslides. And yet the sterile, scowling minerals stayed motionless, stiffened in their barren forms. A different and far more dangerous temptation was that certain things in nature spoke to the mind and others said nothing. This natural aristocracy seemed intolerable to these good citizens. So they organized the external world in such a way that it remained man's greatest conquest. With their heads packed full of their nice square houses, curving crescents, and vast assemblies from which (just like the individual puff of smoke above each man) so many words of wisdom rose, they stripped the world and men of all variable and spontaneous powers. They carefully removed all personal capacities from each object: if that stone, in rolling, was acting—if it was causing a change among its fellows—it would have been subversive to think that it was responsible. All its efficacy it owed to a delegated power. Similarly, the most insignificant voter was well aware that when the dictator declared war, this awesome power of life and death was granted to him from below: "Without me," he thought, "who elected him, could he send me to fight? But could I have caused this great upheaval by myself? It required the cooperation of my comrades."

Power passed from hand to hand up to the hand that tore the treaty into bits. A long chain of meetings and methodical, concerted actions ended up in this decisive gesture, and the power did not properly speaking belong to any one of them. If anyone had been suspected of possessing it as his alone, he would have been immediately executed. Each was only the delegate of another or of all the others; by himself he was nothing but a mineral, a dead stone.

Thus to assume a similar delegation in nature was to be, in respect to the City, lawful and (so to speak) pious: it was to establish a democratic naturalism. In this way, and thanks to a wholly human ingenuity, the great variety of phenomena gave way to an appropriate diversity of delegations. The little men who had been appointed social atoms (and who were, if left to their own devices, more stolid even than an upright burgher) through their solidarity imparted borrowed power to one another and thus gained the sun, the blue sky, and the peacock feather. An elector felt at ease in nature, rejoiced at the morality of the spectacle, and was able to use its beautiful examples to explain the benefits of mutual aid to his son.

At the same time, disturbing mysteries disappeared. Although there had already been, since the death of the Travelers, some relief in the knowledge that there was no longer anyone to speak in shadowy terms of nature's secrets, with how much more reassurance, lightness, and democracy the day rose when it was learned that nature had no more secrets. There was nothing, like an old hatred, that had to be kept hidden at the bottom of the heart because there were no words which could express it. The Republic was completely simple, right down to the infinitely small, a measured movement always coming from without and putting out the same amount of beings it put in. The universe's face was constant, broken only by a delicious multiplicity of smiles. The ghosts slipped back into the hollow trees.

When the conqueror had had the booty of the enemy cast down at his feet, he said: "Be not afraid. All I found beyond the mountains was a big and slightly rusty machine which, although uneconomical in conception, was still in working condition. My role is ended. The task of dismantling its mechanisms falls to others."

Then one saw a pullulation of societies, called Scientific Societies, whose public usefulness was shown by their strictly collective character. Their first members were undoubtedly fanatic democrats who gave up their business or public trust to colonize nature at a distance. In order to be a scientist, it was first necessary to be an upright man and a good citizen, and to possess in the highest degree the spirit of tradition. Each depended on one of his colleagues, who depended in turn on another learned man. The objects of their study felt the repercussion of this fraternity. Nature became a little more fraternal, atomic solidarity increased, and each scientist—bound to the past and his present colleagues like the most bound of atoms— could be penetrated by the idea that he was nothing—nothing without his predecessors, nothing without his descendants—and that his only mission was to do whatever he could to perfect the collective work of mankind.

They never budged from their homes, but had the military bring back from their victorious campaigns great, indistinct, disheveled chunks of nature which they had unloaded in the compounds in the geometric shadows of their buildings.

On these transplanted fragments—dried out by the long hot days of travel, gashed by the jolts, crushed by civilization's fatal mechanisms—they tried out (at random to begin with, then methodically) the most recent wonders of the art of cutlery, blacksmithing, and clockmaking. They poured the fragments into molds, heated them, froze them, mixed them, separated them. They used forces already under their control to break them down, as stool pigeons are used in jails to make guilty prisoners confess. They called the relationships which they established between one of their machines and some natural product "laws." The guilty confessed what they wanted them to confess. What would you have done?

One can read in the works of certain philosophers (a breed we shall be concerned with later) that the mind is all fitted out and carefully compartmented—a well-oiled, smoothly operating, and silent producer of intelligibility and form—but that it needs a fillip to awake it from the deep sleep its complete transparency plunges it into. Without the alien presence—without the one who comes from outside it, opaque and unintelligible—it would simply disappear into its own diaphanous lucidity. But if the formless one is crazy enough to try to cross through the mind's absence, it lays hold of him, stuns him, cuts him up, steam-rollers him, disembodies him, and finally reduces him to burning in his own pure flame.

I have no faith in it, but I think that the philosophers, although born among machines, have done the same thing as the ancients who elevated the familiar objects around them to the level of the gods: what they say about mind is the product of thinking about machines and applies very well to them.

Machines were born long before science, even before truth, from a human idea cast into docile matter. The matter, poor, bare, and undistinguished, was forgotten; but the idea, full-blown, grew fat at its expense. In this way the first temple, the first pot, the first object which was not governed by death were produced. Machines were improved by ways of thinking proper to them, with major and minor ones set in iron or clay. They owed their progress to themselves alone, screening out some inputs from the external world and bending the most docile of them to the requirements of their form. Machines marked the first triumph of the practical idea, of the way of thinking which does not seek to understand but to rule.

The democratic tactic of the Scientific Societies was precisely that of using machines as a means of understanding. Like the magician who draws his audience's attention to his sleeves, which really are empty and innocent, while the goldfish bowl is in his vest, they opened up their heart to everyone who came along, saying, "You see, we let the facts come unto us without discrimination. We have no bias, because we have adopted the contemplative view."

Of course. But by admitting it, they got the chance that they were looking for. Between the inoffensive soul they passively laid bare and the event, they interposed the preconceived idea, the distorting bias, the inhuman and mechanical obstinacy. The machines are watching in the corners. It takes no more than a straw to set their wheels in motion. They snatch up a fly, digest it, spit out a machine. Carefully trained to carry out only one gesture, they take anything as a pretext for carrying it out. The barometer's mercury—weighed, purified, contained—knows how to go up and down, and nothing more. Still, you'll say, there has to be some measure of homogeneity between the machines and certain aspects of nature. Undoubtedly. It is the scientist's business to lend his ear to the slightest murmur and to imagine the apparatus which will divulge its meaning. But earth's murmur and man's rigorous thought, although they're briefly conjugated by coercion, are not really in accord. The earth's slight tremor, when plotted in red ink, is already no longer the same. And if, furthermore, the barometer remains speechless when it's carried here and there under proper precautions, then its stubborn silences are called "constancy."

A servant of the people must have become uneasy about these acts of violence: "Are you sure," he asked the scientists, "that everything is legal?" "Certainly. We are well aware that ungrateful nature has never given us the slightest sign of approval. But she knows very well how to say no when she wants to: her silence is acquiescence." The politician became silent; he recognized in passing one of his own arguments: "You say the Africans are suffering from colonization? But listen, they would say so; they would revolt. Now, you can see them, any time, serious and undisturbed. They're too ungrateful to express satisfaction with our protection publicly. But they say nothing, which comes down to the same thing."

But nature does not say yes or no. She does not know how to think by contraries or contrast. She is silent. Thoughts say no. Machines, those snarling thoughts who guard a scrap of steel or casting in their paws, say no.

To begin with the scientist was free in the virgin realm he had chosen, under two conditions: he had to give an exact account of the results he had obtained by using machines to deal with nature; and his thinking had to show a reasonably civic face from the start. But Scientific Societies are traditionalist, and in the following generation a third condition was added: new theories had to agree with those of defunct colleagues. As the years passed the web tightened: shrouded reasons secretly resisted too personal an undertaking. Then came a critic who brought them to light; the first contradiction tumbled the whole scaffolding down. It was the dead Descartes who convicted Newton of error and not the sun, which unlike men gave no thought to the emission of very small particles or very swift waves.

In more than one case, undoubtedly, the new arrival overthrew his predecessors' claims. This was, it was said, because he had found a new and irreducible fact. But this brings us back to machines; because this fact, as I said, is manufactured by them. Now the scientist can always choose between a theoretical claim and machines; but it is precisely the latter he always chooses, because they are what is most traditional in science. Underneath its official motto, "Save the phenomena," I detect the secret formula, "Save the instruments." This is where the power of Science lies; for it is not in such and such a statement whose author still could be discovered that scientists have placed their trust, but in the most obscure and ancient underpinnings, in procedures, measures, and concepts which are so much a part of science they have become invisible, in short, in what is essential—that which was invented by no man. Everything they reject, in the last analysis, is the work of those men who are not sufficiently forgetful of themselves, the bad citizens.

Thus they kept in check their jealous and furious powers of approbation—pride, anger, blind and violent partiality, injustice—everything which makes adherence an obscene and joyous bacchanal, everything which conditions powerful thinking, including, alas, love. The common herd, the herd alone conjectured to themselves in a dull murmur, and the only way any of them ever considered the thoughts he produced was from the other person's point of view.

The City took care of its orphaned girls, bringing them up with its own pure hands. There isn't anyone who hasn't had a chance to see them regularly, passing row on row through the streets in the disagreeable splendor of their beauty. Everyone who saw them stopped respectfully, letting his eyes wander over their somber uniforms without being able to focus on a single face. But no one ever bent over them tenderly, thinking, "This is my child."

Here I stop. A vast and leaden peace rules over the world, the one that conquering people know how to establish. All is calm. The natives of the distant seas send amber and crimson in tribute. The dry and the moist, the hot and the cold, without distinction pay the tax of Truth. The soldiers and the scientists have no other way of amusing themselves than to seek refinements on the frontiers, the soldiers provoking riots to be able to put them down, the scientists chasing dissident atoms with a green net. The city grows bored amidst its conquests, its glassy eye on that immense and multicolored earth it had twice been able to reduce.

The reader smiles: "You're telling us about child's play in a far-off time. But simple-minded fundamentalists have had their day. Concerning this very subject of scientific truths, everyone today, I'll tell you, has opinions of his own. What you ought to do is sing the praise of progress and the great advancement from the ancient barbarism to our own enlightened age."

I shall. I shall speak of the birth of the probable, truer than the true, with its cortege of philosophers. I shall sing the praises of this late-born son of Truth and Boredom.

But that will be a legend for the grown-ups.

Motion Picture Art

THUMB through the recollections of some contemporary or recently deceased writer, you will surely find a long and fond account of his first contact with the theater. "One whole day long I lived perturbed by fear and hope, consumed by fever, waiting for that unheard-of bliss which just one blow might suddenly destroy. . . . The day the play was due to be performed, I thought the sun would never set. Dinner (of which I swallowed not one mouthful) seemed endless, and I was in mortal terror of getting there late. . . . Finally we did arrive; the usher showed us into a red box. . . . The solemnity of the three opening knocks on the stage and the profound silence following them moved me deeply. The raising of the curtain really was for me a journey to another world."

Now those of you who forty years from now will write memoirs of their own will have a hard time finding comparable expectations and equally overwhelming emotions. That is because you have been going to movie houses since you were very small: many of you were already acquainted with motion pictures before you were five, for it is with motion pictures, not the theater, that one starts out today. Some of us perhaps can still remember the first film we saw, but usually these beginnings are lost in the haze of memory.

Thus that solemn initiation to the rites of the theater, that pomp, those three blows which mark not so much the raising of

This speech was given by Sartre to his students at the *lycée* in Le Havre in 1931 and published as "L'Art cinématographique" in a brochure of the school. See also Vol. 1, 31/7.

the curtain as the passage from childhood to adolescence—all that is gone. We hardly dress up to go to the movies; we don't think about going days ahead of time; we go there any time—in the afternoon, the evening, and for some months now in Paris even in the morning. You have no knowledge of that long wait in a half-empty and gradually filling theater, and of that "journey to another world" which Anatole France spoke about. But you push your way brusquely into a darkened house, still uncertain in the darkness, your eye fixed on the flashlight zigzagging in the usher's hand. The orchestra is playing and does not, as one might expect, stop for you. The picture has been on for a long time; the heroes are there, with their hands or legs going, caught in the thick of action. You are shown your seat; you slip in, bumping knees; you plump down in your seat without having the time to take off your coat. You watch the end of the film and then, after a fifteen-minute wait, the beginning. You don't mind: you know the traitor will be punished and the lovers will get married. Then at the precise moment the heroes reassume the positions you found them in, you get up, bump more knees, and go out without looking back, leaving the heroes frozen with their hands or legs going—perhaps eternally.

This is a very familiar art, an art mixed very closely with our daily life. We dash into movie houses, talk, laugh, and eat there. We have no respect for this popular art. It does not deck itself at all in that majesty which half entered into the pleasure our elders took in the art of the theater. It is good-natured and much closer to us.

Are we losers by the change? Should we regret the vanished solemnities?

If it could be shown that the motion picture really is an art, we would on the contrary need only congratulate ourselves on the change in our customs. It seems to me your total disrespect for motion picture art and your offhand way of dealing with it are much more worthwhile than a mixture of frozen admiration, troubled feelings, and sacred awe. You have heard far too often, unfortunately, that our great classical authors were "artists": you mistrust their fine phrases, which are the pretext for a thousand insidious questions. From your dealings with them, bit by bit and in spite of yourself, you do undoubtedly derive a benefit that you will later on appreciate. But it is good that in certain darkened houses which parents and professors know nothing about, you can find an unpretentious art which has not been dinned into your ears, which no one has dreamed of telling you was an art, concerning which, in a word, you have been left in a state of innocence. For this art will penetrate more deeply into you than the others, and it is this art which will gently shape you to love beauty in all its forms.

It remains to be shown that the motion picture really is an art. The same Anatole France whom we have seen so gently moved when he went to the theater was no doubt differently affected by his first encounter with the motion picture. He said, as a matter of fact, "The motion picture materializes the worst ideals of the masses. . . . The end of the world is not in the balance, but the end of civilization is."

These are very big words; we are going to see if they are justified. Someone will tell me that my investigation is inopportune: if by chance I were to persuade you that there are fine motion pictures, just as there are fine epistles by Boileau and fine funeral orations by Bossuet, you would not go to the movies any more. But that doesn't bother me. I know you will not take the things I tell you seriously, because to have you listen till the end of any speech they made you hear would be unprecedented. Perhaps it also seems ironic to discuss the beauty of mute art just when we are being invaded by talking pictures. But we ought not to pay too much attention to them. Pirandello used to say, and not without melancholy, that the motion picture resembles the peacock in the fable. He silently displayed his marvelous plumage, and everyone admired it. The jealous fox persuaded him to sing. He opened his mouth, gave forth with his voice, and uttered the cry you know about. But what Aesop doesn't say, or Pirandello either, is that after this experience the peacock undoubtedly returned without much urging to his muteness. I think the motion picture is in the process of earning the right to be silent.

So I come back to the question: I claim that the motion picture is a new art with its own laws and its own social means, that it cannot be reduced to theater, and that it should serve your cultivation in the same capacity as Greek or philosophy.

To put it briefly, what's new about motion pictures?

You know that each instant depends narrowly upon those which have preceded it; that any given state of the universe is absolutely explained by its anterior states; that there is nothing which is lost, nothing which is in vain; and that the present goes strictly toward the future. You know this because you have been taught it. But if you look within yourself, around yourself, you do not in the slightest feel it. You see movements arising which, like the sudden stirring of a treetop, seem spontaneous. You see others which, like waves upon the sand, are dying out, and in their dying seem to lose their vital force. It seems to you that the past is bound very loosely to the present, and that everything gets old in an aimless, sloppy, groping way.

Now the aim of the arts of movement is to give the irreversibility of time—the knowledge of which we gain from science, but the feeling of which we would be unable to bear if it inwardly accompanied all of our actions—an outward expression, awesome but still beautiful, in things themselves. There is something fatal in melody. The notes composing it crowd in upon and govern one another with a strict necessity. Similarly, our tragedy presents itself as a forced march toward catastrophe. Nothing in it can turn back: each line, each word, sweeps things a little farther on in this race to the abyss. There is no hesitation, no delay, no hollow phrase which gives a bit of rest; all the characters, no matter what they say or do, advance toward their end. Thus these lost voyagers who have set foot in the swamp's quicksand may struggle as much as they wish; each movement sinks them in a little deeper till they disappear completely.

But music is very abstract. Paul Valéry is right to see it as no more than "interchanging forms and movements." And tragedy, although less intellectual, is still very much so: with its five acts and very pronounced lines, it is still a product of reason, like number and all that is discontinuous.

At the movies the forward movement of the action is still inevitable, but it is continuous. There is no stopping point; the picture is all of a piece. Instead of the abstract and interrupted time of tragedy, one would say that here everyday duration, that humdrum duration of our lives, has suddenly thrown back its veils to stand forth in its inhuman necessity. At the same time, the motion picture is of all the arts the closest to the real world: real men live in real landscapes. The *Montagne sacrée* is a real mountain, and the sea in *Finis Terrae* is a real sea. Everything seems natural except that march toward the end which cannot be stopped.

If there were no more in the motion picture than this representation of fatality, a place would still have to be reserved for it among the fine arts. But there is more.

You will recall that imperative rule which still dominates the theater. The romantics relaxed it, but they were not able to get rid of it, because it is, as it were, what constitutes dramatic art. I want to talk about the third unity, the unity of action. If you take it in its broadest sense, it is applicable to all the arts: the artist must deal with his subject, never be diverted by extrinsic temptations, resist the pleasure of enhancing a development by adding useless touches, and never lose sight of his initial plan.

But this rule has a narrower sense which is applicable to the theater alone: in this sense, the action must be single, spare, and stripped of everything that would only add picturesqueness to the plot. In short, it must be a strict succession of moments so closely tied together that each of them alone explains the following—or better yet, a logical deduction from a few principles established from the start.

But the unity found in music is already different: the composer builds several themes into it. He begins by setting them forth independently while arranging imperceptible movements from one to the other. Then he subtly takes his themes up again, develops them, enlarges upon them, and weaves them into one another. And finally, in the last movement, he gives all these motifs a strict foundation by simply echoing some and bringing others to their most perfect fulfillment.

This unity, which could be called "thematic," could not possibly be appropriate to the theater: it was in vain that a German romantic tried to introduce it. A multiplicity of themes would as a matter of fact require, as it did in Jules Romains's *Donogoo*, the use of short quick scenes. Experience has shown that this technique tends to make people tired. Furthermore, no matter how short the scenes which follow one another in this way might be, they would still not be short enough: the effect of contrast and symmetry would often be lost; one could not leap from one to the other, indicate a resemblance, then come back to the first, insist on some characteristic, and so on in order to stress the more subtle correlations.

Now this is just what the motion picture does. The picture's universe is thematic, because skillful editing can always bring the most diverse scenes together and interweave them: we were in the fields and here we are in town; we thought we would stay in town and the next instant we were taken back to the fields. You know how much can be done with this extreme mobility. Think of Abel Gance's *Napoléon* and that stormy convention accompanied and emphasized by a storm on the Mediterranean. A wave swells and rises up, but before it has broken we are already far away on dry land, among the howling deputies. Robespierre gets up, he is about to speak, but we have left him; we are out on the high sea being tossed about in Napoleon's little boat. A brandished fist. A rolling wave. A threatening face. A waterspout. The two themes accentuate each other, expand upon each other, and finally merge together.

Sometimes, by means of what is technically called a "dissolve," the transition from one motif to another is steady, slow, and imperceptible; sometimes, as the need arises, swift and brutal. It is also possible to develop several themes simultaneously by means of the "multiple exposure." But there is another and much more elegant way to achieve this cinematographic polyphony. Suppose you want to unify two different motifs: all you have to do is use them to bring out a situation which is not reducible to either one but symbolizes with the two together. Look what happens in the classic film, *La Rue sans joie*. In it Pabst shows the postwar destitution of the Viennese people and the dissolute debauchery of a few profiteers. These two themes coexist for a long time without intermingling. Finally the two series of paths meet: one of the profiteers is driving along "the street without joy" on the way to a nearby dive where he is going to finish out the night; in that same street a wretched crowd is standing in line in front of the butcher shop. The profiteer's car brushes by these poor people and disappears; the two momentarily united themes reassume their independence. It seems that everything in all of this is natural and necessary—that it is just a meeting. But that is because you have not really seen the picture. The car's headlights sweep slowly over that bleak and shivering crowd, making hate-filled faces stand out, one by one, from the shadows. That blinding light, these blinking eyes, these squat and worn-out bodies, that powerful, sumptuous car, these gaping shadows; all of this, no doubt, is fated, but in a certain respect it has a stamp all its own: before it fades out, the episode throws a quick, sharp light on the whole picture.

Do not think that these situations, produced by a necessary chain of events yet nevertheless ambiguous and packed with meaning, are rare in motion pictures. On the contrary, motion pictures are what you might call their natural habitat. You'll find throngs of "sign-bearing" objects there, humble utensils on which a theme piled and rolled up onto itself is written in short-hand.

So go admire this supple yet unbending chain of images, this subtle knot wound through events packed full of meaning and determined by both mind and nature, this scattering of actions which makes room, all of a sudden, for striking and soon-broken unions, brief and fleeting flash backs, deep and hidden correspondences between each object and the rest—for such is the world of motion pictures. To be sure, pictures that stay unfailingly at this level are rare; but you will see no pictures that are completely lacking in beauty.

Now I say that you can find your way around this new world very well: you have acquired a certain ability to find your bearings in the mazes of its plots, its symbols, and its rhythms. I have seen cultured men who got lost in them because they had not been going to movie houses. But you who almost live in them, even though you may not be able yet to express your impressions or ideas, are completely at ease there: nothing escapes you; nothing fools you.

Your parents may rest assured; the motion picture is not a bad school. It is an art which seems easy but is really extremely hard and, if it is approached in the right way, very profitable; because by its nature it reflects civilization in our time. Who will teach you about the beauty of the world you live in, the poetry of speed, machines, and the inhuman and splendid inevitability of industry? Who, if not your art, the motion picture . . .

Foods

In Naples I discovered love's vile relationship to Food. Not right away. Naples doesn't show itself at first. It's a town which is ashamed of itself; it tries to make outsiders think that it is peopled by casinos, palaces, and villas. I came in by sea one morning in September, and the town greeted me from afar with dusty lightning flashes. I spent the whole day walking around in its straight, broad streets—the Via Umberto, the Via Garibaldi—and I did not know enough to see the suspect wounds that festered, underneath their scented lotions, in their sides.

By the end of the day I was flopped down at a table outside the Café Gambrinus, in front of an iced drink which I was mournfully watching melt in its glazed cup. I was rather discouraged; all I had gathered in my wanderings were tiny little multicolored facts, confetti. I asked myself: "*Am* I in Naples? Does Naples exist?" I have known towns like that—Milan, for example—false towns which crumble as soon as you enter them. Maybe Naples was only a name given to thousands of ground-level shimmerings, thousands of gleams in thousands of shop-windows, thousands of lonely pedestrians and wind-borne hummings. I turned my head; on my left I saw the Via Roma opening up like a dark armpit. I got up and went in between its high walls. Another disappointment: this vaguely obscene warm shadow was nothing but a hazy curtain one could walk across in fifteen steps. On the other side, I found a long antiseptic passageway which bathed me in its milky light in offering me the

This fragment of a story was published as "Nourritures" in *Verve*, November 15, 1938. See also Vol. 1, 38/20.

splendor of its grocers' shops full of prosciutto, mortadella, and all different kinds of sausages, its neon signs, and the beautiful garlands of lemons the soft drink sellers hang from the tops of their stands. A current carried me away, swept me back up this dazzling boulevard; I rubbed elbows with men dressed in white duck, teeth brushed, eyes bright and tired. I looked at them and, on my left, at their foods flaming up in the shopwindows. I said to myself, "This is what they eat!" It suited them so well: they were clean foods—more than clean, chaste. This prosciutto was muslin; one would have said that this scarlet tongue was sumptuous velvet: these people, who concealed their bodies under brightly colored clothing, lived on dress materials and wallpapers. Glass breadwork too: I stopped in front of the Caflish Pastry Shop; it looked like a jewelry store. Ordinarily, cakes are human; they look like faces. Spanish cakes are ascetic with a swaggering air; they crumble to bits when you bite into them. Greek cakes are greasy like little oil lamps; when you press them, the oil drips out. German cakes have the fat suavity of shaving cream; they are made in order that obese and loving men may eat them with abandon, without savoring their taste, just to fill their mouths with sweetness. But these Italian cakes had a cruel perfection: tiny, very clean—scarcely bigger than teacakes—they gleamed red. Their harsh and gaudy colors took away all desire to eat them; one wanted instead to put them on console tables like painted china. I said to myself, "That does it! Well, the only thing left to do is to go to the movies."

It was then that I discovered, twenty yards from the Caflish Pastry Shop, one of the countless sores of this pock-marked town, a fistula, an alley. I went up and the first thing that I saw, in the middle of a gutter, was another food. Or rather, feed: a slice of watermelon (I still remembered the gaping Roman watermelons, which looked like raspberry and pistachio ice cream dotted with coffee beans) spotted with mud, which was buzzing with flies like rotting flesh and bleeding underneath the dying rays of sun. A child on crutches came up to this rotten meat, took it in his hands, and began to eat it with gusto. Then I thought I saw what the merchants on the Via Roma were hiding behind their alimentary goldsmith's shops: the *truth* about food.

I bore left, then right, then right again; all the alleys were alike. No one paid any attention to me; I was only rarely met from time to time by a blank look. The men did not speak; the women exchanged a few words at long intervals. They gathered together in tight little knots of five or six, and the rags they wore made bright spots on the sooty walls. I had been struck since morning by the Neapolitans' pale color; but now I was no longer astonished: they braised their meat in the shade. The women's flesh especially looked boiled to pieces underneath the dirt. The alley had digested their cheeks: they still clung to their bones, but one could have torn chunks out of them with one's fingers. I was relieved to see a girl's fat mustachioed lips: at least they seemed raw. All of these people seemed to be withdrawn into themselves and not even dreaming: surrounded by their foods—living scraps of meat, fish scales, cabbage stumps, obscene meats, fruits sliced open and soiled—they enjoyed their organic life with sensual indolence. Children clambered over furniture, displaying their bare behinds alongside the fish guts; or else they pulled themselves up the stairway to the upstairs rooms on their stomachs, waving their arms as if they were swimming, scraping their little trembling penises across the stones. I felt digested too: it began with an urge to vomit, a very sweet and sugary one, and then went down into my whole body like a queer tickling. I looked at these meats, all these meats, those which were bleeding, those which were bloodless, the naked arm of an old blind man, the reddish rag which still stuck to a white bone, and it seemed to me there was *something* to be done with it. But what? Eat it? Caress it? Vomit it? At the corner of an alley someone lit an arch of lights which lighted up a Virgin in her niche—a Black Virgin carrying Jesus in her arms. "Is it nighttime?" I raised my head. Above the buildings, above the clothes hanging like dead skins from the windows, very far away and very high I saw the sky still blue.

At the bottom of a hole in the wall there was a shape in a bed. It was a young woman, a sick woman. She was suffering; she turned her head toward the street—her throat made a tender spot above the sheets. I stopped; I looked at her for a long time; I would have liked to run my hands over her skinny neck —I shook myself and strode rapidly away. But it was too late; I was trapped. I no longer saw a thing but flesh: wretched flowers of flesh waving in blue darkness; flesh to palpate, suck, and eat; wet flesh soaked with sweat, urine, milk. Suddenly a man knelt down next to a little girl and looked at her, laughing. She was laughing too and said, "Daddy; my daddy." Then, lifting up the child's dress a little, the man bit into her grey buttocks the way he would a loaf of bread. I smiled: no gesture had ever seemed to me to be so natural, so *necessary*. At this same hour my white-clothed brothers on the Via Roma were buying varnished knickknacks for their dinner. "That's it," I thought; "That's it!" I felt myself falling down into an enormous carnivorous existence; a dirty, pink existence clotting over me. "That's it: I *am* in Naples."

Official Portraits

"I SAW A FAT, WAXEN MAN in a *calèche* being carried away by four horses at a gallop." This sentence, whose author I no longer know, gives a pretty good picture of naïve understanding. What first comes before our eyes is the man, with his bilious fat. He appears in the midst of other men, dignitaries and field marshals; and when we are finally given his right name, he has already disappeared, carried away by his four horses. "*They say* it was Napoleon; it *seems* it was. That I saw the emperor will never be any more than *probable*. But I am *certain* that I saw the man, that wan and yellow flesh." Similarly, Bonaparte's supreme dignity as first consul or emperor was no more than probable for Bonaparte himself. He was not Napoleon at all, but only someone who believed he was Napoleon. And at great cost to his imagination: it is hard work for an important person to reassure himself ceaselessly of his own rights and importance when the mirrors show him the all-too-human insipidity of his own reflection, and when all he finds within himself are confused, melancholy moods. That is why there must be official portraits; they relieve the prince of the burden of thinking about his divine right. Napoleon does not exist and never did exist anywhere except in portraits. This is because the commissioned painter, working in the opposite direction from naïve understanding, goes from knowledge to the object. The man gawking from the sidewalk sees a fat man and thinks, "It

This piece was published anonymously as "Portraits officiels" in a special issue of *Verve* in 1939. See also Vol. 1, 39/28.

looks like Napoleon." But if he looks at the portrait, what he sees first is the first consul or the emperor.

We find sufficient evidence of this in the way painters pile up marks of power around Francis I and Louis XIV. Royalty is what first meets our eye. If we take the time to set aside the hangings and the symbols, we shall (already duly warned and made respectful) discover that little head lying naked at the bottom of its shell, the face. And not so naked at that: a king's face is always dressed. This is because the official portrait aims to justify. It is a matter of suggesting by means of an image that the ruler has the right to rule. Thus it would be out of the question to remember the moving and humiliating countenance of a man crushed by the burden of his office: what is painted is never *fact* but always pure Right. The official portrait doesn't want to have anything to do with weakness or strength; it is only concerned with merit. Because it does not want to show strength—which always offends a little even if it does not terrify—it hides the body as much as it can. Observe the sumptuousness of the materials hiding the limbs of Charles the Bald and Francis I. Do they have bodies? At the end of these materials we see hands, beautiful and anonymous hands, symbols, too, just like the gilded hand on the scepter. But because the painter does not wish to reveal any weakness either, he discreetly trims the flesh of the faces until he has reduced it to simply an *idea* of flesh. Are the cheeks of Francis I cheeks? No; they are the pure concept of cheeks. Cheeks betray kings and are to be mistrusted. With these reservations, the artist will, since he has to, concern himself with the likeness. But here again this likeness must not go too far. This nose of Francis I was long and drooping. And it looks that way in the portrait— only disembodied. In reality it dragged down all the features of his face. In the picture it is carefully detached from the countenance, saying nothing for the face as a whole; it no more disturbs the appearance of the head than it would if it were aquiline. This is because real expressions—trickery, hounded uneasiness, and baseness—have no place in these portraits. Even before the painter has met his model, he already knows what sort of air he must perpetuate on canvas: calm force, serenity, severity, justice. Must the portrait never reassure, persuade, intimidate? The common run of nice people want to be sheltered from naïve impressions, which lead by their very nature to disrespect; nice people are never willingly irreverent. The official portrait functions, furthermore, to produce unity between the prince and his subjects. You will have seen by now that the official portrait, which defends man against himself, is a religious object. That tyrant who hung his effigy from a pole in the main square and ordered that everyone bow down to it was not stupid. On top of a pole like a totem: there's the place for ceremonial paintings. After that, there may be no great need to look at them.

Faces

LIFE IN A SOCIETY OF STATUES would be unrelieved boredom, but it would be in accord with justice and reason. Statues are faceless bodies, blind and deaf bodies, without fear or anger, concerned only with obeying the laws of the just, that is, of equilibrium and motion. They have the regalness of Doric columns, their heads the capitals. In human societies, faces rule. The body is a bondsman. It is wrapped up, disguised. Its role, like a mule's, is to carry a waxen relic around. A body like this bearing its precious burden into a closed hall where men are gathered together is a real procession. It comes forward, bearing on its shoulders, at the end of its neck, the tabooed object. It turns it from one side to the other, displaying it. The other men cast a furtive glance at it and lower their eyes. A woman follows it, her face an erotic altar piled high with dead victims, fruits, flowers, slaughtered birds. On her cheeks, her lips, red markings have been painted. A society of faces, a society of sorcerers. To understand war and injustice and our dark ardors and sadism and history's great terrors, we must go back to these round idols which are paraded through the streets on enslaved bodies or in times of wrath, atop pikestaffs.

This is what psychologists deny: they are only at ease among inert things, and they have made a mechanism of man and an articulate nutcracker of the human face. Besides, they have proved their claims, because they have invented the electric smile. All you have to do is select an unemployed man of

This essay was published as "Visages" in a special issue of *Verve* in 1939. See also Vol. 1, 39/27.

good will or, better yet, a madman hospitalized free of charge in an asylum. Then you delicately stimulate his facial nerve with a low-voltage current; the commissure of his lips rises slightly, the patient smiles. All this is undeniable (there are reports of experiments, calculations, and photographs); and it is thus a proven fact that the play of facial movements is the sum of a series of little mechanical muscle jerks. We still have to explain why the human face moves us so, but this is self-explanatory. According to the psychologists, you have gradually learned to take the signs in and interpret them. You know another person's face by comparison with your own. You have often observed that in anger, for example, you contract the muscles of your eyebrows and the blood rushes to your cheeks. When you find another person with these wrinkled eyebrows and these burning cheeks, you conclude that he is irritated—and that's all there is to it.

The trouble is that I don't see my face—or at least not at first. I carry it in front of me like a secret I am unaware of, and it is, on the contrary, the faces of others which teach me about my own. And then the human face cannot be broken down into its elements. Look at this furious man calming himself; his lips soften, and a smile glows heavy like a drop of water at the bottom of this somber face. Will you speak of local disturbances? Will you dream of adding them up? Only the lips moved, but the whole face smiled. And then anger and joy are not invisible mental events I assume to exist only on the basis of the visible signs of them; they dwell in the face as this red-green dwells in the foliage. To perceive the green of foliage or the sadness of a bitter mouth, no preliminary learning is needed. To be sure, a face is *also* a thing. I can take it in my hands, hold up the warm and heavy weight of a head I love. I can rumple up cheeks like material, pluck off lips like petals, break a skull like an Oriental vase. But it is not merely or even *primarily* a thing. We call "magical" those inert objects—bones, skulls, statuettes, rabbits' feet—which are deep in the rut of their dumb ordinariness and yet possess spiritual properties. Faces are like this: natural fetishes. I am going to try to describe them as absolutely new beings by pretending that I know nothing about them, not even that they belong to souls. I beg you not to take the following considerations for metaphors. I am simply saying what I see.

The face, the outer limit of the human body, must be understood in terms of the body. One thing it has in common with the body is that all its movements are gestures. What this means is that the face creates its own time within universal time. Universal time is made of a linear sequence of instants; it is the time of the metronome, the hourglass, the nail, the billiard ball. We know very well that the billiard ball floats in a perpetual present, its future is external to it and diluted throughout the whole world, its present motion flares out into a thousand other possible displacements. If the cloth wrinkles or the table tips, its velocity will decrease or increase accordingly. I do not even know whether it will ever stop; the end of its motion will be imposed upon it from without, or perhaps it will not be imposed. All of this I see in the billiard ball: I do not see that *it* rolls, I see that it *is rolled*. Rolled by what? By nothing: the motions of inert things are curious mixtures of nothingness and eternity. The time of living bodies stands out against this ground because it is oriented. And once again I do not presuppose this orientation; I see it. The hole of a rat who scampers or runs toward it is the end—the goal and ultimate stopping-point—of his gesture. When I see a running rat or an arm being raised, I know at once where it is going; or at least I know that it is going somewhere. Somewhere, empty and expectant spaces are being hollowed out; around them space is being peopled with expectations, with natural places, and each of these places is a stop, a rest, a journey's end. And so it is with faces. I am alone in a closed room, drowned in the present. My future is invisible; I vaguely imagine it beyond the armchairs, the table, the walls— all these sinister indolences which hide it from me. Someone comes in, bringing me his face; all these things change. Among these slow stalactites of the present, this darting, prying face is always out ahead of my own glance; it hurries toward a thousand particular conclusions, toward the furtive stealing of a glance, the end of a smile. If I want to make it out, I have to lead it, aim at it there where it is not yet, as a hunter does with very swift game. I must set myself up in the future too, right in the middle of its projects, if I want to see it come out to me from the ground of the present. A bit of future has come into the room; a haze of future surrounds the face—*its* future. A tiny little haze, just enough to fill the hollow of my hands. But I can only see men's faces through their future. And that, the *visible* future, is already magic.

But the face is not simply the upper part of the body. A body is a closed form; it soaks up the universe as a blotter soaks up ink. Heat, humidity, and light filter in through the interstices of this pink, porous matter; the whole world passes through the body and impregnates it. Now observe this face with its eyes closed. It is still corporeal yet already different from a belly or a thigh; it has something more, voracity; it is full of greedy holes which suck up everything that comes within reach. Sounds come lapping into the ears and the ears swallow them up; odors fill the nostrils like wads of cotton. A face without eyes is a singular animal, one of those animals encrusted on the hull of ships which stir the water with their legs to draw bits of floating rubbish toward them. But now the eyes are opening and the gaze appears. Things leap backward; behind the sheltering gaze, ears, nostrils—all the vile openings of the head—keep on slyly munching odors and sounds, but no one notices. The gaze is the nobility of faces because it holds the world at a distance and perceives things where they are.

Here is an ivory ball on the table and then, over there, an armchair. There are a thousand equally possible paths between these two inert things, which comes down to saying that there is no path at all, but simply a random distribution of an infinite number of inert things. If I decide to join the ball and chair by a path I trace in the air with my fingertip, the path beads off to bits behind my moving finger: a path exists only in motion. When I now consider these two other balls, my friend's eyes, I immediately notice that there are similarly a thousand possible paths between them and the armchair: this means that my friend is not looking; in relation to the armchair his eyes are still things. But now the two balls are turning in their sockets, the eyes are becoming a gaze. A path is suddenly cleared in the room, a *motionless* path, the shortest, swiftest, and straightest one. The armchair, without leaving its place, is immediately present to these eyes across a heap of inert masses. Even when this presence to the gaze-eyes is twenty steps away from the thing-eyes, I perceive it *in* the armchair as a profound change in its nature. A while ago puffs, couches, sofas, and divans were spread out in a circle around me. Now the living room has lost its focus. According to the wishes of these alien eyes, the furniture and odds and ends in turn are quickened by a centrifugal, immobile swiftness. They are emptied out in back and on the sides. They are relieved of qualities that I never even suspected they had, that I shall never see, and that I know were there within them, dense, piled up, weighting them down, and waiting for another person's glance in order to be born. I begin to understand that my friend's *head,* warm and pink against the back of the easy chair, is not all of his *face;* it is only its nucleus. His face is the furniture's congealed slippage; his face is everywhere; it exists as far as his gaze can carry. And when in turn I contemplate his eyes, I see clearly that they are not stuck over there in this head, as calm as agates. They are created at each instant by what they are looking at; their sense and their conclusion lie beyond them—behind me, above my head, or at my feet. This is the source of the magic charm of old portraits. These faces Nadar photographed around 1860 are long dead. But their gaze remains, and so does the world of the Second Empire, which is eternally present at the end of their gaze.

I may now conclude, because I only intended to deal with the essential. We discover, among things, certain beings we call faces. But they do not exist like things. Things have no future, and the future surrounds the face like a cap. Things are thrown into the world, the world squeezes and crushes them, but for them it is not world at all but only the absurd shove of the nearest masses. The gaze, on the contrary, because it perceives at a distance, suddenly makes the universe appear, and thereby escapes the universe. Things are piled up in the present, shivering but never budging from their place; the face projects itself ahead of itself in space and time. If we call "transcendence" the mind's property of going beyond itself and all things—of breaking free from itself in order to go lose itself outside itself, no matter where but elsewhere—then the meaning of a face is to be *visible* transcendence. Everything else is of secondary importance. Too much flesh may clog up that transcendence. It may happen too that the mechanisms of the ruminating senses prevail over the gaze, and that we are first attracted by the cartilaginous ridges or the moist and hairy openings of the nostrils; and then a model may intervene and fashion the head according to its pointed, round, drooping, or swollen character. But there is no trait of the face which does not first receive its meaning from that primitive witchcraft we have called "transcendence."

Bariona, or the Son of Thunder

*The fact that I took my subject
from Christian mythology does not
mean that the drift of my thinking
changed, even for a moment, during my captivity. All I did was
work with the priests who were my
fellow prisoners to find a subject
which could bring about, on that
Christmas Eve, the broadest possible union of Christians and un-
believers.*

J.-P. Sartre
October 31, 1962

PROLOGUE

A snatch of harmonica music.

THE SHOWMAN: Good people, I am going to tell you about the
strange and wonderful adventures of Bariona, the Son of
Thunder. This story takes place in the days when the Romans
were masters of Judea, and I hope that it will interest you.
While I am telling you the story, you may look at the pictures
behind me: they will help you see things the way they really
were. And if you like my story, pray be generous. Now let the
music play! We're going to begin!

Bariona, ou le fils du tonnerre, Sartre's first play, was written
while he was a prisoner of war in Stalag XII D at Trèves in 1940;
it was performed there by Sartre and his fellow prisoners on Christmas Day of that year. A limited edition was produced by Atelier
Anjou-copies in 1962. As the text has undoubtedly been transcribed
many times, its precision cannot be guaranteed. See also Vol. 1,
62/368.

Harmonica.

Good people, here's the prologue. As the result of an accident, I am blind; but before I lost my sight I gazed a thousand times at these same pictures you'll be looking at, and I know them all by heart because my father was a showman like me and he left me these as my inheritance. This one that you see behind me, the one I am pointing at with my cane, I know is a picture of Mary of Nazareth. An angel has just told her she will have a son who will be Jesus, our Savior.

The angel is immense, with two wings like rainbows. You can see him. I can't see him any more myself, but in my mind I'm still looking at him. He has come sweeping down like a flood on Mary's humble dwelling and is now filling it with his flowing, sacred body and his great floating robe. If you look closely at the scene, you will notice that we can see the furniture in the room right through the angel's body. This was meant to show us his angelic transparency. He is standing in front of Mary, and Mary is hardly looking at him. She is thinking. He didn't have to speak to her in a voice like thunder. Before he had even said a word she sensed it in her flesh. Now the angel is standing in front of Mary, and Mary is numberless and dark like trees in forests in the night, and the good news has gotten lost in her the way a traveler goes astray in the woods. And Mary is full of birds and the leaves' slow rustlings. And a thousand wordless thoughts are wakening inside her, the heavy thoughts of women feeling all the burden of the flesh. And behold, the angel seems abashed at these too human thoughts. He's sorry he's an angel because angels can neither be born nor suffer. And this Annunciation morning, dawning here before an angel's wondering eyes, is the holy day of man, because it is man's turn to be sacred. Watch the picture closely, good people, and let the music play. My prologue is over. The story begins nine months later, December 24, in the mountains of Judea.

Music. New picture.

THE NARRATOR: Now here are some rocks and here's a donkey. The picture shows a very wild mountain trail. The man riding along on donkeyback is a Roman official. He's big and fat, but he's in a foul mood. Nine months have passed since the Annunciation, and the Roman is hurrying through the hollows because night is going to fall and he wants to get to Bethaur before it does. Bethaur is a little town of eight hundred souls located twenty-five leagues from Bethlehem and seven leagues from Hebron. Those of you who know how to read can find it on a map when you get back home. Now you are going to see what this official is up to, for he has just reached Bethaur and entered the house of Levy the Publican.

The curtain rises.

FIRST TABLEAU
At Levy the Publican's.

SCENE I
LELIUS, THE PUBLICAN

LELIUS (*bowing toward the door*): My compliments, Madame. My dear fellow, your wife is charming. Hm! But come, we must think of more serious matters. Please sit down. No, no; I insist; sit down and we shall talk. I have come here for this census.

THE PUBLICAN: Look out, Mister Resident in Chief, look out!

He takes off his slipper and whacks the floor.

LELIUS: What was it? A tarantula?

THE PUBLICAN: A tarantula. But this time of year the cold numbs them quite a bit. That one was dragging along half-asleep.

LELIUS: Lovely. And you have scorpions too, of course. Scorpions who are just as drowsy and who will kill a hundred-and-eighty-pound man on the spot while they are yawning with sleep. The cold in your mountains can benumb a Roman citizen but it cannot manage to make your nasty little beasts die. The young people in Rome getting ready to work in the colonies ought to be forewarned that the life of a colonial administrator is a damned torment.

THE PUBLICAN: Oh come now, Mister Resident in Chief!

LELIUS: I said a damned torment, my dear fellow. For two days now I've been wandering across these mountains on mule-back, and I haven't seen a single human being; not even a plant—or a weed even. Big chunks of red stone beneath this pitiless ice-blue sky, and then this cold, always this cold weighing down on me like a stone, and after miles and miles a little chickenshit village like this one. Brrr! It's cold! Even here in your house. Of course you Jews don't know how to keep yourselves warm. Every year you get surprised by winter just as if it were the first one you had ever seen. You're real savages.

THE PUBLICAN: Could I offer you a spot of brandy just to warm you up?

LELIUS: Some brandy? Hm. I want you to know that the colonial administration is very strict: we're not allowed to accept anything from our subordinates when we're on an inspection tour. Come, I shall have to stay overnight in town. I shall leave for Hebron day after tomorrow. Of course there is no inn?

THE PUBLICAN: The village is very poor, Mister Resident in Chief; no one ever comes here. But if I could be so bold . . .

LELIUS: You would offer me a bed in your home? My poor fellow, you're very kind, but it's the same old story: we are forbidden to sleep at our subordinates' when we're on an inspection tour. What else can you expect? Our regulations were drawn up by bureaucrats who have never left Italy and do not have even the slightest idea of what colonial life is like. Where am I to sleep? Out in the open? In a stable? That isn't in accordance with the dignity of a Roman official either.

THE PUBLICAN: May I take the liberty of insisting?

LELIUS: That's it, my friend. Insist, insist. Perhaps I shall end up giving in to your solicitations. What you mean, if I understand you correctly, is that your dwelling is the only one in the village capable of aspiring to the honor of harboring the representative of Rome? Rrright . . . Oh. Well, after all I'm not exactly on a tour of inspection . . . My dear fellow, I'll sleep at your house tonight.

THE PUBLICAN: How can I ever thank you for the honor you are doing me? I am deeply moved . . .

LELIUS: I believe it, my friend; I believe it. But don't go shouting it from the rooftops: you would hurt yourself as much as me.

THE PUBLICAN: I won't breathe a word to anyone.

LELIUS: Perfect. (*He stretches out his legs.*) Whew! Am I worn out! I've inspected fifteen villages. Listen, you were speaking to me a little while ago about some brandy . . .

THE PUBLICAN: Here it is.

LELIUS: I must drink some of it, by Jove! Since you are offering me a place to sleep, it is only proper that you should also give me food and drink. Excellent brandy. It deserves to be Roman.

THE PUBLICAN: Thank you, Mister Resident in Chief.

LELIUS: Ahh . . . My dear fellow, this census is an impossible business, and I can't imagine what Alexandrian courtier managed to give divine Caesar the idea. All we have to do is take a census of every man on earth. Of course the idea is impressive. And then—go check it out for yourself in Palestine— most of your fellow believers do not even know their birthdate. They were born the year of the great flood, the great harvest, the great storm. Real savages. I'm not hurting your feelings, am I? You're a cultured man even if you are a Jew.

THE PUBLICAN: I had the very great advantage of studying in Rome.

LELIUS: Excellent! It shows in your manners. But look; you people are Orientals. Do you see the difference? You'll never be rationalists; you're a people of witch doctors. In this respect your prophets did you a lot of harm: they got you used to being satisfied with the lazy man's way out—the messiah, the one who shall come and set all things right, who with the flick of a finger shall overthrow the Roman domination of the world and then replace it with your own. And you people eat messiahs up . . . A new one pops up every week, and in one week you get tired of him the same way we Romans tire of pop singers or gladiators. The last messiah they brought before me was an albino and half-way idiotic, but he prophesied dark times just like all the rest. The people of Hebron never got over it. Do you want to know the truth? The Jewish people are still children.

THE PUBLICAN: You're right, Mister Resident in Chief; it would be good if many of our students could go to Rome.

LELIUS: Yes. That would give us the cadres we need. But mind you, the government in Rome, if it were consulted beforehand, would not look unfavorably on the selection of an appropriate messiah. For example, one who came from an old Jewish family, had studied in our country, and would offer guarantees of his respectability. We might even—this is just between the two of us, right?—underwrite the business ourselves, because we're beginning to get tired of Herod, and then in the interest of the Jewish people themselves we want them just for once to straighten themselves out. A real messiah, a man who would show he had a realistic grasp of the Judean situation, would help us.

Hm . . . Brrr . . . brrr . . . It's really cold in your place. Tell me, have you summoned the head of the village?

THE PUBLICAN: Yes, Mister Resident in Chief. He'll be here in a minute.

LELIUS: He has to take charge of this census business; he should be able to bring me the rolls by tomorrow evening.

THE PUBLICAN: Yes sir.

LELIUS: How many are you?

THE PUBLICAN: Around eight hundred.

LELIUS: Is the village rich?

THE PUBLICAN: Unfortunately . . .

LELIUS: Aha!

THE PUBLICAN: One wonders how the people are able to live. There are only a few skimpy pastures, and you have to walk seven or eight miles to get to them. That's all there is. The village is slowly losing its people. Each year five or six of our young people go down to Bethlehem to live. There are already more old people than young ones. Especially because the birthrate is low.

LELIUS: What else can you expect? You can't blame the ones who go into town to live. Our colonials have set up fine factories in Bethlehem. Maybe this is the way you'll come to see the light. A technical civilization, you see what I mean? Well? Listen: I didn't come here just to take a census. What do you rake in here in taxes?

THE PUBLICAN: Well, there are two hundred people on welfare who bring in nothing, and the others pay ten drachmas. Let's say, taking the bad with the good, 5,500 drachmas. A pittance.

LELIUS: Right. Hm! Well, from now on you'll have to try to get eight thousand out of them. The procurator is raising the head tax to fifteen drachmas.

THE PUBLICAN: Fifteen drachmas! It's . . . It's impossible!

LELIUS: Ah, there's a word I'll bet you seldom heard when you were in Rome. Come on, they must have more money than they're willing to admit. And then . . . Hm! You know the government doesn't want to poke its nose in the publicans' business, but still I don't think you'd be any worse off if you did what I say. Right?

THE PUBLICAN: I'm not saying . . . I'm not saying . . . Did you say sixteen drachmas?

LELIUS: Fifteen.

THE PUBLICAN: Yes, but the sixteenth is for my expenses.

LELIUS: Mm . . . Ah . . . (*He laughs.*) This village chief . . . What sort of man is he? . . . His name is Bariona, isn't it?

THE PUBLICAN: Yes; Bariona.

LELIUS: It's a touchy situation. Very touchy. They made a big mistake in Bethlehem. His brother-in-law lived there, there was some kind of complicated business about robbery, and then the Jewish tribunal finally condemned him to death.

THE PUBLICAN: I know. He was crucified. The news reached us about a month ago.

LELIUS: Right. Hm . . . And how did the chief take it?

THE PUBLICAN: He didn't say a thing.

LELIUS: Right. Bad. That's very bad . . . Ah, that's a bad mistake. O.K. Well, what kind of guy is this Bariona?

THE PUBLICAN: Hard to deal with.

LELIUS: Petty feudal chieftain stock. I was afraid of that. These mountaineers are as uncultivated as their rocky land. Is he getting money from us?

THE PUBLICAN: He doesn't want to take anything from Rome.

LELIUS: Too bad. Ah, this doesn't look good. He doesn't like us, I suppose?

THE PUBLICAN: We don't know. He doesn't say anything.

LELIUS: Married? Children?

THE PUBLICAN: He would like some, they say; but he doesn't have any. It's his greatest sorrow.

LELIUS: That's no good! No good at all. There must be a weak point somewhere . . . Women? Honors? No? Well, we'll see.

THE PUBLICAN: There he is . . .

LELIUS: This is going to be tough.

Enter Bariona.

THE PUBLICAN: Good day, my lord.

BARIONA: Get out of here, you pig! You stink up the air you breathe. I don't even want to be in the same room with you. (*The publican leaves.*) My regards, Mister Resident in Chief.

SCENE II

LELIUS, BARIONA

LELIUS: I salute you, great leader, and I bring you the salutations of the procurator.

BARIONA: I am all the more appreciative of this respect as I am wholly unworthy of it. I am a man disgraced, just now, the head of a family that's run dry.

LELIUS: Are you talking about that deplorable business? The procurator has especially instructed me to tell you how much he regretted the Jewish tribunal's severity.

BARIONA: I beg you to tell the procurator that I thank him for his gracious solicitude. It refreshes and surprises me like a salutary downpour in the torrid heart of summer. Knowing that the procurator is all-powerful, and seeing that he allowed the Jews to make such an arrest, I had thought that he approved of what they were doing.

LELIUS: Well, you were wrong. You were all wrong about the whole thing. We tried to get the Jewish tribunal to be merciful, but what could we do? It was adamant, and we deplored its untimely zeal. Do what we did, chief: harden your heart and give up your resentment in the interests of Palestine. Persuade yourself that she has no greater interest—even if it has to involve certain disagreeable consequences for some—than to preserve her traditions and her local administration.

BARIONA: I'm only a village chief, and you must excuse me if I'm no good at your politics. My reasoning is surely more simple-minded. I tell myself that I served Rome faithfully and Rome can do anything. So I must have fallen from its favor for it to let my enemies in town wrong me that way. For a while I thought I could anticipate what it wanted by giving up all my powers. But my fellow villagers, who still had confidence in me themselves, begged me to stay on as their leader.

LELIUS: And you accepted? Good for you. You saw that a chief has to put public affairs ahead of personal grudges.

BARIONA: I bear no grudge against Rome.

LELIUS: Excellent. Excellent. Excellent. Ahem! The interest of your country, chief, lies in letting itself be led in easy stages toward its independence by the firm, benevolent hand of Rome.

Would you like me to give you an immediate opportunity to prove to the procurator that your friendship for Rome is as strong as ever?

BARIONA: I'm listening.

LELIUS: Rome is involved, against its wishes, in a long and difficult war. It would appreciate an extraordinary contribution from Judea, not so much as an aid to defraying the costs of this war as an expression of her solidarity.

BARIONA: You want to increase taxes?

LELIUS: Rome finds that it must.

BARIONA: The head tax?

LELIUS: Yes.

BARIONA: We can't pay any more.

LELIUS: We're only asking you to pay a little more. The procurator has raised the head tax to sixteen drachmas.

BARIONA: Sixteen drachmas! Look here. These old heaps of red mud, chapped, cracked, and furrowed like our hands, are what we live in. They are falling to pieces; they're a hundred years old. Look at that woman going by, bent beneath the weight of her bundle of firewood. Look at that guy with an axe. They're old. They are all old. The village is dying. Have you heard a baby cry since you've been here? There are maybe twenty kids left. Soon they'll leave too. What could keep them here? In order to buy the pitiful plow that the whole village uses, we went into debt up to our ears. The taxes are crushing us. Our shepherds have to walk ten leagues to find patchy little pastures. The village is bleeding. Since your Roman colonists put up those sawmills in Bethlehem, our youngest blood goes flowing out in great gushes, bouncing down like a warm spring from rock to rock to water the lowlands. Our young people are down there, in town. In town, where they're enslaved, paid a starvation wage. In the town that will kill them the way it killed my brother-in-law Simon. This village is dying, Mister Resident in Chief; it smells of death already. And you come to squeeze more blood out of this rotting carcass, you come to demand more gold for your towns, for the plain! Let us die in peace. In another hundred years there won't be a sign of our hamlet left, not on this earth or in the memory of men.

LELIUS: Well, great leader, I am personally very sympathetic with what you have been so kind as to tell me, and I understand your reasons; but what can I do? The man is on your side, but the Roman official has gotten his orders and has to carry them out.

BARIONA: Sure. And suppose we refuse to pay that tax? . . .

LELIUS: That would be extremely unwise. The procurator could not possibly tolerate ill will. I feel qualified to tell you he will be very harsh. Your lambs will be seized.

BARIONA: Soldiers will come into our village the way they came into Hebron last year? They'll rape our women and lead our stock away?

LELIUS: It's your business to see that it doesn't happen.

BARIONA: All right. I'm going to call the Council of the Elders to inform them of your wishes. You can count on our taking prompt action on them. I want the procurator to remember our docility for a long time.

LELIUS: You can be sure he will. The procurator will take into consideration your present hardships, which I shall report to him accurately. Rest assured that if we can help you, we shall not sit still. I salute you, great leader.

BARIONA: My respects, Mister Resident in Chief.

He goes out.

LELIUS, *alone:* This ready obedience doesn't tell me anything worthwhile. This fiery-eyed black rascal is thinking up some low blow. Levy! Levy! (*The publican comes in.*) A little more of your brandy, my friend, for I have to get ready for the worst.

Curtain.

THE NARRATOR: He's right, this Roman official. He's right to be mistrustful. Because Bariona, as he came out of the publican's house, had the trumpets sounded for the Council of the Elders.

The curtain rises.

SECOND TABLEAU

In front of the village walls.

SCENE I

THE CHORUS OF THE ELDERS

Horn notes in the wings; the Elders slowly enter.

CHORUS OF THE ELDERS

This is the way it is:
The horn has blown
We have dressed up in our ceremonial robes

And we have gone out through the great bronze gates
And we are gathered here beside the red dirt wall
The way we always used to do.

Our village is dying and above our houses
Of dried mud
Black flights of crows go wheeling round and round.
What good is it to hold a council meeting
When our hearts have turned to ashes
And our heads keep thinking we have lost
Our manhood?

FIRST ELDER: What do they expect us to do? Why call us together? In the old days, when I was young, the Council's de-
cisions had some effect, and I never backed down, not even
in the face of the boldest resolutions. But now, what's the
use?

CHORUS

What's the use of having us crawl
Out of the holes we've dug ourselves
To die like dying animals?
From the heights of these walls
Once our fathers threw back the enemy,
Now they are cracked and sunbaked ruins.
We do not like to look each other in the eye
For our wrinkled faces tell us of a time gone by.

SECOND ELDER: They say a Roman has come to the village and
is staying with Levy the Publican.

THIRD ELDER: What does he want out of us? Can you squeeze
breath out of a corpse? We don't have any more money and
we'd make mighty poor slaves. Why don't they let us die in
peace?

CHORUS

Here is Bariona, our chief
He is still young, yet
His heart is more wrinkled than ours,
He is coming and his forehead
Seems to drag him down to earth,
He is walking slowly
And his soul is full of soot.

Bariona slowly enters; they rise.

SCENE II

BARIONA: Oh my brothers!

CHORUS: Bariona! Bariona!

BARIONA: A Roman has come out from town, bringing orders from the procurator. It seems that Rome is waging war. From now on we're supposed to pay a sixteen-drachma head tax.

CHORUS: Alas!

FIRST ELDER: Bariona, we can't. We just *can't* pay this tax. Our arms are too weak, our animals are dying, our village is cursed with bad luck. We must not obey Rome.

SECOND ELDER: Great. Then the soldiers will come here and take your lambs the way they did the other winter in Hebron. They'll drag you along the roads by your beard, and the tribunal in Bethlehem will have you beaten on the soles of your feet.

FIRST ELDER: So you're for paying them? Have you sold out to the Romans?

SECOND ELDER: I haven't sold out, but I'm not as stupid as you are and I know how to see things the way they are: when the enemy is stronger, I know you have to bow your head.

FIRST ELDER: Do you hear what I'm telling you, brothers? Have we fallen so low? Up till now we've always given in to force, but now we've had enough: what we can't do we won't do. We'll go look for this Roman at Levy's and we'll hang him from the battlements of the ramparts.

SECOND ELDER: You, a man who doesn't even have a baby's strength any more, you want to rebel? At the first shock of battle your sword would fall right out of your shaky old hand. You're trying to get us all killed.

FIRST ELDER: Did I say I'd fight the war myself? There are still some of us, after all, who aren't even thirty-five.

SECOND ELDER: And you are preaching rebellion to them? You want them to fight so you can keep your skimpy savings?

THIRD ELDER: Be quiet! Listen to Bariona.

CHORUS: Bariona, Bariona, Bariona! Listen to Bariona!

BARIONA: We'll pay that tax.

CHORUS: Alas!

BARIONA: We'll pay that tax. (*A pause.*) But after us no one will ever pay taxes in this village again!

FIRST ELDER: How can that happen?

BARIONA: Because there won't be anyone to pay taxes. Oh my brothers, just look at the fix we're in. Your sons have abandoned you to go down into town and you've decided to stay here because you're proud. And Mark, Simon, Balarm, Jerevah, even though they're still young, have stayed with you because they're proud too. And I, your leader, I did the same as they, the way my ancestors told me to. But this is how it is: the village is like an empty theater after the curtain has gone down and the people have gone home. The mountain's long shadows have crept out across it. I called you together and we're all here, seated in the sunset. Yet each of us is all alone here in the darkness, and silence sits around us like a wall. It's an amazing silence: a baby's slightest cry would shatter it, but even if we pooled our strength and all cried out together, our weak old voices would be shattered by it. We're chained up here on our rock like lousy old eagles. Those of us who still have young bodies have aged underneath, and their hearts are hard as stone because there hasn't been a single thing for them to hope for since the day that they were born. All that's left for them to hope for is to die. Now that's the way it was already in our fathers' time. This village has been dying ever since the Romans came to Palestine, and any one of us who begets children is guilty because he is just prolonging that death agony. Listen! Last month, when they told me about my brother-in-law's death, I went up on Mount Saron. From up above I saw our sunbaked village, and I meditated on the things the closest to my heart. I thought, I have never gone down from my eagle's nest and yet I know the world; because no matter where a man may be, the whole wide world is crowded in around him. My arm is still a young man's arm, yet I am as wise as an old man. Now the time has come to listen to my wisdom. Above my head in the cold sky the eagles were soaring, I looked at our village, and my wisdom said to me, The world is nothing but a limp, unending fall, a lump of earth which never stops its falling. At points along the fall people and things suddenly pop out, and they have no sooner appeared than they are caught up in this universal fall. They start to fall, come apart, go to pieces. Oh brothers, my wisdom told me that life is a defeat. No one ever wins. Everybody always loses. Everything has always turned out very badly, and on this earth the greatest foolishness is hope.

CHORUS: On this earth the greatest foolishness is hope.

BARIONA: Now, my brothers, it is not right for us to be resigned to the fall; for resignation is not worthy of a man. That is why I say to you that we must make up our minds to despair. When I came down from Mount Saron my heart had closed fast on my sorrow like a fist; it held it hard and tight the way a blind man grabs on to his cane. My brothers, close your hearts on your sorrow; hold hard, hold tight; for the dignity of man lies in his despair. Here is my decision. We shall not rebel—if a mangy old dog rebels, he gets kicked back to his kennel. To keep our wives from suffering, we'll pay that tax! But this village is going to bury itself with its own hands. We shall have no more children. I have spoken.

FIRST ELDER: What! No more children!

BARIONA: No more children. We shall have nothing more to do with our wives. We no longer want to perpetuate life or prolong the suffering of our race. We shall beget no more. We shall consummate our lives in meditation on evil, injustice, and suffering. And then, in a quarter of a century, the last of us will all be dead. Perhaps I'll be the last to go. If so, when I feel my time is coming I'll put on my festive clothing and stretch out in the square with my face toward the sky. The crows will pick my rotting body clean and the wind will scatter my bones. Then the village will go back to the earth. The wind will clack the doors of empty houses. Our earthen walls will crumble down like snow in springtime from the mountainsides. There will be nothing left of us upon the earth or in the memory of men.

CHORUS

Is it possible that we shall spend the rest of our days
Without seeing a baby smile?

The bronze silence thickens around us.
Alas, who am I working for then?
Can we live without children?

BARIONA: What? Are you bewailing your lot? Would you still have the nerve to create young lives with your rotten blood? Do you want to provide new blood for the world's unending agony? What fate do you want for your future children? Do you want them to be stuck here all alone like caged vultures, with plucked feathers and staring eyes? Or would you rather that they went down into the towns to become Roman slaves, work at starvation wages, and maybe end up dying on the cross? You'll do what I say. And I only hope that our example shall become known in all Judea and shall mark the founding of a new religion—the religion of nothing—and that the Romans shall remain masters in our deserted villages and our blood shall be upon their heads. Repeat after me the oath I'm going to swear: before the God of Vengeance and of Wrath, before Jehovah, I swear that I shall not beget another child. And if I fail my oath, may my child be born blind, may he suffer from leprosy, may he be a mockery to others and a source of shame and suffering to me. Repeat, Jews, repeat!

CHORUS: Before the God of Vengeance and of Wrath . . .

BARIONA'S WIFE: Stop!

SCENE III

CHORUS OF ELDERS, BARIONA, SARAH

BARIONA: What do you want, Sarah?

SARAH: Stop!

BARIONA: What is it? Tell me!

SARAH: I . . . came to tell you . . . Oh Bariona, you just put a curse on me: you put a curse on my womb and the fruit of my womb!

BARIONA: You don't mean? . . .

SARAH: Yes. I'm pregnant, Bariona. I came to let you know; I'm pregnant by you.

BARIONA: Alas!

CHORUS: Alas!

SARAH: You entered into me and made me fruitful, and I opened myself to you, and together we prayed to Jehovah to give us a son. And now that I am carrying him inside of me and our union is finally blessed, you push me away and you promise our baby to death. Bariona, you lied to me. You have beaten me, you made me bleed, and I have suffered on your bed and taken everything because I thought you wanted a son. But now I see that you were lying to me and were only after your own pleasure. And all the joys my body gave you, all the caresses I gave to you and got from you, all our kisses, all our embraces—now I curse them all.

BARIONA: Sarah! It's not true. I didn't lie to you. I wanted a son. But now I've lost all hope and faith. That child that I wanted so much and you are carrying inside of you, it's *for his sake* that I don't want him to be born. Go to the witch doctor; he'll give you some herb medicine and you'll be barren when you come back.

SARAH: Bariona, please.

BARIONA: Sarah, I'm lord of this village and master of life and death. I've decided that my family will become extinct with me. Go on. And don't regret it: he would have suffered; he would have cursed you.

SARAH: Even if I knew that he would betray me, that he would die on the cross like a thief and cursing me, I would still give birth to him.

BARIONA: But why? Why?

SARAH: I don't know why. I accept his suffering everything that he will suffer even though I know that I shall feel that suffering in my very flesh. There is not a thorn in his path that can stick in his foot without sticking into my own heart. I'll bleed his sorrows in great streams of blood.

BARIONA: And do you think your tears will make his sorrows any easier to bear? No one will be able to suffer his suffering for him; a man always suffers and dies alone. Even if you were at the foot of his cross, he'd have to sweat out his death agony alone. It's for your own joy that you want to give birth to him, not for his. You don't love him enough.

SARAH: I love him already, whatever he may be. You I chose among all others, you I came to, because you were the best looking and the strongest. But the one I'm expecting I didn't choose and I'm expecting him. I love him already, even if he's ugly, even if he's blind, even if your curse covers him with leprosy; I love him already, this nameless, faceless child, my child.

BARIONA: If you love him, take pity on him. Let him sleep the calm sleep of the unborn. Do you want him to have a Judea of slaves for a country? This wind-blown icy rock for a home? This cracked mud for a roof? These bitter old men for brothers? And our dishonored family for a family?

SARAH: I also want to give him sunshine and fresh air and the mountain's purple shadows and young girls' laughter. Please, Bariona, let a child be born, let there be a young chance in the world again.

BARIONA: Be quiet. It's a trap. People always think there's a chance. Every time they bring a child into the world they think he has his chance, and it's not true. The chips are down already. Poverty, despair, and death are there already, waiting for him at the crossroads.

SARAH: Bariona, with you I am like a slave with his master and I owe you my obedience. But I know that you are making a mistake and you are doing wrong. I don't know the art of public speaking, and I can't find any words or reasons that will shake you. But when I'm with you I'm afraid. Here you are, dazzling in your pride and ill will like a rebel angel, like the Angel of Despair, but my heart isn't with you.

Lelius comes forward.

SCENE IV

THE SAME—LELIUS

LELIUS: Madame, gentlemen!

CHORUS: The Roman!

They all rise.

LELIUS: I was passing by, gentlemen, and I overheard your debate. Ahem! Allow me, chief, to support your wife's arguments and give you the Roman point of view. Madame, believe me, shows an exquisite sense of civic realities; and that ought to make you ashamed, chief. She has seen that you were not the only one at stake in this business, and that the first thing to be considered was the interest of society. Rome, Judea's benevolent tutor, is involved in a war which promises to be exceedingly long; and the day will undoubtedly come when she will send forth a call for the support of the natives she protects—Arab, black, and Jewish. What would happen if she found nothing but old men to answer the call? Would you want the rule of law to be overthrown for the lack of men to fight for it? It would be scandalous if Rome's victorious wars had to cease because there weren't enough soldiers. But even if we should live in peace for centuries, don't forget that then it would be industry which laid claim to your children. The great increase in wages during the past fifty years shows that there are not enough manual laborers. And I must add that this obligation to maintain wages at such a high level is a heavy burden for Roman management. If the Jews produce a lot of children, so that the supply of labor finally exceeds the demand, wages can be appreciably reduced and thus we shall free capital which can be more productive in other ways. Produce workers and soldiers for us, chief; that is your duty. This is what Madame felt in a confused way, and I am very happy to have been able to lend her my modest support in clarifying her feelings.

SARAH: Bariona, I'm all mixed up. That isn't what I meant to say at all.

BARIONA: I know. But take a look at what your allies are like and bow down your head in shame. Woman, that child you want to have born is like a new edition of the world. Through him the clouds and the water and the sun and the houses and all the ills that men must suffer will begin again. You are going to recreate the world. It is going to build up like a thick black scab around a little scandalized consciousness which will stay shut up in that scab like a tear. Do you see how outrageously incongruous, how monstrously tactless it would be to run off new copies of this aborted world? To have a child is to approve of creation from the bottom of one's heart; it's to say to the God who is tormenting us: "Lord, all's right with the world and I offer thanks to thee for having created it." Do you really want to sing this hymn? Can you take it upon your-self to say, "If I had to remake this world, I'd make it just the way it is?" Forget it, my sweet Sarah; forget it. Existing is a leprous business which is gradually eating us away, and our parents were wrong to bear us. Keep your hands clean, Sarah, and may you be able to say on your dying day, I am leaving no one after me to perpetuate human suffering. Come on, all of you; swear . . .

LELIUS: I know a good way to put a stop to this.

BARIONA: And how are you going to do it, Mister Resident in Chief? Throw us in jail? That would be the surest way of separating man and woman and making each of them die alone and barren.

LELIUS, *menacing:* I am going to . . . (*Calmed*) Ahem! I am going to refer the matter to the procurator.

BARIONA: Before the God of Vengeance and of Wrath I swear that I shall not beget another child.

CHORUS: Before the God of Vengeance and of Wrath I swear that I shall not beget another child.

BARIONA: And if I fail my oath, may my child be born blind.

CHORUS: And if I fail my oath, may my child be born blind.

BARIONA: May he be a mockery to others and a source of shame and suffering to me.

CHORUS: May he be a mockery to others and a source of shame and suffering to me.

BARIONA: There. We are bound together by oath. Go and be faithful to it.

SARAH: But suppose it were God's will that we beget children?

BARIONA: Then let him give his faithful servant a sign. But he'd better hurry up and send his angels to me before dawn; be-cause my heart is tired of waiting, and once a man has had a taste of despair, it's not a thing he shakes off lightly.

Curtain.

THE NARRATOR: And now it has happened! Bariona has demanded that God show himself. Ah, I don't like that. I don't like it at all . . . You know what they say where I come from? Let sleeping dogs lie. When God is silent, we do have to shift for ourselves, but we're still among men, we get by, we work it out with each other, life is still the way it always is. But if God gets to stirring, pow! It's like an earthquake, and men fall backwards or flat on their face, and afterward it's hard as hell to get back on your feet again; you have to start all over from scratch. And that's just what happened in the story I'm telling you: God got excited about the game. He must not have liked for Bariona to treat him like that. He said to himself, "What's going on here? . . ." and during the night he sent his angel down to earth a few leagues from Bethaur. I'm going to show you the angel; watch closely, and let the music play . . .

See all these guys falling down? They're shepherds who were tending their flocks in the mountains. And of course the angel's wings have been painted with care and the artist did everything he could to make him haughty. But I'm going to tell you what I think: that's not the way it really happened. I believed in that picture for a long time, for as long as I could still see, because it blinded me. But since I stopped seeing, I've thought about it and I've changed my mind. An angel, you see, must not be that ready to show his wings. You've surely met angels in your lifetime, and maybe even some of you are angels. All right, have you ever seen their wings? An angel is a man like you and me, but God has stretched out his hand over him and said, I need you; this time, you'll be the angel . . . And the guy goes wandering off in a daze among his fellow men, like Lazarus brought back from the dead, and he has a funny little expression on his face, a little expression which is neither flesh nor fowl, because he can't get over being an angel. Everybody mistrusts him, because the angel is the one who causes scandal. And I'm going to tell you what I think: when someone meets an angel—a real angel—he thinks at first it's a devil. But to get back to our story. Here's the way I see it: we're on a plateau on the top of the mountain, the shepherds are there around a fire, and one of them is playing a harmonica.

The curtain rises.

THIRD TABLEAU

In the mountains above Bethaur.

SCENE I

Simon is playing the harmonica.

THE PASSER-BY: Good evening, boys!

SIMON: Hey! Who's that?

THE PASSER-BY: It's Peter, the carpenter from Hebron. I'm coming back from your place.

SIMON: Hey pop. Nice night, huh?

THE PASSER-BY: Too nice. I don't like it. I was walking on those hard, barren rocks in the dark, and I thought I was walking through a garden full of great big flowers warmed up by the evening sun. You know, when they fill your whole nose with their sweet smell. I'm glad I found you; I felt more alone in the middle of all that sweetness than I would in the eye of a hurricane. And then on the way I ran into an odor as thick as a fog.

SIMON: What kind of an odor?

THE PASSER-BY: A pretty good one. But it made me dizzy. You'd have said it was alive, like a school of fish. Or a covey of partridges. Or more like those big swarms of pollen that blow about the ripe earth in spring fields and sometimes get so thick they block out the sun. It came down on top of me all of a sudden, and I could feel it quivering all around me. It was sticking to me all over.

SIMON: Lucky you! This odor of yours never made it as far as us. All I can smell is my brothers' natural fragrance, which reminds me more of billy goat and garlic.

THE PASSER-BY: It's no joke! If you'd been in my shoes you'd have been scared the same as me. There was crackling and humming and rustling all around me—on my right, on my left, in front of me, behind me. You'd have said that buds were popping out on invisible trees, that nature had chosen the deserted, icy plateaus just so she could have spring's magnificent celebration all to herself in the middle of winter.

SIMON: Son of a gun!

THE PASSER-BY: There was some kind of magic in it. I don't like it when you can smell spring in midwinter. For every thing there is a time and a season.

SIMON, *aside:* He's gone soft in the head, poor guy. (*Aloud*) So you're coming from Bethaur?

THE PASSER-BY: Yes. Some funny things are happening down there.

SIMON: That so? Sit down and let's hear the whole story. I like to sit and talk around a big fire, but we shepherds never see anyone. Those guys are asleep and these keeping watch with me don't have anything to say. I'll bet it's Ruth, huh? Did her husband catch her with Shalam? I always said that would turn out bad; they don't hide themselves enough.

THE PASSER-BY: You're not with it at all. It's Bariona, your chief. He spoke to God and told him, "Give me a sign before dawn; otherwise I'll forbid my men to have anything to do with their wives."

SIMON: To have anything to do with their wives? Son of a gun. He must have flipped his lid. Still, if what they say is true, he never was a man to sneeze at his own wife's caresses. She must have run around on him.

PASSER-BY: Nope.

SIMON: So what was it?

THE PASSER-BY: Seems it's politics.

SIMON: Oh well! If it's politics . . . But listen, brother, it's mighty poor politics. If my father's politics had been like that, I wouldn't be born.

THE PASSER-BY: That's just what Bariona wants: to stop children from being born.

SIMON: Uh-huh. Well, if I hadn't been born, I'd be sorry. I'm not denying that things don't go the way you'd like every day. But look; there are times which aren't too bad: you pick the guitar a little, drink a little slug of wine, and then on the other mountains all around you see shepherds' fires like this one winking at you. Hey, you guys. Did you hear? Bariona is telling his men they can't sleep with their wives.

CAIPHUS: Yeah? And who will they sleep with?

THE PASSER-BY: No one.

PAUL: Poor bastards. They're going to go crazy!

THE PASSER-BY: And what about you shepherds? It's your business too, because you're from Bethaur.

SIMON: Bah! That won't bother us much. Winter is off season for loving, but in the spring the little girls from Hebron come meet us on the mountainside again. And then, if we did have to rest awhile, I wouldn't mind too much: They always loved me too much to suit me.

THE PASSER-BY: Well, God be with you.

CAIPHUS: Like to have a little drink?

THE PASSER-BY: No thanks! I don't feel any better. I don't exactly know what's going on tonight on the mountain, but I'm in a hurry to get back home. When the elements celebrate, it's not good to be on the road. Good night!

CAIPHUS, PAUL, SIMON: Good night.

CAIPHUS: What's he talking about?

SIMON: How do I know? He smelled an odor, heard some noise . . . Crazy talk.

A silence.

PAUL: Still, he has a good head on his shoulders, old Peter.

CAIPHUS: Bah . . . Maybe he really saw something. People who travel the roads often meet up with strange things.

SIMON: Whatever he saw, I hope it doesn't come up here.

PAUL: Listen, man; play us something.

Simon plays the harmonica.

CAIPHUS: Is that it?

SIMON: I don't feel like playing anymore.

A pause.

CAIPHUS: I don't know what's keeping the lambs awake; I've been hearing their bells ever since nightfall.

PAUL: And the dogs are jumpy; they're baying at the moon and there isn't any moon.

A pause.

CAIPHUS: I can't get over it: Bariona telling his men and women they can't have anything to do with one another. He must have really changed, because he sure was some kind of a lady-killer in the old days, and there ought to be more than one woman on the farms around Bethaur who remembers it.

PAUL: It's a bad business for his wife! He's a good-looking man, Bariona.

CAIPHUS: And what about her! She can put her shoes under my bed any time.

A pause.

SIMON: Hey! There really is some kind of odor around us that doesn't smell like us.

CAIPHUS: Yeah; it smells pretty strong. It's a funny night. Look how close the stars are; you'd say the sky was resting on the earth. But still it's black as pitch.

PAUL: There are nights like this. They bear down on you so hard you think that something big is coming out of them, and then all that comes out is a little bit of wind at dawn.

CAIPHUS: All *you* see is wind. But there are more signs in nights like these than fish in the sea. Seven years ago—I'll never forget it—I was keeping watch on this very spot and it was a night that would make your hair stand on end. It was howling and moaning all over the place, and the grass was lying flat like the wind had stomped it down with its boots, except there wasn't a breath of wind. Well, when I got home the next morning my old lady told me my father was dead.

Simon sneezes.

What is it?

SIMON: It's this sweet smell that's tickling my nose. It's getting stronger and stronger. You'd think you were in an Arab barber shop. So do you think something will happen tonight?

CAIPHUS: Yes.

SIMON: To tell by the strength of this odor, it will really be something. At least the death of a king. I don't feel good at all. Signs from the dead I can do without, and the way I see it kings could just as well depart this life without having it trumpeted from the mountaintops. The death of kings gives lazy people down in town something to do, but up here who needs it?

CAIPHUS: Sh! Be quiet.

SIMON: What is it?

CAIPHUS: It's like we're not alone. I feel a kind of presence, but I couldn't tell you which one of my five senses is warning me. It's all round and soft against me.

SIMON: Oh Lord! Shall we wake the others? There's something warm and tender rubbing up to me; it's like on Sunday when I take our cat on my lap.

CAIPHUS: I have a nose full of some sweet, overpowering odor; its fragrance is swallowing me up like the sea. It's a throbbing odor that's brushing up against me and *looking* at me, a giant sweetness seeping through my pores right into my heart. Some kind of life that isn't mine has chilled me to the marrow of my bones. I don't know what it is. I'm lost at the bottom of another life like at the bottom of a well; I'm smothering, I'm drowning in perfume, I can raise up my head and I don't see the stars any more. All around me enormous pillars of some sort of tenderness I just don't understand are rising right up to the sky, and I feel smaller than a little worm.

PAUL: It's true; you can't see the stars any more.

SIMON: It's going by. The smell isn't so strong now.

CAIPHUS: Yes . . . it's going by; it's going by right now. It's over. How empty the earth and sky are now! Come on; start playing your harmonica again; we're going to start watching again. It's probably not the only marvel we'll see tonight. Paul, put a log on the fire; it's about to go out.

The Angel enters.

SCENE II

THE SAME—THE ANGEL

THE ANGEL: May I warm myself a bit?

PAUL: Who are you?

THE ANGEL: I come from Hebron; I'm cold.

CAIPHUS: Warm yourself if you like. And if you're thirsty, here's some wine. (*A pause.*) Did you come up the goat path?

THE ANGEL: I don't know. Yes; I think so.

CAIPHUS: Did you smell that odor that's prowling around the roads?

THE ANGEL: What odor?

CAIPHUS: An odor . . . never mind; if you didn't smell it, there's nothing to say about it. Are you hungry?

THE ANGEL: No.

CAIPHUS: You're as pale as death.

THE ANGEL: I'm pale because I just had a shock.

CAIPHUS: A shock?

THE ANGEL: Yes. It came like a knock on the head. But right now I must see Simon, Paul, and Caiphus. That's you, isn't it?

ALL THREE: Yes.

THE ANGEL: Yes. Excuse me; the road is long and I don't re- are you Caiphus?

CAIPHUS: Where do you know us from? Are you from Hebron?

PAUL: I swear; he looks like he's out on his feet. (*Aloud*) And you have some business with us?

THE ANGEL: Yes. I looked for you among your flocks, and your dogs howled when they saw me.

SIMON, *aside:* I can see why!

THE ANGEL: I have a message for you.

SIMON: A message?

THE ANGEL: Yes. Excuse me; the road is long and I don't remember any more what I had to tell you. I'm cold. (*Bursting out*) Lord, my mouth is bitter and my shoulders are bowed beneath your enormous weight. I bear you, Lord, and it's as if I were bearing the whole earth. (*To the others*) I scared you, didn't I? I walked toward you in the night, the dogs howled for the dead as I passed, and I'm cold. I'm always cold.

SIMON: It's a poor crackpot.

CAIPHUS: Be quiet. And you, give us your message.

THE ANGEL: Message? Oh yes; the message. Here it is: wake your brothers and get going. You will go to Bethaur and you will tell everyone the good news.

CAIPHUS: What news?

THE ANGEL: Hold on a minute; it's in Bethlehem, in a stable. Just hold on a minute and be still. There's a great void and a great expectancy in heaven, because nothing has happened yet. And there's this cold in my body like the cold in heaven. Right this minute there is a woman lying on straw in a stable. Be still, because heaven has become completely empty like a great big hole; it's empty and the angels are cold. Ah! Are they cold!

SIMON: That doesn't sound like good news at all.

CAIPHUS: Be quiet.

A long silence.

THE ANGEL: There. He's born! His infinite and sacred spirit is imprisoned in the soiled body of a child, and is astonished to be suffering and ignorant. That's it: our Master is no longer anything but a child. A child who can't speak. I'm cold, Lord; how cold I am. But that's enough weeping about the angels' sorrow and the immense emptiness in the heavens. On earth, mild odors are darting everywhere, and it's the turn of human beings to rejoice. Do not be afraid of me, Simon, Caiphus, and Paul; awaken your brothers.

They shake the sleepers.

FIRST SHEPHERD: Huh! What is it?

SECOND SHEPHERD: Let me sleep. I was dreaming that I had a pretty little maiden in my arms.

THIRD SHEPHERD: And I was dreaming I was eating.

ALL

Why wake us up?
And who's this guy with the long pale face
Who seems, like us, to be just waking up?

THE ANGEL: Go to Bethaur and cry out everywhere: The Savior is born. He is born in a stable, in Bethlehem.

ALL: The Savior.

THE ANGEL: Tell them: go down in a throng into the city of David to worship Christ, your Savior. And this shall be a sign unto you; you shall find the babe wrapped in swaddling clothes, lying in a manger. You, Caiphus, go find Bariona who is suffering and whose heart is full of gall and say to him, "Peace on earth to men of good will!"

ALL: Peace on earth to men of good will.

SIMON: Come on, you guys; let's hurry up and get the people of Bethaur out of bed, and we'll have fun seeing the astonished look on their faces. Because nothing's more fun than giving someone good news.

PAUL: And who's going to watch over our sheep?

THE ANGEL: I'll watch over them.

ALL: Let's go! Let's go quick. Paul, you bring your jug; and Simon, you bring your harmonica. The Savior is with us. Hosanna! Hosanna!

They go out jostling one another.

THE ANGEL: I'm cold . . .

Curtain.

FOURTH TABLEAU

A square in Bethaur, early in the morning.

THE SHEPHERDS

We have left our mountain peak
And come down among men
For our hearts were full of gladness.
Down there in the town with flat roofs and white houses
That we do not know and can scarcely imagine
In a great mass of men who lay sleeping stretched out on their
    backs
His little white body piercing the maleficent shadows of the dark
    night of cities
        Of the night of crossroads
And coming up from the depths of nothingness
As a silver-bellied fish comes up from the deeps of the sea
        The Messiah was born unto us!
The Messiah, the King of Judea, He whom the prophets promised
    us
The Lord of the Jews was born, bringing joy to our earth.
Henceforth the grass will grow on mountaintops
        And the sheep will graze by themselves
        And we'll have nothing more to do,
And we shall stretch out on our backs the livelong day,
We shall caress the most beautiful girls
And we shall sing hymns of praise to the Lord.
That is why we've drunk and sung on the roads
And are drunk with a lighthearted drunkenness
Like that of the goat-footed dancing girl
Who has whirled and whirled about to the sound of the flute.

> *They dance. Simon plays the harmonica.*

CAIPHUS: Hey there, Jerevah! Gird up thy loins and come hear
the good news.

ALL: On your feet! On your feet, Jerevah!

JEREVAH: What's up? Are you off your rocker? Can't a man
sleep in peace any more? I had cast off my cares with my
clothes at the foot of my bed, and I was dreaming I was young
again.

ALL: Come on down, Jerevah; come on down! We bring you the good news.

JEREVAH: Who are you people? Ah! It's the shepherds from Mount Saron. What are you doing in the village, and who's watching your sheep?

CAIPHUS: God is watching them. He'll take care that none strays, for this night above all is blessed; it is as fruitful as a woman's womb and as young as the world's first night, for everything is starting over from the start and all the men on earth are going to get a new chance.

JEREVAH: Have the Romans pulled out of Judea?

PAUL: Come on down! Come on down! You'll find out everything. But we'll wake the others.

SIMON: Shalam! Shalam!

SHALAM: Yes! I'm getting out of bed and I can hardly see. Is there a fire?

SIMON: Come on down, Shalam, and come join us.

SHALAM: Are you crazy, waking a man up at this hour? Don't you know how impatiently we people in Bethaur wait each day for our sleep, a sleep like death?

SIMON: From now on, Shalam, you won't want to sleep any more, you'll frisk like a kid on the mountainsides—even at night—and you'll pick flowers to make yourself a crown.

SHALAM: What kind of jazz is that? There aren't any flowers on the mountainsides.

SIMON: There will be. Lemon and orange trees are going to grow on the mountaintops, and all we'll have to do is stretch out our hand to pluck golden oranges as big as grapefruits. We bring you the good news.

SHALAM: Have they discovered a new fertilizer? Have they raised the price of agricultural products?

SIMON: Come on down! Come on down! And we'll tell you everything!

> *The people come slowly out of their houses and gather*
> *in the square.*

THE PUBLICAN, *appearing on his stairs:* What's up? Are you drunk? I haven't heard cries of joy in the streets for forty years. And the day you pick to cry for joy has to be the one day I have a Roman in my house! It's scandalous.

PAUL: We're going to run the Romans right out of Judea with big boots in the ass, and we'll hang the publicans upside down over hot coals.

THE PUBLICAN: It's the Revolution! It's the Revolution!

LELIUS, *coming out in pajamas with his helmet:* Ahem! What's up?

THE PUBLICAN: It's the Revolution! It's the Revolution!

LELIUS: Jews! Remember that the government . . .

CAIPHUS: Villagers and shepherds, let's sing and dance because the golden age has returned!

ALL, *singing:* The Eternal reigns! Let the whole earth jump for joy, and all the islands rejoice!
   Great clouds and darkness surround him; justice and judgment are the firm foundation of his throne. Fire radiates from him and burns his enemies everywhere to a crisp.
   Stars shine everywhere. The world and the earth tremble at his sight.
   The mountains melt like wax in the presence of the Eternal, the presence of the Lord of all the earth.
   The heavens manifest his justice, and all peoples bear witness to his glory.
   Zion heard him and rejoiced, and the daughters of Judah thrilled with gladness.
   Let the sea proclaim his joy, and the earth and all those who dwell in it.
   Let the rivers clap hands and the mountains sing.
   For the Eternal is come to judge the earth: he shall judge the world with justice and the peoples with his truth.

BARIONA, *enters:* Pigs! Are you only happy when somebody tricks you with honeyed words? Don't you have enough guts to look truth in the eye? Your songs are breaking my eardrums and your drunken women's dances are making me throw up in disgust.

THE CROWD: But Bariona, Bariona! Christ is born!

BARIONA: Christ! You poor fools! You poor blind fools!

CAIPHUS: Bariona, the Angel told me, "Go find Bariona, who is suffering and whose heart is full of gall, and tell him, Peace on earth to men of good will."

BARIONA: Ha! Good will! The good will of the poor who starve to death without a whimper underneath the rich man's stair! The good will of the slave who says Thank you when they beat him! The good will of the soldiers who are led like sheep to slaughter and fight without knowing why! Why isn't he here, this angel of yours; and why doesn't he run his own errands? If he were here, I'd tell him, "There's no peace on earth for me, and I want to be a man of ill will."

The crowd mutters.

Yes, ill will! Against the gods, against men, against the world. I've shielded myself with a threefold armor. I shall ask no favors and I shall give no thanks. I shall not bend my knee before any man, I shall put all my dignity in my hatred, and I shall keep precise account of all my sufferings and the sufferings of all other men. I want to be the witness and the judge of all men's sorrow; I welcome it and keep it in my heart like a blasphemy. Like a pillar of injustice, I want to rise up against the sky; I shall die alone and unrepentant, and I want my soul to rise toward the stars like a great brassy clamor, a clamor of irritation.

CAIPHUS: Watch it, Bariona! God gave you a sign and you refuse to hear it.

BARIONA: Even if the Eternal had shown me his face in the clouds I would still have refused to listen to him, because I'm free, and not even God himself has any power over a free man. He can grind me to dust or set me on fire like a torch, he can make me writhe in pain like a snake in a fire, but against that pillar of bronze, that inflexible column—a free man—he is powerless. But where did you get the idea that he gave me a sign anyway, you fools? You'd believe anything, wouldn't you? Those guys have hardly finished telling you their story before you're leaping to believe them like they'd asked you to put your savings in the bank downtown. Let's see. You, Simon, the youngest shepherd, come up here. You look more innocent than the others and you'll tell me best the way it really was. Who gave you the good news?

SIMON: Uh! Lord, it was an angel.

BARIONA: How do you know it was an angel?

SIMON: Because I was so scared. When he came up to the fire I thought I was going to fall on my tail.

BARIONA: Right. And what was this angel like? Did he have big spread-out wings?

SIMON: Good night, no. He acted like he didn't know how to act, and his knees were knocking together. And he was cold. Man, was he cold, that poor rascal!

BARIONA: A great messenger from heaven, no doubt about it. And what proof did he give you for what he said?

SIMON: Well . . . He . . . He . . . He didn't give any proof at all.

BARIONA: What? Not the tiniest little miracle? He didn't turn the fire into water? Or even make flowers grow out of the top of your staffs?

SIMON: We never thought about asking him for one, and I'm sorry we didn't because I've got real bad rheumatism that's killing my hip and since he was there I should have asked him to get rid of it. He didn't feel like talking. He told us, "Go to Bethlehem, look in the stable, and you'll find a babe wrapped in swaddling clothes."

BARIONA: Why sure! That's all he had to say. There's a big crowd of people in Bethlehem now because of the census. The inns are turning people away in droves; there are lots of folks sleeping out in the open and in the stables. I'm willing to bet that you'll find more than twenty babes in the manger. You'll have more than enough to choose from.

THE CROWD: But it's still true.

BARIONA: So? What did he do after that, this angel of yours?

SIMON: He went away.

BARIONA: Went away? Disappeared, you mean? Went up in smoke the way angels always do?

SIMON: No, no. He left on his own two feet, limping a little, in a very natural way.

BARIONA: And that's your angel for you, you melon heads! So all it takes is some boozed-up shepherds running across some half-cracked guy in the hills who drivels Lord knows what nonsense about Christ's coming for you to be drooling for joy and throwing your hats in the air?

FIRST ELDER: Alas, Bariona; we've been waiting so long!

BARIONA: Who are you waiting for? A king. One of the lords of the earth who will appear in all his glory and streak across the sky like a comet, preceded by a blast of trumpets. And what do they give you? Some poor beggars' child, all covered with crap, squalling in a stable, with bits of straw sticking out of his diapers. Ah, what a fine king! Go ahead, go on down, go on down to Bethlehem; it will be worth the trip for sure.

THE CROWD: He's right! He's right!

BARIONA: Go back home, good people, and in the future show better judgment. The Messiah hasn't come. The world is an endless fall, and you know it. The Messiah would be someone who'd stop the fall, who'd suddenly reverse the course of things and make the world bounce back up in the air like a ball. Then we'd see the rivers flow backwards from the sea to their sources; the flowers would grow on rocks; and men would have wings and we'd be born old men and then get younger until we were newborn babes. The universe you're dreaming of is a madman's. There's only one thing I'm sure of, and that's that everything will always fall: the rivers will always fall into the sea, old nations will always fall under the domination of young ones, human undertakings will always fall apart, and people like us will always fall into vile old age. Go back home.

LELIUS, to the publican: I don't think any Roman official has ever found himself in such an embarrassing situation. If I don't straighten them out, they're going to descend en masse on Bethlehem and kick up a racket down there that will get me in hot water. And if I do straighten them out, they're going to persist all the more in yesterday's abominable error and produce no more children. What shall I do? Hm! The best thing is to say nothing and let things take their natural course. Let's go back and pretend we heard nothing.

JEREVAH: Come on, let's go back home! We still have time to sleep a little. I'll dream that I'm rich and happy. And no one will be able to steal my dreams.

Day slowly breaks. The crowd gets ready to leave the square.

Music.

CAIPHUS: Wait a minute, you all, wait a minute! What's that music? And who is that coming toward us decked out so beautifully?

JEREVAH: They're kings from the east, all bedizened with gold. I've never seen anything so beautiful.

THE PUBLICAN, *to Lelius:* I saw kings like them at the colonial exposition in Rome almost twenty years ago.

FIRST ELDER: Move back and make room for them. Their retinue is coming this way.

The Three Wise Men enter.

MELCHIOR: Good people, who is in charge here?

BARIONA: I am.

MELCHIOR: Are we still far from Bethlehem?

BARIONA: It's twenty leagues from here.

MELCHIOR: I'm glad I've finally met someone who can give me some information. All the towns around here are empty, because the people who live in them have left to worship Christ.

ALL: Christ? Then it's true? Christ is born?

SARAH, *who has mingled with the crowd:* Oh tell us, tell us that he's born and warm our hearts. The divine child is born. There really has been a woman that lucky. Oh doubly blessed woman.

BARIONA: You too, Sarah? You too?

BALTHAZAR: Christ is born! We saw his star rising in the east and we followed it.

ALL: Christ is born!

FIRST ELDER: You were tricking us, Bariona, you were tricking us!

JEREVAH: You no-good shepherd, you lied to us. You wanted to let us die out on this barren rock, didn't you, while the people in the lowlands were enjoying our Lord to their hearts' content.

BARIONA: You poor fools! You believe these guys just because they're all decked out in gold.

SHALAM: And what about your wife? Look at her; look at her! And tell us that she doesn't believe. Because you tricked her same as you tricked us.

LELIUS, *to the publican:* Ha, ha! Things are going badly for our Arab vulture. I did the right thing not getting mixed up in it.

THE CROWD: Let's follow the Wise Men! Let's go down to Bethlehem with them!

BARIONA: You won't go! As long as I'm your leader, you won't go!

BALTHAZAR: What? Are you stopping your people from going to worship the Messiah?

BARIONA: I don't believe in the Messiah any more than I believe any of your jive. You rich people, you kings, I see through your little game. You're fooling the poor people with a bunch of bull to keep them quiet. But you're not going to fool me. People of Bethaur, I don't want to be your leader any more, because you doubted me. But I'm telling you again for the last time, look your misfortune squarely in the eye, because man's dignity lies in his despair.

BALTHAZAR: Are you sure it doesn't lie in his hope instead? I can see from your face that you've suffered, and I can also see that you've enjoyed it. Your features are noble but your eyes are half-closed and your ears seem stopped up. Your face has that kind of heaviness you find in blind and deaf people's faces. You look like one of those tragic, blood-smeared idols pagans worship. A ferocious idol, with lowered eyelashes, blind and deaf to human speech, who won't listen to any advice except what comes from his own pride. But look at us; we've suffered too, and among men we're wise. But when that new star rose, we didn't hesitate to leave our kingdoms and follow it, and we are going to worship our Messiah.

BARIONA: Well go ahead and worship him. Who's stopping you, and what's that got to do with me?

BALTHAZAR: What's your name?

BARIONA: Bariona. So what?

BALTHAZAR: You're suffering, Bariona.

Bariona shrugs his shoulders.

You are suffering, and yet your duty is to hope. Your duty as a man. It's for you that Christ came down to earth. For you more than for anyone, because you're suffering more than anyone. An angel doesn't hope at all, because he has his joy and God gave him everything ahead of time. And a stone doesn't hope either, because it lives dully in a perpetual present. But when God created human nature, he joined hope and care together. A man, you see, is always much more than he is. You look at this man here, all weighed down by his flesh, rooted to the spot by his two big feet, and you say, stretching forth your hand to touch him, he's there. And that's not true: wherever a man happens to be, Bariona, he's always *somewhere else*. Somewhere else, beyond the purple mountaintops you see from here. In Jerusalem. In Rome. Beyond this icy day. Tomorrow. And all these other men around him, they haven't been here for a long time either. They're in Bethlehem in a stable, gathered around a baby's little warm body. And all that future which man is shaped by—all those mountaintops, all those purple horizons, all those wonderful towns he haunts without ever having set foot in them—all of that is hope. Hope. Look at these prisoners all around you here, living in the mud and cold. Do you know what you'd see if you could follow their souls? Rolling hills, a softly winding river, cornfields, and the southern sun. Their fields and their sun. That's where they are; down there. And for a prisoner who's shivering with cold and crawling with bugs and rats, the green fields of summer are hope. Hope and what's best in them. And what you want to do is take away their summertime and fields and sunlight on those far-off hills. You want to leave them nothing else but mud and lice and cold potatoes. You want to make them live in terror in the present like an animal. Because that's what your despair is: chewing over the time going by like a cow, looking down stubbornly at your feet like a dumb jackass, cutting your soul off from the future and locking it up in the present. And if you do that, Bariona, you won't be a man any more; you'll be a hard black stone by the side of the road. Wagon trains keep moving down that road, but the stone just lies there, resentful in a lump beside it.

BARIONA: You're talking like a fool, old man.

BALTHAZAR: Bariona, it's true we're very old and very wise and know all there is to know about the bad things on this earth. But when we saw that star in the sky, our hearts jumped for joy like children's and we set forth; because we wanted to do our duty as men, which is to hope. The man who loses hope, Bariona, is the man who'll be hounded out of his village. People will curse him and the stones on his path will be harder and the thorns sharper and the burden he carries will be heavier and all the bad things will swarm down on him like stirred-up bees and everyone will mock him and shout at him. But for the man who has hope, everything comes up smiles and the world is his oyster. Come on now, the rest of you and tell me if you think you ought to stay here or come along with us.

ALL: We'll come with you.

BARIONA: Stop! Don't leave! I have some more to say to you.

They go out shoving against each other.

Hey, Jerevah! You were my brother in the old days and you always believed what I said. Don't you trust me any more?

JEREVAH: Leave me alone; you tricked us.

He goes away.

BARIONA: And you, old man; you were always on my side in our councils.

THE ELDER: You were the leader then. Now you're nothing. Let me get by.

BARIONA: All right; leave then. Go ahead, you poor fools. Come on, Sarah; we'll stay here by ourselves.

SARAH: Bariona, I'm going with them.

BARIONA: Sarah! (*A pause.*) My village is dead, my family is dishonored, my brothers are abandoning me. I didn't think I could suffer any more and I was wrong. Sarah, the hardest blow came from you. You didn't love me, then?

SARAH: I love you, Bariona. But understand me. Down there there's a happy woman who has everything she wants, a woman who gave birth for every mother, and it's like a permission she gave me—permission to bring my own baby into this world. I want to see her—*see her*—this happy, sacred mother. She saved my baby, he will be born, I know that now. It doesn't matter where. Beside the road or in a stable like his. And I also know that God is with me. (*Timidly*) Come with us, Bariona.

BARIONA: No. You do what you want to.

SARAH: Well, farewell then!

BARIONA: Farewell. (*A pause.*) They're gone, Lord. You and me, we're alone. I've known a lot of suffering, but I had to live to this day to taste the bitter taste of being left alone. Oh how alone I am! But you won't hear a word of complaint from my lips, God of the Jews. I want to live a long time here on this barren rock they've left me on, me who never asked to be born; and I want to be your remorse.

Curtain.

FIFTH TABLEAU

In front of the witch doctor's house.

SCENE I

BARIONA, *alone:* A god who becomes a man! What a fairy tale! I don't see anything in our life that would make him want to do it. The gods stay in heaven, with plenty to do just enjoying one another. And if they did come down among us, they'd come in some bright and fleeting shape, like a purple cloud or a stroke of lightning. A god who'd turn into a man? The Almighty in all his glory would contemplate these lice swarming on the crust of this old earth and say, "Me want to be one of these vermin? What a laugh." A god who'd tie himself down to being born, to being a bloody strawberry for nine months? They'll get there late at night because the women will slow them down . . . Well let them go and laugh and cry beneath the stars and wake up sleeping Bethlehem. It won't be long before the Roman's bayonets begin to prick their ass and cool their blood a little.

Lelius enters.

SCENE II

LELIUS, BARIONA

LELIUS: Ah! Here's chief Bariona. I'm glad to see you, chief. Yes, yes; very glad. Political disagreements came between us, but for the moment we're the only two left in this deserted village. The wind has risen and is making the doors rattle. It makes you shiver. We have every reason to get together again.

BARIONA: I'm not afraid of rattly doors, and you've got Levy the Publican to keep you company.

LELIUS: No—this will make you laugh—old Levy borrowed my donkey and followed your men. I'll have to go home on foot. (*Bariona laughs.*) Yes; hm! It is very funny. And . . . what do you think of all this, chief?

BARIONA: Mister Resident in Chief, that's just what I was going to ask you.

LELIUS: Oh, me . . . They threw you out, huh?

BARIONA: The choice to follow them or not was all mine. Are you going to keep on with your trip, Mister Resident in Chief?

LELIUS: Bah! It's not worth it any more, since it seems that all the villages on the mountain have been emptied of their people. The whole mountain is visiting Bethlehem. I'm going back home on foot. And what about you? Are you going to stay here alone?

BARIONA: Yes.

LELIUS: It's an unbelievable experience.

BARIONA: There's nothing unbelievable except human stupidity.

LELIUS: Yes. Uh; you don't believe in this Messiah, do you? (*Bariona shrugs his shoulders.*) No; of course not. Just the same I'd like to go have a look at that stable. You never know; those Wise Men seemed so sure.

BARIONA: So you let yourself be impressed by uniforms too? And yet you Romans should be used to them.

LELIUS: Ahem! You know in Rome we have an altar to unknown gods. It's a prudent measure which I've always approved of and which guides my present conduct. One more god can't hurt us, we have so many already. And there are enough oxen and goats in our empire for all the sacrifices.

BARIONA: If a god had become man *for me,* he'd be the only one among them all I'd love. There would be sort of a blood brotherhood between him and me, and not even my whole lifetime would be long enough for me to shout my gratitude to him. Bariona isn't ungrateful. But what god would be crazy enough to do that? Certainly not ours. He has always been pretty distant.

LELIUS: In Rome they say that Jupiter takes on human form from time to time when he spies some nice young maiden from the top of Olympus. But I don't have to tell you that I don't believe it.

BARIONA: A god-man, a god made of our humiliated flesh, a god who would agree to know that salty taste we have in the back of our mouths when the whole world abandons us, a god who would agree ahead of time to suffer what I'm suffering today . . . Come on; it's too crazy.

LELIUS: Yes. Ahem! I'm going to have a look down there just the same; you never know. And then the two of us especially are going to need the gods, because after all you've lost your job and I'm risking mine.

BARIONA: You're risking yours?

LELIUS: Ha! You bet. Just imagine that avalanche of bandy-legged hillbillies streaming down into the streets of Bethlehem. It pains me just to think of it. The procurator will never forgive me.

BARIONA: As a matter of fact, it will be funny. What are you going to do if they boot you out?

LELIUS: I'll retire to Mantua; it's my home town. I'll admit I really want to; it'll just happen a little sooner than I thought, that's all.

BARIONA: And Mantua is surely a very big Italian city, all surrounded by factories?

LELIUS: What are you talking about! No; it's a very small town. It's all white, in the valley, on the edge of a river.

BARIONA: What? No factories? Not even the least little sawmill? But you're going to be bored to death. You'll miss Bethlehem.

LELIUS: Shoot no. Look; Mantua is famous all over Italy for the bees we keep there. My grandfather's bees knew him so well that they didn't sting him when he came to take their honey. They flew out to meet him and settled on his head and in the folds of his toga; he didn't wear either gloves or a hood. And I admit I'm pretty good at it myself. But I don't know whether my bees will know me when I come back to Mantua. I haven't been there for six years. We make good honey, you know, green, brown, black, and yellow. I've always dreamed of writing a treatise on beekeeping. Why are you laughing?

BARIONA: Because I'm thinking of the speech that old fool made: man is always somewhere else; man is hope. You too, Mister Resident in Chief, you have your elsewhere, you have your hope. Ah, the charming little blue flowers, and how well it suits you! All right, go ahead, Mister Resident in Chief; go ahead and make your honey in Mantua. My best regards.

LELIUS: Good bye.

The witch doctor comes out of his house.

SCENE III
THE WITCH DOCTOR, LELIUS, BARIONA

THE WITCH DOCTOR: My kind regards, your Lordships.

BARIONA: Are you still here, you old soak? You didn't leave with the others?

THE WITCH DOCTOR: My old legs are too weak, your Lordship.

LELIUS: Who is it?

BARIONA: It's our witch doctor, a sharp old man who knows his business. He predicted my father's death two years before it happened.

LELIUS: Another prophet. That's all there is in your neck of the woods.

THE WITCH DOCTOR: I'm no prophet and I'm not inspired by God. I read cards and coffee grounds, and my science is completely natural.

LELIUS: Well, then tell us what this Messiah who's cleaning out all the mountain villages like a vacuum cleaner is.

BARIONA: No, by God! I don't want to hear any more talk about this Messiah. That's my brothers' business. They abandoned me and I'm abandoning them.

LELIUS: Leave him alone, my dear fellow; let him go on. He can give us useful information.

BARIONA: If you want him to.

LELIUS: Go on; say what you have to say. And you shall have this money if I'm satisfied.

THE WITCH DOCTOR: I don't feel too good talking about divine things; it's not my line. I'd rather have you ask me whether your wife is faithful, for example; that's more up my alley.

LELIUS: Ahem! My wife is faithful, my good man. That's an article of faith. The wife of a Roman official must be above suspicion. Furthermore, if you knew her, you'd know she spends all her time playing bridge, doing social work, and chairing meetings.

THE WITCH DOCTOR: That's good, your Lordship. In that case, I'll try to talk about the Messiah. But excuse me; I have to go into a trance first.

LELIUS: Will it take long?

THE WITCH DOCTOR: No. It's just a little formality. Only takes the time to dance a little and get high on the tom-tom.

He dances while he beats the tom-tom.

LELIUS: Real savages.

THE WITCH DOCTOR: I see! I see! A child in a stable.

LELIUS: And then what?

THE WITCH DOCTOR: And then he's growing up.

BARIONA: Naturally.

THE WITCH DOCTOR, *annoyed:* It's not so natural. There's a lot of infant mortality among the Jews. He is going down among men and telling them, "I am the Messiah." He is addressing himself above all to the children of the poor.

LELIUS: Is he preaching rebellion to them?

THE WITCH DOCTOR: He's telling them, "Render unto Caesar that which is Caesar's."

LELIUS: There's something I like very much.

BARIONA: And I don't like it at all. Your Messiah has sold out.

THE WITCH DOCTOR: He isn't taking money from anyone. He's living very modestly. He's performing a few little miracles. He's changing water into wine at Cana. I could do that; all you need is a few powders. He's raising a certain Lazarus from the dead.

LELIUS: An accomplice. And then what? A little hypnotism, no doubt?

THE WITCH DOCTOR: I guess. There's some business about loaves and fishes.

BARIONA: I see the kind of thing he's doing. And then what?

THE WITCH DOCTOR: That's all for the miracles. He doesn't seem to want to work them.

BARIONA: No kidding. He must not know how to do them right. And then what? What's he saying?

THE WITCH DOCTOR: He's saying, "He who would gain his life must lose it."

LELIUS: Very good.

THE WITCH DOCTOR: He's saying that his father's kingdom is not of this earth.

LELIUS: Perfect. That makes people patient.

THE WITCH DOCTOR: He's also saying that it is easier for a camel to pass through the eye of a needle than for a rich man to enter the kingdom of heaven.

LELIUS: That's not so good. But I excuse him: if you want to make out with the lower classes, you have to make up your mind to get in a few knocks at capitalism. The main thing, though, is for him to leave the kingdom of the earth to the rich.

BARIONA: And what happens to him next?

THE WITCH DOCTOR: He suffers and dies.

BARIONA: Like everyone.

THE WITCH DOCTOR: More than everyone. He's being arrested, dragged before a tribunal, stripped naked, whipped, mocked by everyone, and, finally, crucified. The people are crowding around his cross and telling him, "If thou be the King of the Jews, save thyself." And he isn't saving himself; he's crying out in a loud voice, "My God, my God, why hast thou forsaken me." And he dies.

BARIONA: And he dies? No kidding! The great Messiah. We've had better ones who have all been forgotten!

THE WITCH DOCTOR: This one won't be forgotten so fast. On the contrary, I see a great indwelling of nations around his disciples. And his word is carried across the seas to Rome itself and farther on up to the shadowy forests of Gaul and Germany.

BARIONA: What are they so joyful about then? His useless life or his shameful death?

THE WITCH DOCTOR: I think it's his death.

BARIONA: His death! Damn, if we could only keep it from happening . . . No; let them shift for themselves. They asked for it. (*A pause.*) My brothers! My brothers folding their big knotty fingers and going down on their knees in front of a slave dying on the cross. Dying without even a cry of rebellion as he breathes out a soft astonished reproach like a sigh. Dying like a rat in a trap. And my men, my own men are going to worship him. Come on; give him his money and get him out of here. Because I guess you don't have anything else to tell us, right?

THE WITCH DOCTOR: Nothing else, your Lordship. Thank you, your Lordships.

The witch doctor goes out.

LELIUS: How come you're so upset all of a sudden?

BARIONA: Don't you see that it's a matter of the liquidation of the Jewish people? If you Romans had wanted to punish us you wouldn't have done anything different. Come on; tell the truth. Is he one of your people, this Messiah? Is Rome paying him?

LELIUS: Remember that at this moment he has existed for twelve hours. He's a little young to have sold out already.

BARIONA: I can see Jerevah as he used to be—the solid, brutal Jerevah, more a fighter than a shepherd, and my lieutenant in the old days in our struggles against Hebron—and I can just imagine him all perfumed and pomaded with that religion. He's going to bleat like a lamb . . . Ah! What a laugh . . .
. . . Witch doctor! Witch doctor!

THE WITCH DOCTOR: Your Lordship?

BARIONA: Did you say the mob will adopt his teachings?

THE WITCH DOCTOR: Yes, your Lordship.

BARIONA: Oh humiliated Jerusalem!

LELIUS: What in the world is the matter with you?

BARIONA: I know one alone who is crucified—Zion. The Zion that your people, the copper-helmeted Romans, nailed with their own hands to the cross. And we who are not Romans, we have always believed that the day would come when Zion would tear her martyred hands and feet free from the stake and march forth, bloody and proud, against her enemies. And that was our belief in the Messiah. Ah, if only that man with his unbearable gaze had come all armored in sparkling steel, if only he had put a sword in my right hand and said to me,

"Gird up thy loins and follow me!" How I would have followed him in the din of battles, making Roman heads fly off the way you cut the heads off poppies in the field. We grew up with that hope. We gritted our teeth, and if a Roman happened to come through our town, we used to like to stare at him and whisper behind his back, because the sight of him fed the hate in our hearts. I'm proud! I'm proud because I never accepted slavery and I never once stopped stoking up the burning fire of hatred in me. And lately, seeing that our bloodless village didn't have enough strength any more to rebel, I preferred having it wipe itself out to seeing it bow beneath the Roman yoke!

LELIUS: Beautiful! That's the kind of speech a Roman official is exposed to when he's sent to inspect a godforsaken village. But I don't see what this Messiah has to do with all this.

BARIONA: That's because you don't want to see. We were expecting a soldier and they sent us a mystical lamb who preaches resignation to us and tells us, "Do as I do; die on your cross uncomplainingly and cautiously, so that you won't upset your neighbors. Be gentle. Gentle like children. Lick your suffering with little licks the way a beaten dog licks his master so that he'll be forgiven. Be humble. Think that you have merited your sufferings. And if they seem too great to bear, imagine they are trials which will make you pure. And if you feel a human anger boiling up inside of you, push it down again. Say Thank you, always say Thank you. Thank you when they slap you. Thank you when they kick you. Have children so that there'll be new tails to kick in the future. Old people's children who'll be born resigned and who'll pamper their little old wrinkled sufferings with the proper humility. Children who'll be born just to suffer the way I do; I was born for the cross. And if you're good and humble and contrite, if you've made your breastbone hum like the skin of an ass by beating it diligently, then maybe you'll have a place in the kingdom of the humble people, which is in Heaven . . ." Is that what my people are to become, a people who go willingly to their own crucifixion? What has happened to you, Jehovah, God of Vengeance? Ah, Romans, if this is true, you won't have done a quarter of the harm to us that we're going to do to ourselves. We're going to poison the living springs of our strength; we're going to sign the order for our own arrest. Resignation will kill us; and I hate it, Roman, more than I hate you.

LELIUS: Whoa; whoa down there, chief; you've lost your common sense. And in your wildness you're saying things you'll be sorry for.

BARIONA: Shut up! (*To himself*) If I could only keep it from happening . . . Keep the pure flame of rebellion burning in them . . . Oh my brothers! You've abandoned me and I'm not your leader any more. But at least I'll do this for you. I'll go down to Bethlehem. The women are slowing them down and I know short cuts they don't: I'll be there before they are. And it won't take long, I guess, to wring the frail neck of a baby, even if he is the King of the Jews!

Bariona goes out.

LELIUS: Let's follow him. I'm afraid he'll go to the worst extremes. But that's the life of a colonial administrator.

Curtain.

THE SHOWMAN: Good people, I refrained from coming out to interrupt the scenes you've just been seeing so that events could take their own course. And you see that the plot has thickened, because here's our Bariona running over the mountain to kill Christ.

But now we have a little break, because all our characters are on the road, some having taken the mule drivers' road and the others the goat paths. The mountain is swarming with men rejoicing, and the wind is carrying the echoes of their joy all the way up to the wild animals who live on the mountaintops.

I'm going to take advantage of this break to show you Christ in the stable, because otherwise you won't see him: he doesn't appear in the play, nor does Joseph or the Virgin Mary. But since it's Christmas today, you have the right to insist that you be shown the manger. Here it is.

Here is the Virgin and here is Joseph and here is the baby Jesus. The artist put all his love into this picture, but maybe it will seem a little simple-minded to you. See; the people have pretty clothes but they look stiff: you'd think they were puppets. They surely weren't like that. If your eyes were closed like mine . . . But listen; all you have to do is close your eyes and listen to me, and I'll tell you how I see them inside myself.

The Virgin is pale and she's looking at the child. What you ought to paint on her face is an anxious amazement which has been seen only one time on a human face. Because Christ is her child, the flesh of her flesh and the fruit of her bowels. She carried him nine months and she'll give him her breast and her milk will become God's blood. And at times the temptation is so great she forgets that he is God. She hugs him in her arms and says, My little baby! But other times she's all flabbergasted and she thinks, God is there—and she feels overcome by a religious horror at this silent God, this terrifying child. Because all mothers are pulled up short that way sometimes in front of that rebellious bit of their flesh which is their child, and they feel like exiles even though they're just a step away from this new life that has been made out of their life, and that houses a stranger's thoughts. But no other child has been more cruelly and quickly torn from his mother, because he is God and he far surpasses anything she can imagine.

And it's hard on a mother to be ashamed of herself and ashamed of being human when she's with her son.

But I think there are other times too, quick gliding ones, when she feels *at the same time* that Christ is her son, her own little one, and that he's God. She looks at him and she thinks, "This God is my baby. This divine flesh is my flesh. He's made of me; he has my eyes and this shape of his mouth is the same shape as mine. He looks like me. He's God and he looks like me."

And no woman has had her God just for herself that way. A tiny little God you can take in your arms and cover with kisses, a God all warm and smiling and breathing, a God you can touch, who's alive. And it's in one of these moments that I'd paint Mary if I were a painter, and I'd try to show the air of tender boldness and timidity with which she stretches out her finger to touch the soft little skin of that child-God whose lukewarm weight she feels on her lap, and who is smiling at her.

And that's that for Jesus and the Virgin Mary.

And what about Joseph? I won't paint Joseph. I'll only show a shadow at the back of the barn and two shining eyes.

Because I don't know what to say about Joseph, and Joseph doesn't know what to say about himself. He worships and is happy worshipping, and he feels a little out of it.

It think he's suffering without admitting it. He's suffering because he sees how much the woman he loves resembles God, how close she already is to God. Because God has burst into the closeness of this family like a bomb. Joseph and Mary are separated forever by this burst of light. And Joseph's whole life, I guess, will be for the sake of learning to accept.

Good people, that's it for the Holy Family. Now we're going to take up Bariona's story again, because you know he wants to strangle this baby. He's running, he's hurrying up, and here he is in Bethlehem. But before I show him to you, here's a little Christmas song.

Let the music play.

SIXTH TABLEAU

Bethlehem, in front of a stable.

SCENE I

LELIUS, BARIONA, *with lanterns*

LELIUS: Unh! I'm worn out and out of breath. You ran across that mountain in the middle of the night like a will-o'-the-wisp. And all I had to light my way was this puny little lantern.

BARIONA, *to himself:* We got here before they did.

LELIUS: A hundred times I thought I'd break my neck.

BARIONA: I wish to God you were at the bottom of a cliff with all your bones broken. I would have pushed you down there myself if I hadn't had my mind on something else. (*A pause.*) Well here it is. You can see a circle of light filtering under the door. You can't hear a sound. He's there on the other side of the wall, the King of the Jews. He's there. We'll take care of that business right now.

LELIUS: What are you going to do?

BARIONA: When they get here, they'll find a dead baby.

LELIUS: Do you really mean it? Are you really thinking about going through with this awful business? Isn't it enough for you to have wanted to kill your own child?

BARIONA: Isn't it the death of the Messiah they're supposed to worship? Well, I'm going to set it ahead thirty-three years, that death. And I'll spare him those humiliating death pangs on the cross. A little blue corpse on the straw! Let them kneel before that if they want. A little corpse in swaddling clothes. And that will put an end forever to all this fine preaching about resignation and the spirit of sacrifice.

LELIUS: Your mind is really made up?

BARIONA: Yes.

LELIUS: Then I'll spare you my speeches. But at least let me leave. I don't have enough strength any more to stop this murder. Besides, you'd cut my throat too, and it's beneath the dignity of a Roman citizen to spend the night on a road in Judea with his throat slit. But I can't sanction such an abomination with my presence either. I'll apply the rule of my leader, the procurator: let the Jews shift for themselves. My regards.

> *He goes out; Bariona, left alone, goes up to the door. He's about to go in; Mark appears.*

SCENE III[1]

MARK, BARIONA

MARK, *with a lantern:* Hey there, fellow. What are you doing here?

BARIONA: Is that your stable?

MARK: Yes.

BARIONA: Are you sheltering a man named Joseph and a woman named Mary in there?

MARK: A man and a woman came to me day before yesterday asking for hospitality. As a matter of fact, they are asleep in there.

1. Mistake in numbering.

BARIONA: I'm looking for my cousins from Nazareth who were supposed to come here for the census. The woman was pregnant, wasn't she?

MARK: Yes. She's a very young woman with a modest air and the smiles and curtsies of a child. But there's a pride in her modesty I never saw in anyone. Did you know she had a baby last night?

BARIONA: Really? I'm glad, if it's my cousin. Is the baby all right?

MARK: It's a son. A beautiful little boy. My mother tells me I looked like him at that age. How much they seem to love him! The mother had scarcely had him before she washed him and took him on her lap. She's there, very pale and leaning against a post, looking at him without saying anything. And the man, he isn't real young anymore, right? He knows that this baby is going to go through all the suffering he's already been through. And I imagine he must be thinking, maybe he'll succeed where I tried and failed.

BARIONA: I don't know. I don't have a son.

MARK: Then you're like me. And I'm sorry for you. You'll never have that look, that luminous and slightly comical look, of a man who hangs back, very embarrassed by his big body and sorry he didn't suffer labor pains for his son.

BARIONA: Who are you? And why are you talking to me this way?

MARK: I'm an angel, Bariona. I'm your angel. Don't kill that baby.

BARIONA: Get out of here.

MARK: Yes. I'm going. Because we angels can't do anything to stop human freedom. But think about that look on Joseph's face.

He goes out.

SCENE IV

BARIONA, *alone:* I've had enough of angels! It's time, because the others will be here soon. And that's what Bariona's last great act will be: strangling a baby. (*He opens the door a crack.*)

The lamp is smoking; the shadows are rising up to the ceiling like great moving pillars. The woman has her back turned to me and I can't see the baby; he's on her lap, I guess. But I can see the man. It's true: the way he's looking at her! With such eyes! What can there be behind these two unclouded eyes, unclouded like two empty places in that tangled, furrowed face? What hope? No; it isn't hope. And what clouds of horror would rise up from the depths of him and cover over these two patches of sky if he saw me strangle his child? All right; I haven't seen this baby, but I know already that I won't lay a hand on him. If I was going to get up the nerve to crush that young life between my hands, I shouldn't have seen him first at the bottom of his father's eyes. All right; I'm beaten. (*Shouts of the crowd.*) There they are. I don't want them to recognize me.

He hides his face with the edge of his cloak and keeps himself to the side.

SCENE V

BARIONA, THE CROWD

THE CROWD: Hosanna! Hosanna!

CAIPHUS: Here's the stable!

A great silence.

SARAH: The child is there. In that stable.

CAIPHUS: Let's go in and fall on our knees before him to worship him.

PAUL: And we'll tell his mother we're just ahead of the Wise Men's procession.

SHALAM: I'll kiss his little hands and be made young again as if I'd dipped my old bones in a fountain of youth.

CAIPHUS: Hey, you people! Get your gifts together and let's be ready to give them to the Holy Mother to honor her. Me, I'm going to bring him some lamb's milk in my gourd.

PAUL: And me, two big hanks of wool I sheared off my sheep's backs myself.

FIRST ELDER: And me this old silver medal my grandfather won in a rifle match.

THE PUBLICAN: And me, I'll give him the donkey that brought me here.

FIRST ELDER: Your present won't have cost you much; it's the Roman's donkey.

THE PUBLICAN: All the more reason. The one who has just freed us from Rome couldn't help liking a donkey stolen from the Romans.

PAUL: And you, Simon; what are you giving our Lord?

SIMON: Today I won't give him anything, because I've been caught short. But I've written him a song that tells him all the gifts I'll give him later.
My sweet Jesus, for your feast . . .

THE CROWD: Hurrah! Hurrah!

FIRST ELDER: Be quiet and let's go in in an orderly way and hold your hats in your hands. If the wind and the trip have mussed up your clothes, smooth them out again.

They file in.

BARIONA: Sarah is there with the others. She's pale . . . I hope that long walk didn't wear her out. Her feet are bleeding. Ah, how joyful she looks! There isn't the least little memory of me back of those shining eyes any more.

The crowd has come into the stable.

What are they up to? You can't hear any noise at all any more; but this silence isn't like the silence in our mountains, that icy silence of the high thin air which rules our granite halls. It's a silence deeper than the silence of the forests. A silence rising up toward heaven and rustling against the stars like a big old tree whose hair is soothed by the wind. Have they fallen on their knees? Ah if I could be there with them, invisible; because the spectacle really must not be any ordinary one, with all those tough, serious men, out to work and make a buck, down on their knees before a crying baby. Shalam's son, who left him when he was fifteen because he'd been whacked on the head too much, would really get a laugh out of seeing his old man worshipping a little brat. Are the children going to rule over their parents? (*A silence.*) They're in there in that lukewarm stable, simple and happy after their long hike in the cold. They've folded their hands and they're thinking, something has begun. And they're wrong, of course, and they've fallen into a trap and it will cost them dearly later on; but just the same they will have had this moment. They're lucky to be able to believe that something's beginning. What is there that moves a man's heart more than the beginning of a world and the ambiguous features of youth and the beginning of a love, when everything is still possible, when the sun is there like a fine dust in the air and on our faces without having come up yet, and the raw freshness of the morning gives us a hint of the day's heavy promise?

In that stable, a day is breaking . . . In that stable, it's morning. And here outside it's nighttime. Nighttime on the road and in my heart. A starless night, deep and full of tumult like the high seas. That's it; I'm being tossed about by the night the way the waves toss a barrel, and the stable is behind me, shut up in its light. It's wandering through the night like Noah's ark, holding the morning of the world. The world's first morning. Because there never had been any morning before. It had fallen from the hands of its unworthy creator and it was falling in a fiery furnace, in the darkness, and the great flaming tongues of that hopeless night were licking over it, covering it with blisters and making swarms of lice and bedbugs fester on it. And me, I dwell in the earth's great night, in the tropical night of hatred and calamity. But for my brothers—O deceitful power of faith—thousands of years after the creation, in that stable, by the light of a candle, the world's first morning is rising.

The crowd sings a Christmas carol.

They're singing like pilgrims who've set out in the cool of the night with their knapsacks, staffs, and sandals and who are beginning to see the first gray streaks of dawn in the distance. They're singing and that child is there between them like the pale eastern sun, the early morning sun that you can still look at. A little naked child the color of the rising sun. Ah what a beautiful lie. I'd give my right hand to be able to believe it even for a second. Is it my fault, Lord, that you have made me like a night creature and cut into my flesh that terrible secret: It will never come morning? Is it my fault if I *know* that your Messiah is a poor beggar who'll die on the cross like an animal, and that Jerusalem will always be enslaved?

Second Christmas carol.

There. They're singing and I'm keeping to myself on the threshold of their joy, blinking my eyes like an owl frightened by the light. They've abandoned me and my wife is with them and they're rejoicing, having forgotten that I even exist. I'm on the road on the side of the world that's ending, and they're on the side of the world that's beginning. I feel more alone on the edge of their joy and their prayer than I do in my deserted village. And I'm sorry I came down among men, because I don't find enough hate in me any more. Alas, why is man's pride like wax, and why does it take no more than the first rays of dawn to melt it? I'd like to tell them, "You're going toward vile resignation, toward the death of your courage; you'll be like women and slaves, and if you're slapped on one cheek you'll turn the other." And I remain silent, I don't move, I don't have the heart to take away their blessed confidence in the power of the morning.

Third Christmas carol.

The Three Kings enter.

SCENE VI

BARIONA, THE THREE KINGS

BALTHAZAR: Is that you, Bariona? I thought I'd find you here.

BARIONA: I didn't come to worship your Christ.

BALTHAZAR: No; you came to punish yourself and keep to yourself on the edge of our happy crowd, like the men who flocked to his cradle of straw tonight. They'll betray him the way they betrayed you. Right now they're showering him with gifts and tenderness, but there's not one of them—not one, you hear—who wouldn't abandon him if he knew the future. Because he'll disappoint them all, Bariona. They're expecting him to run the Romans out, and the Romans won't be run out; to make flowers and fruits grow from the rocks, and the rocks will stay barren; to put an end to human suffering, and people will still be suffering a thousand years from now just the way they are today.

BARIONA: That's what I told them.

BALTHAZAR: I know. And that's why I'm speaking to you now, because you're closer to Christ than all of them and your ears can be opened to receive the real good news.

BARIONA: And what is this good news?

BALTHAZAR: Listen: Christ will suffer in the flesh because he is man. But he is God too and in his divinity he is *beyond* that suffering. And we men made in the image of God are beyond all our own suffering to the extent that we are like God. Look: until tonight man had his eyes stopped by his suffering the way Tobias' eyes were stopped with bird droppings. All man saw was his suffering, and he took himself for a wounded animal drunk with pain who went leaping through the woods to escape his wound and took his hurt with him wherever he went. And you, Bariona, you too were a man of the old dispensation. You looked upon your suffering with bitterness and said, I'm mortally wounded; and you wanted to lie down on your side and spend the rest of your life meditating the injustice that had been done to you. Now Christ came to redeem you; he came to suffer and to show you how to deal with suffering. Because we mustn't mull over it, or think our honor consists in suffering more than the others, or resign ourselves to it either.

Suffering is a common thing, a natural fact, that you ought to accept as if you had it coming to you; and it is unbecoming to talk about it too much, even to yourself. Come to terms with it as soon as possible, snuggle it down nice and warm in the middle of your heart like a dog stretched out by the fire. Don't think anything about it, unless it's that it's there, as that stone is there in the road, as the night is there all around us.

Then you will discover that truth which Christ came to teach you and which you already know: you are not your suffering. Whatever you do and however you look at it, you surpass it infinitely; because it means exactly what you want it to. Whether you dwell on it as a mother lies down on the frozen body of her child to warm it up again, or whether on the contrary you turn away from it indifferently, it is you who give it its meaning and make it what it is. For in itself it's nothing but matter for human action, and Christ came to teach you that you are responsible for yourself and your suffering. It is like stones and roots and everything which has weight and tends downward; it's because of it that you weigh heavily on the road and press against the earth with the soles of your feet. But you, you are beyond your own suffering, because you shape it according to your will. You are light, Bariona. Ah, if you knew how light man is. And if you accept your share of suffering as your daily bread, then you are *beyond*. And everything that is beyond your lot of suffering and your cares, all of that belongs to you—all of it—everything that's light, I mean the world. The world and your own self, Bariona, because you are for yourself a perpetually gratuitous gift.

You are suffering and I have no pity at all for your suffering, for why wouldn't you suffer? But there is this beautiful inky night around you, and there are these songs in the stable, and there is this beautiful hard dry cold as merciless as a virtue, and all of this belongs to you. It is waiting for you, this beautiful night swollen with shadows across which fires are darting like fish cutting through the sea. It is waiting for you by the side of your road, timidly and tenderly; because Christ has come to give it to you. Fling yourself toward the sky and then you shall be free, O expendable creature among all the expendable creatures, free and breathless and astonished to exist at the very heart of God, in the kingdom of God who is in heaven and also on earth.

BARIONA: Is that what Christ came to teach us?

BALTHAZAR: He also has a message for you.

BARIONA: For me?

BALTHAZAR: For you. He has come to tell you, let your child be born. He will suffer, it's true. But that isn't any of your business. Don't pity his suffering; you have no right to. It will be his business alone, and he'll make exactly what he wants of it, because he will be free. Even if he is lame, even if he has to go to war and lose his arms or legs there, even if the woman he loves betrays him seven times, he is free, free to rejoice eternally in his existence. You were telling me before that God has no power over human freedom, and it's true.

But so what? A new freedom is going to shoot up toward heaven like a great pillar of bronze. Would you have the heart to stop it? Christ is born for all the world's children, Bariona, and each time a child is born, Christ will be born in him and through him to be forever mocked, along with him, by all the pains of life, and in him and through him, to escape all those pains. Forever. He is come to tell the blind, the disabled, the unemployed, and the prisoners of this world, "You should not keep from having children. For even for the blind and the disabled and the unemployed and the prisoners there is joy."

BARIONA: Is that all you had to tell me?

BALTHAZAR: Yes.

BARIONA: All right then: Go into that stable too and leave me alone, because I want to meditate and talk things over with myself.

BALTHAZAR: I'll be seeing you, Bariona, O first disciple of Christ.

BARIONA: Leave me alone. Don't say any more. Get out.

Balthazar goes out. Bariona is left alone.

SCENE VII

BARIONA, *alone:* Free . . . Ah, you heart of mine clenched tight around your denial, you ought to loosen your fingers and open yourself up; you ought to accept . . . I ought to go into that stable and get down on my knees. It would be the first time in my life. I'd go in, keep apart from the others who betrayed me, on my knees in a dark corner . . . and then the icy wind of midnight and the infinite empire of this sacred night would belong to me. I'd be free, free. Free against God and for God, free against myself and for myself . . . (*He takes a few steps; there's a chorus from the stable.*) Ah, how hard it is!

SEVENTH TABLEAU

SCENE I

JEREVAH: They won't be able to get away. Troops are coming from the south and north and squeezing Bethlehem in a vise.

PAUL: We could tell Joseph to go up into our mountains. He'd be safe up there.

CAIPHUS: Impossible. The mountain road meets the highway a good seven leagues from here. The troops coming from Jerusalem will be there before us.

PAUL: Then . . . Unless there's a miracle . . .

CAIPHUS: There won't be any miracle: the Messiah is still too little; he doesn't understand yet. He'll smile at the man in his coat of mail who's going to lean over his cradle to stick him through the heart.

SHALAM: They'll go into all the houses and grab the newborn by their feet and split their heads open against the wall.

A JEW: Blood, still more blood, alas!

THE CROWD: Alas!

SARAH: My child, my God, my little one. You whom I already loved as if I were your mother and worshipped as if I were your servant. You whom I would have liked to give birth to in pain, O God who made yourself my son, O son of all women. You were mine, mine; you were already more a part of me than this flower of flesh which is blooming in my flesh. You were my child and the destiny of this child who's sleeping in the depths of me, and here they are on the way to kill you. Because it's always the males who tear us apart, when they feel like it, and make our little ones suffer. O God the Father, Lord who sees me, Mary is still happy and sacred in the stable, and she can't pray to you to keep her son safe from harm because she doesn't suspect anything yet. And the mothers in Bethlehem are happy, all nice and warm in their homes; they're smiling at their little children, unaware of the danger marching up toward them. But me, me here on the road alone and still childless, look upon me; for in this instant it is me you've chosen to sweat out the agony of all the mothers. O Lord, I'm suffering and writhing like a chopped worm, my anguish is enormous like the ocean. Lord, I am all the mothers and I say to you, take me, torture me, poke out my eyes, tear out my fingernails, but save him! Save the King of Judea, save your son, and save our little ones too.

CAIPHUS: Come on! You were right, Bariona. Everything always has gone badly and it still is. We just begin to see a little light and then it's snuffed out by the mighty of the earth.

SHALAM: Then it wasn't true that the orange trees were going to grow on the mountaintops and we'd have nothing left to do and I was going to get young again?

BARIONA: No; it wasn't true.

CAIPHUS: And it wasn't true that there would be peace on earth to men of good will?

BARIONA: Oh yes! That was true. If you only knew how true it was!

SHALAM: I don't understand what you mean. But I know that you were right the other day when you urged us not to have any more children. Our people have a curse on them. Look; the women in the lowlands gave birth and they came and cut their newborn babies' throats while they were holding them in their arms.

CAIPHUS: We should have listened to you and never come down to town. Because what happens in towns just isn't for us.

JEREVAH: Let's go back to Bethaur; and you, Bariona, you tough but farsighted guide, forgive us our trespasses and be our leader again.

ALL: Yes, yes! Bariona! Bariona!

BARIONA: O men of little faith. You betrayed me for the Messiah and now at the first breath of ill wind you are betraying the Messiah and turning back to me.

ALL: Forgive us, Bariona.

BARIONA: Am I your leader again?

ALL: Yes, yes.

BARIONA: Will you carry out my orders blindly?

ALL: We swear!

BARIONA: All right then; listen to what I'm ordering you to do. You, Simon, go warn Joseph and Mary. Tell them to saddle up

Lelius' donkey and follow the road up to the crossroads. You'll show them the way. You'll have them take the mountain road up to Hebron. Then they're to go down again toward the north; the road is open.

PAUL: But Bariona, won't the Romans be at the crossroads before they are?

BARIONA: No, because the rest of us are going to go out to meet them, and we'll make them retreat. We'll keep them busy long enough for Joseph to get through.

PAUL: What are you saying?

BARIONA: Don't you want your Christ? All right then, who's going to save him if you don't?

CAIPHUS: But they're going to kill us all. All we have is poles and knives.

BARIONA: Tie your knives to the end of your poles and you can use them for pikestaffs.

SHALAM: We'll all be massacred.

BARIONA: All right, we will! I think we will all be massacred. But listen; I *believe* in your Christ now. It's true; God has come to earth. And what he is asking of you right now is this sacrifice. Are you going to refuse to make it for him? Are you going to keep your children from hearing his teaching?

PAUL: You, Bariona, the skeptic who refused so long to follow the Wise Men, do you really believe that this child? . . .

BARIONA: I'm telling you the truth: that child is the Christ.

PAUL: Then I'm with you.

BARIONA: And you, brothers? You always used to miss the bloody street fights we fought against the people up in Hebron when we were young. Now the time to fight has come again, the time of red harvests and berries of blood beading up on the lips of wounds. Are you going to refuse to fight? Would you rather die of old age and poverty up there in your eagle's nest?

ALL: No! No! We'll follow you; we'll save Christ. Hurrah!

BARIONA: Oh my brothers, I've found you again and I love you. All right now, leave me alone a while because I want to think about a plan of attack. Run through the town and pick up all the arms you can find.

ALL: Long live Bariona!

They go out.

SCENE II

BARIONA, SARAH

SARAH: Bariona . . .

BARIONA: My sweet Sarah!

SARAH: Forgive me, Bariona!

BARIONA: I don't have anything to forgive you for. Christ called you and you took the royal road to him. Me, I took the back roads. But we ended up finding each other again.

SARAH: Do you really want to die? Christ requires us to live.

BARIONA: I don't want to die. I don't want to die at all, I'd like to live and enjoy this world which has been revealed to me and help you raise our child. But I want to stop them from killing our Messiah and I really think I don't have any choice: I can only defend him by giving my life.

SARAH: I love you, Bariona.

BARIONA: Sarah! I know you love me and I also know you love the child you're going to have even more than me. But I don't want any bitterness, Sarah; we're going to leave one another without any tears. You must rejoice instead, because Christ is born and your child is going to be born.

SARAH: I can't live without you . . .

BARIONA: Sarah! Instead you must cling to life avariciously, ruthlessly, for the sake of our child. Raise him without hiding any of the world's miseries from him, and arm him against them. And I'm making you responsible for a message for him. Later, when he has grown up, not right away, not at the first pangs of love, not the first time he's disappointed, but much later, when he knows how immensely left alone and lonely he is, when he tells you about a certain taste of gall in the back of his mouth, tell him, "Your father suffered everything you're suffering and he died joyfully."

SARAH: Joyfully.

BARIONA: Joyfully! I'm overflowing with joy like a cup that's too full. I'm free; I hold my fate in my hands. I'm marching against Herod's soldiers and God is marching at my side. I'm light, Sarah, light. Ah, if you only knew how light I am! Oh joy, joy! Tears of joy! Farewell, my sweet Sarah. Hold up your head and smile at me. You must be joyful: I love you and Christ is born.

SARAH: I will be joyful. Farewell, Bariona.

The crowd comes back on stage.

SCENE III

The Same—the Crowd

PAUL: We're ready to follow you, Bariona.

ALL: We're ready.

BARIONA: My brothers, soldiers of Christ, you look determined and ferocious and I know you'll fight well. But I want more from you than this somber determination. I want you to die joyfully. Christ is born, oh my brothers, and you are going to fulfill your destiny. You're going to die like fighters just the way you dreamed of dying when you were young, and you're going to die for God. It would be indecent if you kept these sullen faces. Come on, drink a little slug of wine, I give you permission, and let's march against these mercenaries of Herod. Let's march, drunk with songs and wine and hope.

THE CROWD: Bariona, Bariona! Noel! Noel!

BARIONA, *to the prisoners:* And you prisoners, this is the end of this Christmas play which was written for you. You are not happy, and maybe there is more than one of you who has tasted that taste of gall in his mouth, that bitter salty taste I'm talking about. But I think that for you, too, on this Christmas day—and every other day—there'll still be joy!

Herman Melville's *Moby Dick*

GIONO'S SALUTE TO MELVILLE—a peasant saluting a sailor. I confess that I was curious to hear a landlubber—one of those landlubbers Melville had such contempt for—speak to us about this seaman. Would Giono find—among his arsenal of firmly rooted painted images, borrowed from the country landscape's patient shapes, among his store of animistic images (the animism of small-town tales)—the proper ways of speaking of the sea's unending new beginnings and of those geometric skies which spin above our heads like a circle whose center is nimble and circumference elastic? I confess I was disappointed. Giono became a tiller of the fields through a conscious decree, a little like the way Barrès became a Lorrainer—and he is still a tiller of the fields. Like a tiller of the fields he looks at the sky to see if the weather will be good tomorrow. If he talks about the sea he does so as a peasant: "He painfully plows and replows the immense fields of the South Seas." (What real sailor could think that he's "plowing" this great barren metal?) Even when he elevates his tone, he is still a rustic poet, completely surrounded by "living beings" and frozen once and for all into his arrested, anthropomorphic mythology. He'll say that Melville "straddles iron thunderstorms." And when he writes "the sea currents' monstrous mane," he's less like a rustic than a small-town

This review of Jean Giono's translation of *Moby Dick* was published as "*Moby Dick* d'Herman Melville: Plus qu'un chef-d'oeuvre, un formidable monument" in *Comoedia*, June 21, 1941. See also Vol. I, 41/32.

scholar, a notary public dreaming over a map and its big blue-colored spaces.

Luckily we have *Moby Dick* for every useful bit of information we could want. Let's not call *Moby Dick* "this masterpiece." Let's call it instead—as we call *Ulysses*—"this imposing monument." If you enter this world, what will strike you first is its total absence of color. It's a furrowed, battered, bristly world of rugged places and reliefs, enormous fixed or moving waves. But the sea in it is neither green nor blue; it is gray, black, or white. White above all, when the boats are dancing on "the curdled milk of the whale's dreadful wrath." The sky is white, the nights are white, the icicles hang from the ship's poop "like the white tusks of a giant elephant." In Melville's work, whiteness returns like a leitmotiv of demoniacal horror. Ahab, the accursed captain, says of himself, "I leave a white and troubled wake of pallid cheeks and waters everywhere I sail." It's that "nature doesn't fail to use whiteness as an element of terror." Colors are only secondary qualities, *trompe-l'oeil*. Melville suffers from a very special kind of color blindness: he is condemned to strip things of their colored appearance, condemned to see white. Giono tells us that this sailor "has a precision of gaze which fastens onto every place where there is nothing: in the sky, in the sea, in space. . . ." And it's true that Melville's vision is strangely precise. But it isn't nothingness he's looking at but pure being, the secret whiteness of being; he "looks upon . . . the universe's leprous skin, the gigantic white shroud that wraps all things, with a naked eye." I am reminded of that contrary yet identical expression of Audiberti's, "the secret blackness of milk." Black and white are the same here, in a Hegelian identity of opposites. The reason is that "the whole of divine nature is painted simply." At their center, on the level of their sheer existence, beings are indifferently black or white: black in their compact and stubborn isolation, white when they are struck by the light's great emptiness. It is on the level of this massive, polar indistinction of substance that the deeper drama of *Moby Dick* is played out. Melville is condemned to live at the level of being. "All objects," he writes, "all visible objects are no more than cardboard dummies. But in each event . . . in living being . . . behind the incontestable fact, something unknown and reasoning reveals itself, behind the dummy which does not itself reason." No one more than Hegel and Melville has sensed that the absolute is there all around us, formidable and familiar, that we can see it, white and polished like a sheep bone, if we only cast aside the multicolored veils with which we've covered it. We haunt the absolute; but no one, to my knowledge, no one except Melville, has attempted this extraordinary undertaking of retaining the indefinable taste of a pure quality—the purest quality, whiteness—and seeking in that taste itself the absolute which goes beyond it. If this is one of the directions in which contemporary literature is trying in a groping way to go, then Melville is the most "modern" writer.

That is why we should stop seeing a symbolic universe in the tales he tells and in the *things* he describes. Symbols are attached retrospectively to ideas we begin with, but to begin with Melville has no idea to express. He is acquainted only with things, and it is in the depths of things that he finds his ideas. I am sure that he began by thinking that he would tell the best story of a whale hunt he could. This accounts for a first, heavily documentary aspect of his book. He tries to make even the slightest detail precise; he piles up knowledge and statistics to such a degree that he comes to seem insanely erudite and we think at first—as a result of his naïvely didactic concerns, the slow peaceful pace of his narrative, and also a certain humor typical of the period—that we are in the presence of some eccentric Jules Verne novel. *Twenty Thousand Leagues Across the Sea, or The Adventures of A Whale Hunter.* And then, little by little, a cancerous proliferation begins to swell and warp the clean and easy style of this American Jules Verne, just as *Crime and Punishment* is basically only a cancer eating away *Les Mystères de Paris.* The documentary comes apart at the seams. What happened was that Melville suddenly realized that there was an idea in the whale hunt; he saw "in a white heat" that strange tie between man and animal, the *hunt.* A relationship of dizziness and death. And it is this relationship that is revealed abruptly at the end of the first hundred pages. Hatred. *Moby Dick's* romantic subject is the exact opposite of that of *Une Passion dans le désert:* not an animal's love for a man but a man's hatred for an animal. Ahab, the captain of the *Pequod,* has lost his leg in "the ivory jaws" of a white whale which has escaped his harpoon. Since then he has been consumed with hatred for this monster; he pursues him everywhere across the seas. This demoniacal character, whose role is to bring out what might be called the zoological side of man's fate, man's animal roots, his carnivorous nature, his nature as the scourge of animals, remains in spite of everything at the level of a somewhat outmoded romanticism: Ahab inveigles his harpooners into a solemn oath which reminds us a little of the casting of the bullets in *Der Freischütz* and of Weber's music. But this novel of hatred swells and then bursts beneath the thrust of a different cancer. With it, even the novelistic form of the narrative disappears; for there is an idea of hatred just as there is an idea of whiteness or of the whale hunt, and this idea involves the whole man, the whole human condition. From now on the novelist's technique seems to Melville to be insufficient to catch this idea. All means are going to seem legitimate to him: sermons, courtroom oratory, theatrical dialogues, interior monologues, real or seeming erudition, the epic—the epic above all. The epic because the volume of these sumptuous marine sentences, which rise up and fall away like liquid mountains dissipating into strange and superb images, is above all epic. In his best moments, Melville has the inspiration of a Lautréamont. And then, finally, he becomes conscious of writing an epic. He amuses himself writing it, he multiplies invocations to the democratic god and prosopopoeias, he entertains himself by presenting the harpooners as Homeric heroes. But when the reader has finally gotten the idea, when he finds himself at last face to face with the unaccommodated fate of man, when he sees man as Melville sees him—this fallen transcendence in his horrible abandonment—it's no longer an epic he thinks he has read but an enormous *summa*, a gigantic, monstrous, gently antediluvian book which could only be compared, in its unmeasured hugeness, to Rabelais's *Pantagruel* or James Joyce's *Ulysses*. And after that it would be rather tactless to reread the salute which Giono, a minor rural prophet, tosses to the major prophet Melville.

Sick at Heart

June 10

AT SIX IN THE MORNING we leave Mommenheim by motorcar. The regiments of footsloggers we pass on the road have knocked off more than forty kilometers during the night. It seems they're coming from Wissemburg, and they've made big detours. They watch us go by, not angry but very surprised. Actually, we've had to grunt just like everybody else, but the fact remains that we're being shipped by motorcar.

"I wonder what they think of us?" Pierné, a socialist, asks.

"Not much. They're thinking, There are some guys being shipped by motorcar."

We reach Haguenau toward eight. The town has been evacuated for a month. It had been bombarded May 12 without any damage other than a few scratches on the brand-new façade of a Gothic house and a shell hit on a tumble-down cottage. The order to evacuate was given that very evening. We saw the tumble-down cottage as we went by: a tile roof caved into a garden full of iris. It doesn't look like a war casualty. If it weren't for the iris—so fresh, so blazingly fresh and looking so much like "nothing special" that it makes you uneasy—you'd think it died of old age. And then there's that buckled floor sticking up in the air that you see through a big hole in the wall.

These pages from Sartre's wartime journal were written in 1940 and published as "La Mort dans l'âme" in the volume *Exercice du silence* (Brussels: Jean Annotiau, 1942). See also Vol. 1, 42/33.

11 A.M.

In the cellar of the city hall. We've just come down Indian file, each of us with a straw mattress on his back. Dust, the winy smell of plaster. Every now and then an airhole. We're going to have to live in here.

"It really smells!" Dupin says.

"Yeah. Seems they want to set up offices in here too."

"Sure. And why not bring down the field kitchens too? And the trucks."

We throw down our bedrolls and sit down on them. Swirls of white dust fly up to the ceiling. I have asthma. We're there in our overcoats with our knees against our chins, not even thinking about putting down our helmets and our packs. We're plumped on the ground like hunks of lead as if we had to spend the rest of the war here. We need roots: for some time now we've felt so light we're afraid the wind will blow us away. No smoking, of course.

Lieutenant Monique appears at the head of the stairs, all smoky with a golden light clinging and drifting up around him like a vapor. He leans over, hot and red-faced from the sun, with the light shining through his ears, and tries to make out our pale bodies and blue faces in the shadows.

"Hey, Sarge!"

"Here, lieutenant."

"Chaubé, muster your men and come back up on the double."

Chaubé musters us and we go back up—six administrative assistants, four men from the records section. We reload the truck in the courtyard and start out again, leaving our buddies in the cellar.

The sergeant major is still keeping to himself. Our officers, meek and shifty-looking and mistrustful, have set up quarters away from the rest in a Catholic girls' school. It's an old building made out of pink sandstone; two century plants in green boxes flank the door. A pink-paved courtyard in front, a garden out back. We'll sleep in the kindergarten classroom. We look at one another; we're glad we got out of the cellar.

On the walls there are gilded blue pictures—the Virgin, the baby Jesus; on the shelves, male and female saints in little plaster gardens. It smells of tisane and the good sisters. A big linden tree full of birds thrusts its branches through the open window into the room, and the light filters through its leaves. A soft green flickering light, a tisane of light. On the desk there are two piles of pink notebooks. I thumb through them. French composition notebooks. They all stop on May 10, 1940: "Your mamma is ironing. Describe her."

The birds in the linden tree are doves; they coo all day long.

June 11

Outside, a sun of death and glory, the same sun that's making decaying carcasses steam in Flanders. Inside the school, a cool light of slightly stagnant holy water. We don't have anything to do. We never have anything to do any more; it's a bad sign. Luberon is playing waltzes on the harmonium. Sergeant Chaubé, chief administrative assistant and an office worker in civilian life, is walking around making his shoes crackle pensively and voluptuously, the way you make cigars crackle between your thumb and forefinger. Each time they crackle he smiles, loving it. The war hasn't bothered him; he's living in the middle of files and gluepots just the way he did in peacetime. When he went on leave he said he was going on vacation.

Five alarms today. Strange alarms, howling like animals being slaughtered, that mount skyward toward the planes like cries of terror and fall on deaf ears in the dead town. The planes fly very low; they're on a milk run. They're masters of the skies, of course; no antiaircraft or French fighters. The orders are to take cover when you see them, so that the town will still look like a graveyard from the air.

"It sure as hell is quiet," Dupin says. Right. A vegetable silence which is not the absence of noise: there are these doves in the thick green foliage like crickets way down in the grass, these airplane motors roaring and sparkling—you'd say it was the noise of the sun—and then this town all around us at the end of the garden on the other side of the wall, this forbidden city. Dupin gets up:

"Shit! I'm going to take a look around this burg."

"It's against orders."

"What the hell do I care."

Dupin is a tradesman. He loves towns with a passion. It excites him to feel one on the other side of the wall, even a dead one: a town at any rate means shopwindows and street corners.

He jams his cap on his head and looks at us through the big window-glass horn rims he wears "because in business you have to look impressive." Pierné says to him:

"If you find a newspaper . . ."

"A newspaper?" Moulard says. "Are you out of your ever-lovin' mind? There's not even a cat left in this hole."

Dupin smiles complacently.

"Don't get excited. If there's anything to scrounge, I'll get it; don't worry."

He's gone. Four or five guys are sleeping on the ground, wrapped up in their overcoats with their caps down over their noses to keep the flies off. Chaubé starts strolling around the room again. Moulard is writing to his wife, and I read over his shoulder, "my little doll." Moulard is twenty-five and he looks twenty. Women like him. He worships his wife and runs around on her innocently. He has blue eyes, frizzly hair, and buckteeth. He has a little trouble talking; the words always seem to be a little too big to come out, and he shakes his head to make them fall out of his mouth.

Pierné asks abruptly:

"So what the fuck are we doing here? Anybody know?"

Silence. He insists:

"Chaubé?"

Chaubé sometimes overhears what the officers are saying. He shakes his head:

"I don't know."

"Will we be here long?"

"I don't know."

"They said this is the new HQ for this sector."

Foulon, the motorcycle sergeant, who was trying to sleep, raises his head and says with an effort:

"I don't think so. It's too far from the lines."

Pierné, thin and wiry with steel-rimmed glasses, looks irritated and unhappy. He's a mathematics teacher. Is that why he can't live without landmarks? Last winter he had to take his bearings every day. He devoured the newspapers when there were any, or he walked fifteen kilometers in the snow to go listen to the news in the radio truck. He needs to be anchored. He was anchored during this whole rotten war. He knew the exact distance separating him from his wife, how long he was going to stay in a sector, what his number on the leave list was. For some days now they've hauled anchor, and he's drifting. We're all drifting with him, by the way. A whole flotilla drifting in the fog.

Pierné keeps on, hesitantly:

"Would you say they wanted to combine our sector with the one in Lauterbourg? . . ."

"Could be."

"Some guys," Foulon says, "say too that it was just a staging area and we'll go take up positions on the Marne."

"The Marne?" Fay straightened up his little yellow skinhead. "The Germans crossed the Marne a long time ago."

"What do you know about it?" Chaubé says.

"At the rate they were going at."

"We don't know anything."

We stop talking, with heavy hearts. It's true. We don't know anything. Where are the Germans? Outside Paris? In Paris? Are they fighting in Paris? We haven't had a newspaper or a letter for five days. One image obsesses me. I see a café on the place Saint-Germain-des-Prés where I used to go sometimes. It's packed and the Germans are inside. I don't see the Germans— since the beginning of the war I've never been able to *imagine* the Germans—but I know they're there. The other customers look wooden. Each time the image comes back to me it's like a knife blow.

Since day before yesterday I have hundreds of memories. Golden memories of Paris, light as haze. I see the quays of la Rapée, a patch of sky over Ménilmontant, a street in La Villette, la place des Fêtes, les Gobelins, la rue des Blancs-Manteaux, everything I love. But these memories have been struck dead; someone has killed them. They smell of death like this town crushed with heat on the other side of the wall.

We are silent, numbed by silence. The turtledoves are cooing, and the mosquitoes are waking up. A little afterward we hear noisy footsteps in the hall; it's Dupin coming back. He comes in wiping his forehead. He has a funny look—and empty hands.

"Well?"

"Well, I saw the whole town. You can go anywhere you want; nobody's there."

"So? What's it like?"

He hesitates:

"It must have been nice before the war . . ."

"Sure . . . and what about now?"

"Now . . ."

He hesitates. He has sat down and begun to wipe the lens of his glasses. He blinks his eyes and pushes out his fat lips with an air of tortured happiness, naked happiness. But he's not quite that good. He says:

"It's funny . . ."

"Funny?"

"Yeah, well, not funny funny."

I say:

"Come on, four eyes; you're going to show us."

"Were there any papers?" Pierné asks.

"Sure there were. There's not even a cat."

I say:

"You guys coming?"

Chaubé pretends he doesn't hear; he knows we don't want him.

The four of us—Moulard, Pierné, Dupin, and I—go out. We go down one empty street, and then another, and then another. Suburban streets. Houses with two, three, stories at most, little gardens, grillwork, and black doors with gold bells. I'm not too surprised to find them empty: it's always that way in the suburbs. Only I'd like to get into the heart of town, and I have the impression it's running away from me. I go ahead, I make the others hurry up, and it retreats; we can't manage to get out of the suburbs. The town is down there, always down there, at the end of these hot, chalky streets.

"You see," Dupin says. "It's kind of empty."

"Yeah! Too damn bad."

We suddenly come out on a square. Beautiful tall houses with painted façades—blue, white, green, and pink—and turrets, gables. Big shops. The iron curtains aren't even lowered; the windows sparkle. Except they took off the door latches when they left. No more doubt about it; we're downtown. We look all around, a little at a loss, and then it suddenly starts to be Sunday. A Sunday afternoon, a Sunday in the country and the summertime, truer than life. We aren't alone any more; the people are all there, behind their drawn blinds in the shadow. They've just had dinner; they're having a nap before their evening stroll. I say to Moulard:

"You'd think it was Sunday."

"Sort of," he says vaguely.

I shake myself. I try to tell myself, "It's Wednesday and its morning; all those abandoned rooms behind the curtains are empty and dark." No; it's no use; Sunday won't budge. In Haguenau there's just one day for the whole week, one hour for the whole day. Sunday has slipped into my most muffled, most intimate expectations. Sunday is my future. I'm waiting for the sounds of Sunday dishes, the lazy distant sounds which come regretfully from houses' bellies. I'm waiting for the dusty roads on the outskirts of town, the flags and shouts in stadiums. I'm waiting for the movies and the smell of mild tobacco. I'm waiting for the crisp rub of clean linen against my skin and that Sunday lassitude which grabs you in the back or in the shoulders when you've walked among the crowd too long. I'm waiting to feel in my body, like a memory of my dead life, the placid despair of summer afternoons.

"It's true," Dupin says, "you'd expect there'd be bells ringing."

Yes. Vespers. It's a completely ordinary Sunday; it wouldn't take much for it to go unnoticed. Only there's something a little stiffer, a little more chemical, than usual in it. It's too silent; you'd say it was embalmed. And then, it can glow all it wants to, but when you've been inside it for a minute you realize that it's full of secret stagnancies already. When the inhabitants of Haguenau come back they'll find a rotten Sunday flopped down on their dead town. Dupin has come up to a big wool shop; he's nodding his head in appreciation of the art with which the display has been "done." But the multicolored balls of wool so skillfully arranged in the window are yellowing; they look old. And the layettes and the shirts in the neighboring shop look old too; they're wilting and a floury dust is gathering on the counters. It's a festival for flies. I don't know how they managed to get in, but they're buzzing by the thousands behind the big windows streaked with long trains of white like trails of tears. Dupin turns around abruptly:

"This gives me the blues."

He runs his hand lightly over the windowpane. He caresses it with a kind of competent love, the way a musician does his instrument. He shakes his head:

"It must be like this now where I come from."

He has talked to us often about his store. "Bobby's," it's called. Women's lingerie and hats. The prettiest one in the neighborhood. It has all its lights on at night; it lights the street by itself.

"Your wife will have had time to put away the displays and lower the iron curtains."

"It's my brother-in-law who stayed. I don't trust him."

He stays a moment longer in front of the window, his head lowered. He looks unhappy.

Moulard, who has become impatient, tugs at his arm:

"Come on; let's go. We're not going to stand in front of these leftovers forever. You're getting on our nerves."

"That's because you're not in trade. Even if I don't have a piece of the action, it breaks my heart to see merchandise wasted."

We lead him away through bourgeois streets, a public garden in flower, the paths of the railroad station. Wherever we go, on windows, doors, and fronts of buildings we read the word *Death*. It's a sinister little obsession. Up close we see, "Pillaging evacuated houses is punishable by DEATH. Sentence will be carried out immediately." But all that is in small letters; all you see is *Death*. Death: a dead war, death in the sky, a dead town, and these thousands of colors dying in the store windows along with this fine putrid summer, full of flies and misfortune, and our hearts, which we killed last winter out of fear of suffering. Dupin looks at me timidly:

"Say . . ."

"What?"

"If they enter Paris do you think they'll pillage everything?"

"What do you think they're going to pillage in the Twentieth Arrondissement," Moulard says irritated. "They'll go into the good neighborhoods."

Dupin doesn't answer. He licks his lips and sighs. A corner, a brand new street. At the very end of the street, a soldier runs away when he sees us, like a lizard startled by the approach of men. A marauder we've disturbed. Or a dogface, out walking like us, who took us for officers.

"Great," Moulard says looking up; "here it comes! It's been a long time."

Sure enough, here it does come: a noisy ripping tearing through the sky from north to south, and then the long bellow of the empty town, and then the plane, very small, shining in the sun.

"A Stuka," Moulard says.

"Let's take cover," Dupin says prudently. We get under the awning of a butcher's shop. The plane is still shining; how slow it seems! Strange impression: this little twinkle of metal is the only living thing in the sky, with a dense metallic life which belongs with the heat of this pitiless blue and with the sun's heavy flames. And on earth we living beings are the only living beings, whom great hollow stones surround with their shadows and their mineral silence. I do not know why this brilliant burst of steel tracing its furrow up above has made me feel so keenly that I have been abandoned in the midst of war. But a close tie, a blood tie, has been forged between it, this glorious living being in the sky, and us, the living beings flattened out in the earth's shadow. It seems that it is looking for us on the crust of this cooling star, among the tombs, in this Sunday cemetery; just for us in the whole town. It's there just for us. Since it has been roaring up above me, the silence all around me has seemed more oppressive, more planetary; I feel like running out into the street and signaling to it with a handkerchief like a castaway signaling a rescue ship. Signaling to him to drop his whole bomb load on the town: that would be a resurrection. This funereal Sunday would shred open like a fog. The town would ring with enormous noises, the noises of a forge, the way it did not long ago when it was in labor, and beautiful red flowers would climb up the walls toward the sky.

The plane goes by. It will go relieve itself over Haguenau forest or some road covered with our trucks. It obviously didn't see us, or even look at us. The alert is over; we return to our solitude.

Here's Luberon. He comes out of an alley with a paper bag in his hand.

"Hi. Is that some stuff to eat?"

Luberon is always eating. He looks at us, blinking his eyes. He's not too happy to meet us: he must have been waiting for us to leave so he could slip out. He stares at us perplexedly. He's an albino. His floury eyelashes blink over his big pale eyes. Finally he cracks open his sack and immediately closes it. But we have time to see golden crusts.

"Croissants! Shit! Where'd you find 'em?"

Luberon smiles and says with a normal air:

"At the bakery."

"There's a bakery? We thought everyone had left."

He points out a store down the street on the left.

"So?" Dupin says, irritated because he didn't find the bakery all by himself. "It's closed."

"No it isn't. The iron curtain is pulled down and the latch is off; but if you lean on the door you go in. It starts ringing and this lady comes up. She serves you in the dark, by God; I wonder how she's able to see. They're not supposed to sell to soldiers but they manage."

Dupin starts to run and we watch him. We see him go into the bakery and Luberon goes on:

"It seems there are twenty who've come back. As soon as they heard there were troops here, you know. They reopened on the sly—a grocer, a bookseller. Especially because of the officers. Before the evacuation the officers bought anything at any price they asked; the people in Haguenau did good business."

Dupin comes back with a big bag under his arm.

"Are there cafés open?"

"That's what they say."

"We'll see."

We go from café to café pushing on the doors. Finally there's one that gives way; we go into an arched, low-ceilinged, completely dark room. There's a man at the counter we can barely make out.

"Can we have a drink?"

"Come in quickly then. And shut the door; I'm not supposed to serve soldiers. Go into the back room."

The back room is well lighted and gay; it opens onto a courtyard. It used to be reserved for banquets, weddings, and sports clubs. There are three large copper cups in a glass cabinet. The Cycle Club and Pedaling Club of Haguenau won them. The owner comes toward us. With his long swept-back hair and black mustache he looks Italian. He's wearing slippers and shuffling his feet. Veiled eyes, cruel smile.

"What'll you have?"

"Four schnapps."

Pierné asks:

"Do you have newspapers?"

The guy has broadened his smile:

"No more newspapers."

He waits a while and adds:

"There won't be any papers from Paris any more."

A chill. He goes to get the schnapps. "Maybe there's some news on the radio," Pierné says, squirming on his chair. I tell him:

"Shut up. If you ask him something, he'll soft-soap you. He doesn't look like a guy who's too fond of Frenchmen."

"Right."

We drink our schnapps without enjoying it much. The owner comes and goes noiselessly. He keeps his eye on us like an ogre. How he must hate us. Pierné can't contain himself any more: he's dying to ask him for news. If he does, I'll pop him one in the mouth. If we asked the guy questions, he'd be only too happy. Dupin calls him:

"How much?"

"One hundred sous."

He's leaning on the table. He says:

"Was the schnapps good, boys?"

"Very good."

"Just as well. You won't drink any more any time soon."

A pause. He's waiting for us to ask questions, but we don't want to ask any. He waddles around a bit, watching us, and his look fascinates us. He has it in for us, and what gets me is that I can't get mad at him. I can't because he's smiling. He says bluntly:

"You're leaving tomorrow morning."

I turn my head so I won't see his smile any more. Dupin shrugs his shoulders and says a little too loudly:

"Maybe. We aren't in on it."

Pierné's eyes shone. I feel like telling him, "Forget it. Will you forget it?" But he has taken the bait. He tries to look unconcerned but his voice is trembling with the urge to know.

"And where are we going, since you know so much?"

The guy gestures vaguely.

"To the Italian front?" Pierné asks.

I kick at him under the table. The guy pretends to hesitate and then answers brusquely:

"You won't go far."

I have the feeling that he wanted to give his voice a menacing tone of suggestion. I get up:

"What do you say? Shall we shove off?"

In the other room the door opens, creaking. Authoritative footsteps. The guy goes to have a look, without haste; I hear him say in a purposely loud voice:

"Yes, lieutenant. Right, lieutenant."

He comes back into our room and takes a bottle of cassis out of the cabinet. Silently, he moves his head to show us the door at the end of the room. We're out in half a minute.

"We're still going to eat the croissants," Luberon says.

Drieu la Rochelle, or Self-Hatred

THERE ARE SOME LITERARY MEN of easy virtue nowadays who write for the slavish press, go to Germany to drink to Goethe's honor with champagne stolen from the cellars of Epernay, and are trying to establish a "European" literature—the one in which, according to M. de Chateaubriant in *La Gerbe*, Hitler's speeches are the brightest jewels. We're not in the least surprised to find the drunkard Fernandez and the pederast Fraigneau among their number. But there are others who seem more decent. What could have led them to join forces with this gang? The lure of profit? But some of them are rich, and then the Germans pay badly. The truth is that they have more hidden, more disturbing motives than the healthy cupidity of classical traitors. Look at Drieu la Rochelle: a lyrical writer, he never stops talking about himself; he fills the pages of *La Nouvelle Revue française* with his little fits of anger and hysteria, and, since that's still not enough, he republishes his old writings with new prefaces in which he speaks about himself some more. All we have to do is put together what he has confided to us and we shall very swiftly understand the reasons for his choice.

He's a long, tall, sad kind of guy with a great big battered head and the faded look of a young man who didn't know how to grow old. Like Montherlant, he fought for kicks in 1914. His patrons in high places sent him to the front when he asked them to and had him pulled back as soon as he began to worry about

This article was published as "Drieu la Rochelle ou la haine de soi" in an underground issue of *Les Lettres françaises*, April, 1943. See also Vol. 1, 43/40.

getting bored. He ended up by going back to women again and being even more bored. The fireworks at the front had kept him from paying attention to himself for a while. When he came back home it was inevitable that he should make a scandalous discovery—he thought nothing, felt nothing, loved nothing. He was soft and cowardly, with neither physical nor moral resiliency, a "hollow man." His first move was to run from himself. He caroused and took drugs—moderately, from lack of courage. And then, just as his hate-filled stupor at himself was threatening to take a tragic turn, he found the gimmick that enabled him to bear himself. It wasn't his fault if he was a bad little boy in a man's body. It was just that our epoch was one of great failures. He wrote, "I found myself confronted with a crushing fact: decadence." Now there's a good piece of work for you. It is always easier to be the innocent victim of a social upheaval than simply an individual who just couldn't make it himself. Thus from 1914 to 1918 millions of French peasants and workers got themselves killed defending their native soil, and from 1918 to 1939 millions of French peasants and workers tried courageously and patiently to live, but M. Drieu la Rochelle, who was bored, declared that France had failed.

The rest needs no further explanation. Gilles, his wretched hero, tries at the end of the novel to heal his incurable boredom with the blood of others. Drieu wanted the Fascist revolution the way certain people want war because they don't dare break up with their mistresses. He hoped that an order imposed from without and upon everyone would succeed in disciplining these weak and ungovernable passions that he had been unable to conquer, that a bloody catastrophe would succeed in filling the inner void he had been unable to fill, that the restlessness of power (like the sounds of battle in the past) would divert him better than morphine or cocaine from thinking about himself. And he has in fact since that time been speaking, getting excited, making a tiny little noise in the silence. He questions, exhorts, preaches to, and insults Frenchmen who are bound and gagged. The universal silence doesn't bother him. All he wants to do is talk. He writes that he is a naturally prophetic writer, that he prefers the German occupation to the prewar Jewish occupation. In part out of hatred for men, in part out of a taste for gossip, he denounces Free Zone writers to the Vichy government and threatens those in the Occupied Zone with prison. He enjoys himself as well as he can, wretchedly. But these little distractions are no more capable of tearing him away from himself than drugs; he's still hooked. When a journal in the ex-Free Zone digs into him, when the defunct *Esprit* takes the liberty of calling *La Nouvelle Revue française* the N.R.B.,[1] he howls and fills his journal with hysterical tantrums. This is not a man who has sold out: he doesn't have the untroubled cynicism which that takes. He has come over to nazism through an elective affinity: at the bottom of his heart, as at the bottom of nazism, there is self-hatred—and the hatred of man it engenders.

1. I.e., *La Nouvelle Revue boche* [The New Boche Review].

A More Precise Characterization of Existentialism

NEWSPAPERS—including *Action* itself—are only too willing these days to publish articles attacking existentialism. *Action* has been kind enough to ask me to reply. I doubt that many readers will be interested in the debate: they have many more urgent concerns. Yet if, among the persons who might have found principles of thinking and rules of conduct in this philosophy but have been dissuaded by these absurd criticisms, there were just one I could reach and straighten out, it would still be worth writing for him. In any case I want to make it clear that I am replying in my own name only: I would hesitate to involve other existentialists in this polemic.

What do you reproach us for? To begin with, for being inspired by Heidegger, a German and a Nazi philosopher. Next, for preaching, in the name of existentialism, a quietism of anguish. Are we not trying to corrupt the youth and turn it aside from action by urging it to cultivate a refined despair? Are we not upholding nihilistic doctrines (for an editorial writer in *L'Aube,* the proof is that I entitled a book *Being and Nothingness.* Nothingness; imagine!) during these years when everything has to be redone or simply done, when the war is still going on, and when each man needs all the strength he has to win it and to win the peace? Finally, your third complaint is that existentialism likes to poke about in muck and is much readier to show men's wickedness and baseness than their higher feelings.

This article was published as "A propos de l'existentialisme: Mise au point" in *Action,* December 29, 1944. See also Vol. 1, 44/59.

I'll give it to you straight: your attacks seem to me to stem from ignorance and bad faith. It's not even certain that you have read any of the books you're talking about. You need a scapegoat because you bless so many things you can't help chewing out someone from time to time. You've picked existentialism because it's an abstract doctrine few people know, and you think that no one will verify what you say. But I am going to reply to your accusations point by point.

Heidegger was a philosopher well before he was a Nazi. His adherence to Hitlerism is to be explained by fear, perhaps ambition, and certainly conformism. Not pretty to look at, I agree; but enough to invalidate your neat reasoning. "Heidegger," you say, "is a member of the National Socialist Party; thus his philosophy must be Nazi." That's not it: Heidegger has no character; there's the truth of the matter. Are you going to have the nerve to conclude from this that his philosophy is an apology for cowardice? Don't you know that sometimes a man does not come up to the level of his works? And are you going to condemn *The Social Contract* because Rousseau abandoned his children? And what difference does Heidegger make anyhow? If we discover our own thinking in that of another philosopher, if we ask him for techniques and methods that can give us access to new problems, does this mean that we espouse every one of his theories? Marx borrowed his dialectic from Hegel. Are you going to say that *Capital* is a Prussian work? We've seen the deplorable consequences of economic autarky; let's not fall into intellectual autarky.

During the Occupation, the slavish newspapers used to lump together the existentialists and the philosophers of the absurd in the same reproving breath. A venomous little ill-mannered pedant named Albérès, who wrote for the Pétainist *Echo des étudiants,* used to yap at our heels every week. In those days this kind of obfuscation was to be expected; the lower and stupider the blow, the happier we were.

But why have you taken up the methods of the Vichyssoise press again?

Why this helter-skelter way of writing if it's not because the confusion you create makes it easier for you to attack both these philosophies at once? The philosophy of the absurd is coherent and profound. Albert Camus has shown that he was big enough to defend it all by himself. I too shall speak all by myself for existentialism. Have you even defined it for your readers? And yet it's rather simple.

In philosophical terminology, every object has an essence and an existence. An essence is an intelligible and unchanging unity of properties; an existence is a certain actual presence in the world. Many people think that the essence comes first and then the existence: that peas, for example, grow and become round in conformity with the idea of peas, and that gherkins are gherkins because they participate in the essence of gherkins. This idea originated in religious thought: it is a fact that the man who wants to build a house has to know exactly what kind of object he's going to create—essence precedes existence—and for all those who believe that God created men, he must have done so by referring to his idea of them. But even those who have no religious faith have maintained this traditional view that the object never exists except in conformity with its essence; and everyone in the eighteenth century thought that all men had a common essence called *human nature*. Existentialism, on the contrary, maintains that in man—and in man alone —existence precedes essence.

This simply means that man first *is*, and only subsequently is this or that. In a word, man must create his own essence: it is in throwing himself into the world, suffering there, struggling there, that he gradually defines himself. And the definition always remains open ended: we cannot say what *this* man is before he dies, or what mankind is before it has disappeared. It is absurd in this light to ask whether existentialism is Fascist, conservative, Communist, or democratic. At this level of generality existentialism is nothing but a certain way of envisaging human questions by refusing to grant man an eternally established nature. It used to be, in Kierkegaard's thought, on a par with religious faith. Today, French existentialism tends to be accompanied by a declaration of atheism, but this is not absolutely necessary. All I can say—without wanting to insist too much on the similarities—is that it isn't too far from the conception of man found in Marx. For is it not a fact that Marx would accept *this motto of ours for man: make, and in making make yourself, and be nothing but what you have made of yourself?*

Since existentialism defines man by action, it is evident that this philosophy is not a quietism. In fact, man cannot help acting; his thoughts are projects and commitments, his feelings are undertakings, he is nothing other than his life, and his life is the unity of his behavior. "But what about anguish?" you'll say. Well, this rather solemn word refers to a very simple everyday reality. If man *is* not but *makes himself,* and if in making himself he makes himself responsible for the whole species—if there is no value or morality given a priori, so that we must in every instance decide alone and without any basis or guidelines, yet *for everyone*—how could we possibly help feeling anguished when we have to act? Each of our acts puts the world's meaning and man's place in the universe in question. With each of them, whether we want to or not, we constitute a universal scale of values. And you want us not to be seized with fear in the face of such a total responsibility? Ponge, in a very beautiful piece of writing, said that man is the future of man. That future is not yet created, not yet decided upon. We are the ones who will make it; each of our gestures will help fashion it. It would take a lot of pharisaism to avoid an anguished awareness of the formidable mission given to each of us. But you people, in order to refute us more convincingly, you people have deliberately confused anguish and neurasthenia, making who knows what pathological terror out of this virile uneasiness existentialism speaks of. Since I have to dot my *i*'s, I'll say then that *anguish, far from being an obstacle to action, is the very condition for it, and is identical with the sense of that crushing responsibility of all before all which is the source of both our torment and our grandeur.*

As for despair, we have to understand one another. It's true that man would be wrong *to hope.* But what does this mean except that hope is the greatest impediment to action? Should we hope that the war will stop all by itself without us, that the Nazis will extend the hand of friendship to us, that the privileged of capitalist society will give up their privileges in the joy of a new "night of August 4"? If we hope for all of this, all we have to do is cross our arms and wait. Man cannot will unless he has first understood that he can count on nothing but himself: that he is alone, left alone on earth in the middle of his infinite responsibilities, with neither help nor succor, with no other goal but the one he will set for himself, with no other destiny but the one he will forge on this earth. It is this certainty, this intuitive understanding of his situation, that we call despair. You can see that it is no fine romantic frenzy but the sharp and lucid consciousness of the human condition. *Just as anguish is indistinguishable from a sense of responsibility, despair is inseparable from will.* With despair, true optimism begins: the optimism of the man who expects nothing, who knows he has no rights and nothing coming to him, who rejoices in counting on himself alone and in acting alone for the good of all.

Are you going to condemn existentialism for saying men are free? But you need that freedom, all of you. You hide it from yourselves hypocritically, and yet you incessantly come back to it in spite of yourselves. When you have explained a man's behavior by its causes, by his social situation and his interests, you suddenly become indignant at him and you bitterly reproach him for his conduct. And there are other men, on the contrary, whom you admire and whose acts serve as models for you. All right then, that means that you don't compare the bad ones to plant lice and the good ones to useful animals. If you blame them, or praise them, you do so because they could have acted differently. The class struggle is a fact to which I subscribe completely, but how can you fail to see that it is situated on the level of freedom? You call us social traitors, saying that our conception of freedom keeps man from loosening his chains. What stupidity! When we say a man who's out of work is free, we don't mean that he can do whatever he wants and change himself into a rich and tranquil bourgeois on the spot. *He is free because he can always choose to accept his lot with resignation or to rebel against it.* And undoubtedly he will not be able to avoid great poverty; but in the very midst of his destitution, which is dragging him under, he is able to choose to struggle—in his own name and in the name of others—against all forms of destitution. He can choose to be the man who refuses to let destitution be man's lot. Is a man a social traitor just because from time to time he reminds others of these basic truths? Then the Marx who said, "We want to change the world," and who in this simple sentence said that man is master of his destiny, is a social traitor. Then all of you are social traitors, because that's what you think too just as soon as you let go the apron strings of a materialism that was useful once but now has gotten old. And if you didn't think so, then man for you would be a thing—a bit of carbon, sulfur, phosphorus, and nothing more—and you wouldn't have to lift a finger for him.

You tell me that I work in filth. That's what Alain Laubreaux used to say, too. I could refrain from answering here, because this reproach is directed at me as a person and not as an existentialist. But you are so quick to generalize that I must nevertheless defend myself for fear that the opprobrium you cast upon me will redound to the philosophy I have adopted. There is only one thing to say: I don't trust people who claim that literature uplifts them by displaying noble sentiments, people who want the theater to give them a *show* of heroism and purity. What they really want is to be persuaded that it's easy to do good. Well, no! It isn't easy. Vichyssoise literature and, alas, some of today's literature would like to make us think it is: it's so nice to be self-satisfied. But it's an outright lie. Heroism, greatness, generosity, abnegation; I agree that there is nothing better and that in the end they are what make sense out of human action. But if you pretend that all a person has to do to be a hero is to belong to the *ajistes*, the *jocistes*, or a political party you favor, to sing innocent songs and go to the country on Sunday, you are cheapening the virtues that you claim to uphold and are simply making fun of everyone.

Have I said enough to make it clear that *existentialism is no mournful delectation but a humanist philosophy of action, effort, combat, and solidarity*? After my attempt to make things clear, will we still find journalists making allusions to "the despair of our eminent ones" and other claptrap? We'll see. I want to tell my critics openly: it all depends on you now. After all, you're free too. And those of you who are fighting for the Revolution, as we think we're fighting too: you are just as able as we are to decide whether it shall be made in good or bad faith. The case of existentialism, an abstract philosophy upheld by a few powerless men, is very slight and scarcely worthy. But in this case as in a thousand others, depending on whether you keep on lying about it or do it justice even as you attack it, you will decide what man shall be. May you grasp this fact and feel a little salutary anguish.

The Liberation of Paris:
An Apocalyptic Week

THESE DAYS, if a man isn't willing to say that Paris liberated itself, he is taken for an enemy of the people. And yet it seems quite clear that the city could not have even dreamed of rising up in revolt if the Allies had not been very close. And since they in turn could not have even dreamed of disembarking if the Russians had not kept in check and beaten the major part of the German divisions, it must be concluded that the liberation of Paris, an episode in a war of universal dimensions, was the common work of all the Allied forces. One does not, furthermore, drive out people who are leaving of their own free will, and by the time the insurrection first broke out the Germans had already begun to evacuate the city.

The goal of the members of the Resistance was just the opposite of that which is imputed to them today: they tried to slow down the enemy retreat and close Paris in on the occupying troops like a trap. And then, above all, they wanted to show future conquerors that the Resistance was not, as people outside the country still seemed all too ready to believe, a myth. In the eyes of governments who had dreamed for a time of having the liberated territories administered by their officers, they wanted to affirm the sovereignty of the French people; and they understood that the only means they had of legitimizing the power of the people was to shed their own blood.

Thus their undertaking owes its greatness to its limitations.

This article was published as "La Libération de Paris: Une Semaine d'apocalypse" in *Clartés*, August 24, 1945. See also Vol. 1, 45/78.

The destiny of Paris was at stake fifty kilometers away; it was the German and the American tanks that would settle the issue. But the men of the Resistance did not want to be bothered with it. They did not even want to know the outcome of the struggle they had undertaken. In giving the signal for the uprising, they had unleashed vague and powerful forces capable from one moment to the next of crushing them. And that's what gave this week in August the appearance of an antique tragedy. But fate was just what these men meant to deny. Whether or not the Germans blew up the Senate and a whole part of the city with it did not depend on them. Whether the retreating divisions fell on Paris and made another Warsaw of our city did not depend on them. But what did depend on them was to bear witness by their actions—and regardless of the outcome of the unequal struggle they had undertaken—to the will of the French people. So each of them refused to put his hope in anyone besides himself. The Parisians who were not fighting asked from hour to hour with anguish if the Allied troops would not be here soon. The fighters never thought about it, and it even seemed there was a tacit agreement which forbade them to talk about it: they were doing what they had to do. One afternoon during that week, as I was going to see a friend who ran a Resistance newspaper in the place he had just taken over, someone came to tell him about German infiltrations around the building. "If they attacked to-night," he told me, "we'd be trapped like rats. There are only two ways out of here and both are guarded." "Do you at least have arms?" He shrugged his shoulders and replied, "No." Thus, surrounded by obscure dangers brushing them, these journalists did what they had to do, which was to print a paper. About everything else—that is, about everything concerning their personal security, their chances of coming out of the adventure alive—they didn't want to think. Since they were unable to influence the outcome of these things by their actions, they figured that none of it was any of their business.

This accounts for that other aspect of the Paris uprising, the festive air it never ceased to have. Whole sections of the city dressed up in their Sunday best. And if I ask myself just what they were celebrating, I see that it was man and his powers. It is reassuring that the anniversary of the Paris uprising fell so close to the first appearances of the atomic bomb. What the bomb represents is the negation of man. Not only because it risks destroying the whole of mankind, but above all because it makes the most human qualities—courage, patience, intelligence, the spirit of initiative—vain and ineffectual. Most of the FFI, on the contrary, had in August, 1944, an obscure sense of fighting not only for France against the Germans but also for man against the blind powers of the machine. We had been told often enough that the revolutions of the twentieth century could not be like those of the nineteenth, and that it would take only one plane, only one big gun to put down a rebellious mob. We had been warned enough about the ring of guns the Germans had surrounded Paris with! We had been shown often enough that we could do nothing against their machine guns and tanks. Well, during that month of August the fighters you met in the streets were young people in shirtsleeves. All they had for weapons were revolvers, a few rifles, a few grenades, bottles of gasoline. Facing an enemy boxed in steel, they became intoxicated with the feeling of the freedom and the lightness of their movements. The discipline which they invented with each passing moment won out over discipline which had been learned. They tried—and made us try—the naked power of man. And we couldn't help thinking of what Malraux calls, in *Man's Hope*, the rehearsal of the apocalypse. Yes, it was the triumph of the apocalypse, of that apocalypse which is always defeated by the forces of order and which for once, within the narrow limits of this street fight, was victorious. The apocalypse: that is to say a spontaneous organization of revolutionary forces. All Paris felt, during that week in August, that man still had a chance, that he could still win out over the machine; and even if the battle had ended with the crushing of the Resistance forces, as it did in Poland, these few days would have been enough to prove the power of freedom. So it makes very little difference that the FFI did not, strictly speaking, liberate Paris from the Germans: at each instant, behind each barricade and on each street, they exercised freedom for themselves and for each Frenchman.

So what we're going to commemorate each year, officially and in an orderly manner, is the explosion of freedom, the disruption of the established order, and the invention of a spontaneous and effective order. It is to be feared that the festival will quickly lose its meaning. Yet there is a certain aspect of the insurrection which may endure in our ceremonies. When the mob of 1789 invaded the Bastille, they did not know the meaning, the consequences, of their gesture; it was only afterward and by degrees that they became conscious of it and raised it to the level of a symbol. What was striking in August, 1944, was that the symbolic character of the uprising was already established even while its outcome was still uncertain. Choltitz, in hesitating to destroy Paris; the Allies, in agreeing to advance the date of their entry into the capital; the members of the Resistance, in choosing to fight their big battle there—all of them decided that the event would be "historic." All of them were remembering Paris' great days of wrath. All of them considered it one of the essential things at stake in the war. And each FFI, in fighting, felt that he was writing history. The whole history of Paris was there, in that sun, on those naked streets. That is why this tragedy, this risky affirmation of human freedom, was also something like a "ceremony." A pompous and bloody ceremony whose ordering was carefully controlled and that ended fatally in deaths, something like a human sacrifice. It is this triple aspect of tragedy denied, apocalypse, and ceremony that gives the insurrection of August, 1944, its deeply human character and its continuing power to move us deeply. Is it not even, today, one of our best reasons for hoping? It is vain and useless for us to imagine and proclaim that we liberated ourselves with our forces alone. Would you like to meet Maurras on some side street and drivel on with him the absurd "France, France, alone. . ."? And similarly it is useless to stamp our feet, strike lofty poses, and insist daily on a place in the concert of nations we are daily denied. But is it not the insurrection of 1944 which, set against the inordinate powers the war brought into being, shows us our true strength? In that ceremonious and disproportionate battle, Paris affirmed, in opposition to the German tanks, the power of human beings. Is it not still our task today to defend the human, without great illusions and without too much hope, before the young and slightly inhuman forces which have just won the victory?

N-Dimensional Sculpture

As long as men were concerned with making the human form eternal, they put their trust in eternity's empirical image, stone. But the eternal has slid back behind the world now, we are no longer unaware that we are historical, and marble is suddenly revealing its flaw. Although it seems inalterable, it is actually undermined by a hidden sinkhole: this pure condensation of space is composed of *separable* parts. In this eternal crumbling, if one tries to inscribe the unity of a face, it breaks down. Even worse: since the artist has to shape an indefinitely divisible substance part by part, he has to break down his own perception of his model before he even starts to work. Achilles spends his life trying to catch the tortoise; the sculptor is afraid of spending his trying to finish the end of this nose. The drama of today's sculpture lies in its struggle against its own nature.

David Hare has found his personal way of solving the conflict between space and idea. He knows that animals and men are ambiguous realities: indefinitely divisible as cadavers and, when they are living, indecomposable presences. When they are living—that is, when they are running, crying out, and fighting, but equally when *we* are living them. In love and hate, lover and enemy are integrally present. And then the emotional universe unfolds in a space without distance: this face crushed up against the window and frightening me is not five meters or

This article was published as "Sculptures à n dimensions" in *Exposition David Hare: Catalogue*, the catalogue of a 1947 show at the Maeght Gallery. See also Vol. 1, 47/123.

[165]

even two meters away from me; it is *upon* me. Even objects, if I make use of them, suddenly take on an organic unity. It is my gestures which gather together these little bits of wood, glass, and leather and align them around me, which change them into doors, windows, and armchairs. A staircase scatters when it's nothing but the rigid other side of a climb. Hare has chosen to sculpt presences.

The other day somebody told me that in the diggings recently begun at Marseille they have found "a charming breast." A charming breast: it rolled like a ripe fruit; it barely clung to the branch. What need do we have for the body of the goddess? We can dream it into being from this breast. But if, a few centuries from now, bits of one of Hare's statues are found, these fragments won't go to take their place in our museums between the invalids of Samothrace and Milo. It's all or nothing. Break the legs off Apollo and he is still at least a stumpless cripple; but if Hare's statue isn't whole, there's nothing there but a stone. That's what he means by saying that his sculpture is nonrepresentational.

This classification needs some clarification. For, after all, his art is not abstract, nor is it writing. No doubt he did have a short brush with symbolism. His first statue represented a young girl whose sexual organ was the keyhole of a lock surrounded by quills, and perhaps a trap for prowlers too. But he saw the danger: symbolic sculpture just postpones the problem without eliminating it. Although you don't represent the object you at least represent its symbol. You haven't gotten anywhere. Today Hare has freed himself from all ideological formulas: he does not try to signify, he gives us the thing.

Of course there is no question of this provoking horror by a faithful rendering of the gorilla; but he sculpts the horror and the gorilla is in it. He brings us both the passion and its object, the labor and the tool, the religion and the sacred object. Paulhan, who amused himself by translating (or creating) Chinese proverbs, asks us in one of them, "Which is more abstract, fish or swimming? It's the fish, because many other animals swim. Which is more abstract, birds or flying? It's the bird, because there are flying fish. That's why we have to say that swimming fishes and flying birds." In this sense, we could say that Hare's gorilla is "a horror which gorillas," that is, the gorilla is a certain special condensation of our horror.

And yet there is no question of idealism either. It's just that the passion is form and the object matter. The passion does not analyze, does not observe: the object suddenly springs forth in its universe, compact, twisted, indecomposable; we see what's horrible in a face, not the color of the eyes. That is why Hare's figures, even though he does not want to *represent* anything, are always like a confused mess of contradictory representations, soured, kneaded, and packed down by emotion.

If one wished to define his sculpture, it would be better to say that it is not *observable*. For observation takes apart and puts together again, goes from the whole to the parts and from the parts to the whole in infinite comings and goings each one of which brings enrichment. But put yourself in front of the dead elephant. At first your eyes will lose themselves in the floating fixity of a stony fog; ambiguous forms—pads, ears, a trunk —will solicit them for an instant only to vanish immediately in the mist. And then, suddenly, the *thing* is going to leap out at you as it does in those puzzles where you have to find the hunter's cap and rifle. It is there, without parts, impenetrable, mysterious, fully lighted, and completely given—but given comprehensively without your being able to do anything about it. After that, look at it as much as you like and you won't see anything more. It would be useless for you to try to observe its details; it has no details. Hare creates indivisible sculptures.

His is a reflexive art in that it presents the object through man's work or emotion. Not things, but the shadow of man on things: these statues are neither forsaken nor natural; I touch myself on the stone. It is also an instrumentalist and very American art: the world it seeks to render is the world of tools, dangers, the sacred, human relations. Today the scientists say that the experimenter is part of the experimental system. Hare could say for his part that the sculptor is part of every sculptured whole. But this reflexive sculpture is not intellectual: I grasp the object through my deepest and most secret movements; the unity which I impose upon it is a unit of groveling, abduction, or flight. An animal heat broods in these figures: each form is like a noiseless gesture, soft and swift, sensual, sexual. Hare's imagination is vitalist.

When a sculpture is representational, it is hard to make a clear distinction between the real and the imaginary. At the Musée Grévin the gentleman you ask for directions is made out of wax. Even if it's a plaster king, the resemblance entices us with such a soft, persuasive power that we cannot be sure it does not belong to our space. It points its index finger toward an unseen regicide, and we can't help believing that it's pointing at us. Thereupon they take it down and carry it off to the museum. What is more ridiculous than a king bumping through crowded streets on a wagon and pointing out the passers-by?

Hare wants the gesture to close in on the statue; he wants the work to have its own space distinct from any other and clearly imaginary. You can move his sculptures around without their raising their arms to *our* heaven to be their witness. Movement is not a translation which leaves what moves unchanged; it's a little fever which erodes it from within. Hare sculpts feverish figures. He integrates behavior to form. The gesture is everywhere present but nowhere represented; it dwells in the whole statue like residual magnetism, still a resemblance, but diffuse and elusive in the manner of that air of *déjà vu* which so disturbs us in certain faces. A quality of the object, an alteration of its substance, the movement which haunts the stone is given as a whole. Matter's eternity is the frozen moment: classical sculpture cuts some instantaneous position from the gesture. In *The Duelists* or *The Man at the Drum*, Hare brings in past, present, and future. His characters are present during the complete duration of their act. But this is still not enough: Hare, like Calder, introduces real movement into his sculpture. The man at the drum is lightly balanced like the gorilla's jaw. But Calder, who is an engineer, retains the reality of real movement. Hare makes it unreal. He uses it not to represent the model's gesture but to suggest immobile realities and even, at times, abstractions. So the drummer's movement, which one would expect to be vertical by analogy to the movement of the drumsticks which strike the drumhead, becomes horizontal. Hare uses it to suggest grovelings and the sacred, to introduce, in short, religion into the object's syncretism. Thus the movement is form in the unreal, as the form in the unreal is movement. Since the movement does not retain any representational autonomy, the total form governs and corrupts it. The movement does not disrupt the unity of the imaginary; on the contrary, it intensifies it by permeating the stone with a subtle change. The essential characteristic of this art is to use the motionless to suggest mobility and to use mobility to suggest the motionless. Hare's sculpture is in its essense transubstantiation.

It isn't difficult after this to understand the dialectic which led Hare to his latest investigations, which aim to integrate the landscape into the statue. I imagine he considers classical statuary an abstract art, since it isolates its model from the human universe and from true duration. For him, the goal he gets closer to every day is the concrete absolute: man or the living animal in his entirety. But we know now that our milieu is a part of ourselves: it transforms us and we transform it. If we are to present this concrete totality, man in situation, we have to surround him with his true landscape. As far as I know, Hare has not yet given any answer to these new questions. What we can say in any case is that he will not "situate" his figures in a fragment of geometrical extension: if he wants to show the presence of the forest around the stroller, he will not shape separate trees we can *count*. For some years now the psychologists have talked about a "hodological" space, furrowed with roads and currents, contracted or dilated by our gestures, tinted by our passions, and sticking to us like a cloak. It is this space that Hare will close in upon his figures like a box. Then everything will be settled: each figure will have secreted its shell, a living and personal space which will protect it against our space. Hare will have attained the constant object of his plastic concern, life—animal and human life as it appears when it is refracted in a human milieu. He will have made out of each of his figures a real *event*, that is, a living form moving through a space-time in which time functions as the unification of space. They will be eternal figures not because they carry an indivisible particle of duration from one century to another, but because they have closed up like a fist on the whole of their own duration. They will be purificatory figures: in inscribing horror, the sacred, and desire in stone, they will free us from them. Comedy also frees us from our passions by showing them to us from without. Is it this intimate relation to the comic which gives Hare's sculptures their black, elusive humor? Let's recognize, as a matter of fact, that classical statuary is related to tragedy because it is a party to our passions and aims to provoke them (a statue by Praxiteles or Donatello springs forth *within* the human world); and Hare's sculpture, on the contrary (like Giacometti's), shows us man from without. It tries to dehumanize our gaze in the manner of Kafka, who shows us transcendence inside out.

We thereby step right into the realm of magic, which Alain defined as "mind dragging along in things." In soaking up human meanings like a blotter, the object becomes isolated and ceases to be natural. It's a good opportunity to push on into the very heart of magic. If Hare did in fact stop short at this point, his art, even though it is not representational, would nonetheless be limited to giving us the world. Undoubtedly a world richer than that of ancient sculpture—which has been already seen, loved, and assimilated by man—but just the same, in spite of everything, the world as it *is*. But the ambiguity of art is that it has always made us see what is, and at the same time created, beyond what is, what is not. In even the most naturalistic sculpture, creation and imitation are intimately related. A moment comes when Hare's sculpture offers itself for its own sake, in its sculptural *autonomy*. But to those who look at it in this light it never offers itself as pure plastic form. The human, living world always remains in the background; and this is the world from which it borrows forms shot through with meanings, and with which it amuses itself by setting one against the other in a primitive syncretism. Hare is all the more at ease on this ground because the integral space of the emotions is already magical, and magical, too, is the distanceless presences it reveals. The syncretism he makes use of is the key to this ambiguity. It is *realistic*, since it is a syncretism of fear and love; but it also leaves room for all the transmutations, since it comes down to creating ambivalent and contradictory structures. Movements and forms, densities and figures ceaselessly destroy each other. Each object makes a fake appeal to representation: these are eyes, breasts. But we are barely on the road to recognition when suddenly another form abruptly rises up, begins to haunt the first and confuses our judgment. These eyes are also arms, thighs; they're eye-arms, breast-thighs. And even this interpretation is challenged by a form more vast and indivisible which envelops all the others. Thus there are created, in the very movement which is trying to present the world to us, qualities and forms which are not of this world. Hare told me one day that he wanted to render by properly sculptural means natures analogous to the one Audiberti reveals in his famous phrase, "the secret blackness of milk." Are these inventions or discoveries? Destructions or creations? The works of Hare oscillate perpetually between these different terms. As Audiberti's phrase does too. For after all it's true that the secret blackness of milk *exists*, and it is also true that the *word* "blackness" gratuitously destroys the *essence* of milk. People will speak of a surrealist influence here. But the surrealists work their destructions at the level of conventional representation. Thus the magic is present first, at the level of common sense. In Hare's works it is, so to speak, on the far side of sculpture; it is a way of suggesting that man is always ahead of himself and the world is both entirely given and entirely to be made. Gracious and comical, mobile and rigid, realistic and magical, indivisible and contradictory, expressing simultaneously mind become thing and mind's perpetual transcendence of things, Hare's works, in their ambivalence, have the disturbing and malicious look of entrancing bad-luck pieces.

We Write for Our Own Time

WE SAY, in opposition to these critics and authors, that salvation is won on this earth, that it is the salvation of the whole man by the whole man, and that art is a meditation on life, not death. It is true that only talent counts as far as history is concerned. But I'm not inscribed in history yet, and I do not know how I shall be: by myself, as part of an anonymous crowd, or as one of those names they put in the footnotes to literature texts. In any case I don't have to be concerned about the judgments that the future will make of my work, because I can't do anything about them. Art cannot be reduced to a dialogue with the dead and the yet unborn; that would be both too hard and too easy, and I see it as a final remnant of the Christian belief in immortality. Just as man's stay here below is presented as a brief time of testing between limbo and hell or heaven, so a book is supposed to pass through a transitional period which coincides roughly with the period of its effectiveness, and subsequently—disembodied and gratuitous, like a soul—it enters eternity. But for Christians at least it is this journey through the world that settles everything, and ultimate blessedness is no more than a sanction; whereas it is commonly believed that the

This fragment of *Qu'est-ce que la littérature*, although omitted from the final version of that work, was printed as "Ecrire pour son époque" in a number of European and American journals between 1946 and 1948. According to Rybalka and Contat, this article seems to have been written as a reply to criticisms evoked by the article setting forth the position of *Les Temps modernes* [translator's note]. See also Vol. 1, 46/114.

path our books take after we have ceased to exist reflects back upon our life to justify it. This is true from the viewpoint of Objective Mind. In Objective Mind people are classed according to talent. But our grandchildren's view of us merits no special privilege, since others will come after them and judge them in turn. It goes without saying that we all write from a need for the absolute; and in fact a work of the mind is indeed an absolute. But people make a twin mistake in this respect. To begin with, it is not true that a writer raises his sufferings or flaws to the level of the absolute by writing about them; it is not true that he redeems them. People say that this unhappily married man who writes with such talent about marriage has made a good book *out of* his conjugal misery. That would be too easy: the bee makes honey *out of* the flower because it works *real* transformations in vegetable matter; the sculptor makes a statue *out of* marble. But it is out of words, not his troubles, that the writer makes his books. If he wants to keep his wife from being nasty, he is wrong to write about her; he would do better to beat her. One no more *puts* his troubles in a book than one puts his model on canvas: one gets his inspiration from them, and they stay just the way they are. Perhaps one gains a momentary relief in rising above them to write about them, but once the book is finished, there they are again. Bad faith begins when the artist, wanting to give his misfortunes meaning as a sort of immanent finality, persuades himself that they are there *in order that* he may speak of them. When he uses this dodge to justify his own sufferings, he is asking to be laughed at; but if he tries to justify the sufferings of others, he is simply odious. The finest book in the world will not redeem the suffering of a child. One does not redeem evil, one fights it. The finest book in the world redeems itself, and it redeems the artist. But not the man. No more than the man redeems the artist. We want the man and the artist to be redeemed together, the work to be an act as well, conceived expressly as a weapon in the struggle men are waging against evil.

The other error is no less serious: there is in every human heart such hunger for the absolute that eternity, which is allegedly a timeless absolute, has often been confused with immortality, which is only a perpetual reprieve and a long chain of vicissitudes. I can see why people want the absolute. I want it too. But why go so far to look for it? It is there all around us, beneath our footsteps, in each of our gestures. We produce the absolute the way M. Jourdain produced prose. You light your pipe and it's an absolute; you hate oysters and it's an absolute; you join the Communist Party and it's an absolute. Whether the world is matter or mind, whether God exists or not, whether the judgment of future centuries will be favorable or hostile to you, nothing will ever prevent your having passionately loved this painting, this cause, this woman, or having lived this love from day to day—lived it, willed it, undertaken it—or having been involved completely in it. Our grandfathers were right to say, as they drank their glass of wine: "Here's one more the Prussians won't get." Neither the Prussians nor anyone else. They can kill you, they can take away your wine until your dying day, but neither God nor man can take away this final gliding swallow of Bordeaux across your tongue. Nor relativism. Nor "the eternal course of history." Nor the dialectic of the sensible world. Nor the disassociations of psychoanalysis. It is a pure event, and we too, at the depths of historical relativity and our insignificance, are inimitable and incomparable absolutes, and our choice of ourselves is an absolute. All these vital and impassioned choices which we are and which we make perpetually with or against others, all these common undertakings which we throw ourselves into from birth to death, all these ties of love or hate which unite us one to another and which exist only to the extent that we feel them, all these immense combinations of movements which reinforce or annul one another and which are all lived through, all this discordant and harmonious life comes together to produce a new absolute which I would call a *time*. A time is intersubjectivity, the living absolute, the dialectical other side of history. It brings to birth in pain events that will be labeled later by historians. The meanings they will cull through their reasoned labors a time lives blindly, in rage and fear and rapture. Each spoken word, before it becomes a historic word or the recognized source of a social process, is in its time an insult or an appeal or a confession. Economic phenomena themselves, before they become the theoretical causes of social upheavals, are suffered in humiliation or despair. Ideas are tools or evasions; facts arise from intersubjectivity and upset it, as emotions arise from the individual soul. History is made out of dead times. Each time, when it dies, becomes relative, takes its place in line beside the dead throughout the centuries, and is illumined by a new light, challenged by a new understanding.

The dead time has its problems solved for it. Its most passionate investigations are shown to have been doomed to failure, and the lofty undertakings it was so proud of are shown to have had consequences just the opposite of those it had anticipated, so that its limitations and its lack of understanding suddenly appear. But this is because it *is* a dead time. "At the time," its limitations and its lack of understanding did not exist. We do not live a lack. Or, rather, the time then was a perpetual transcending of its limitations toward a future which was *its* future and which died with it. At the time it was *this* daring, *this* lack of prudence, *this* ignorance of its ignorance. To live is to foresee in the short run and muddle through with the means at hand. Perhaps with a little more understanding our fathers would have seen that such and such a problem was insoluble, that such and such a question had been badly put. But the human condition makes us choose in ignorance; it is ignorance that makes morality possible. If we knew all the conditioning factors, if we were gambling on a sure thing, risk would disappear, but along with risk, courage and fear, expectation, effort, and ultimate joy. We would be languishing gods, but certainly not men. The bitter Babylonian disputes about portents, the bloody and passionate Albigensian and Anabaptist heresies, all seem erroneous to us today. At the time, man was completely involved in them, and by expressing them at the risk of his life he made truth exist through them, because truth never reveals itself directly but appears only through errors. In the dispute over universals, or over the Immaculate Conception or transubstantiation, the fate of human reason was at stake. And the fate of reason was also at stake during those big suits certain American states brought against the professors who taught evolution. In each time it is wholly at stake in relation to doctrines which the following time will reject as false. It is possible that evolutionary thinking will someday seem to be our century's greatest insanity; yet in bearing witness to its truth in opposition to the churches, the American professors *lived* the truth and lived it passionately and absolutely, at their own risk. Tomorrow they will be wrong; today they are absolutely right: the time is always wrong when it is dead, and always right while it is living. People may condemn it later all they want to, but it has already had its own passionate way of loving itself and tearing itself to pieces, against which future judgments are powerless. It has had its taste which it alone has tasted, and which is just as incomparable, just as irremediable, as the taste of wine in our mouth.

A book has its absolute truth in its own time. It is *lived through* like a riot or a famine. With far less intensity, of course, and by fewer people, but in the same way. It's an emanation of intersubjectivity, a vital bond of fury, hate, or love between those who have produced it and those who receive it. If it succeeds in making itself felt, thousands of people reject it and deny it: to read a book, as we well know, is to rewrite it. *At the time* it is panic or evasion or courageous affirmation to start with; at the time it is good or bad *action*. Later, when the time has died out, it will become relative, become a message. But the judgments of posterity will not annul the ones made of it while it lived. People have often said to me about dates and bananas, "You can't say anything about them: to know what they're like you have to eat them right away, just after they've been picked." And I have always thought of bananas as dead fruits whose true taste escaped me. The books which carry over from one time to another are dead fruits. They have had, in another time, another taste, a tart and vivid one. We should have read *Emile* or *The Persian Letters* when they had just been picked.

So we have to write for our own time, the way the great writers did. But that doesn't mean we have to shut ourselves up in it. Writing for the time doesn't mean passively reflecting it. It means wanting to keep it the way it is or to change it, and thus going beyond it toward the future. And it's this attempt to change it that makes you so profoundly a part of it, for then it can never be reduced to a dead heap of tools and customs but is a constant movement of transcendence in which the concrete present and the living future of the men who make it up are one and the same. If, among other characteristics, Newtonian physics and the theory of the Happy Savage help sketch the appearance of the first half of the eighteenth century, we must not forget that the former represented a consistent attempt to snatch shreds of truth from the slough of ignorance in order to approach an ideal science, beyond the present state of knowledge, in which phenomena could be deduced mathematically from the principle of gravitation, and that the latter involved an attempt to restore, beyond the vices of civilization, the state of nature. Both of these theories outlined a future; and even though it's true that this future never did become a present—

that men gave up the Golden Age and the attempt to make science a strict logical deduction—the fact remains that these vital and profound aspirations outlined a future beyond men's daily cares, and that in order to make out the meaning of this daily life we have to come at it *from* that future. A man could never be a man or get to be a writer if he did not trace a vanishing line beyond his present horizon, but in every case this self-transcending is finite and singular. We do not transcend *in general* and simply for the proud pleasure of transcending: Baudelairean dissatisfaction represents only the abstract image of transcendence, and since it is dissatisfaction with everything it ends up being dissatisfaction with nothing. Real transcendence requires that we want to change certain definite aspects of the world, and transcendence is colored and characterized by the concrete situation it aims to change. A man puts all of himself into his project to free the Negroes or to restore the Hebrew language to the Jews in Palestine; he puts all of himself into it and at the same time realizes the human condition in its universality, but always in connection with a singular and dated undertaking. And if someone like M. Schlumberger tells me that we also transcend our time when we aim at immortality, I shall answer that it is a false transcendence: instead of wanting to change an insupportable situation, we try to escape it and seek refuge in a future that is wholly alien to us, since it is not the future *we are making* but the concrete present of our grandchildren. We have no means of acting on that present; our grandchildren will live it for their own sake and the way they want to, situated in their time as we are in ours. If they make use of our writings it will be for the sake of ends of their own which we have not foreseen, they way you pick up stones from the road to throw them at someone who's attacking you. Any attempt we made to shift the responsibility for prolonging our existence to them would be futile; they have neither the duty nor the desire to prolong it. And since we have no way of acting on these strangers, we'll come before them like beggars and implore them to give us a semblance of life by hiring us to do any old sort of job. If we are Christians we shall humbly let them use us as witnesses to the inefficacy of faith, if only they will still keep talking about us. If we are atheists we'll be very happy that they are still concerned with our anxieties and failings, even if it is to prove that man without God is miserable. Would you be satisfied, M. Schlumberger, if after the Revolution our grandchildren considered your writings the most striking example of the conditioning of art by economic structures? And if you have no literary destiny, you'll have a different but scarcely better one: if you escape dialectical materialism, it will be perhaps to bear the costs of some psychoanalysis. In any case our grandchildren will be abusive orphans, so why should we bother with them? Maybe Céline will be the only one of us who endures. It is highly improbable but theoretically possible that the twenty-first century will remember Drieu's name and forget Malraux's. In any case it won't take up our squabbles again; it won't even mention what we call today the treason of certain writers—or if it does it will be without our anger and contempt. But what do we care? It is what Malraux and Drieu are for us that's absolute. In certain of our hearts there is an absolute contempt for Drieu and friendship for Malraux that a hundred posthumous judgments could not touch. There has been a living Malraux, a weight of warm blood at the heart of the time; there will be a dead Malraux, the prey of history. Why should the living concern themselves with establishing the image of the dead man he will be? Of course he lives ahead of himself; his gaze and cares extend beyond his bodily death. What measures a man's weight and *presence* is neither the fifty or sixty years of his organic life nor the borrowed life that he will lead in the minds of strangers in the course of centuries; it is the choice he himself will have made of the temporal cause that transcends him. It is said the runner from Marathon was dead an hour before he got to Athens. He was dead and he kept on running; he was running dead; as a dead man he announced the Greek victory. It's a beautiful myth; it shows that for a little while longer the dead act as if they were living. A little while—one year, ten years, maybe even fifty, but in any case a *finite* period—and then they're buried a second time. This is the standard we offer for the writer: as long as his books provoke anger, embarrassment, shame, hatred, love—even if he is no longer anything but a shade—he shall live! Afterward, the deluge. We are for a morality and an art of the finite.

The Historical Process

*Existentialism has no awareness
of the historical process.*
Pravda, January 23, 1947

I'VE BEEN EXPECTING an attack like this for a long time. I had put some questions to the Communist intellectuals in my magazine, *Les Temps modernes,* and they had been unable to answer. On the other hand, M. Ehrenburg had on his return from America severely criticized my books, and I had made him admit that he had not read them, which he did graciously and without being in the least disturbed. What was needed, evidently, was an encyclical to straighten everything out. It is clear that M. Zaslavski hasn't read the existentialist works either. But he talks about them more, and more noisily. I am greatly embarrassed to have to reply to him: one replies to someone, but M. Zaslavski is not someone. For the time being, *Pravda's* editorial writer and (in his own words) the "historical process" speak through his mouth. Tomorrow, perhaps, the historical process will turn away from him, he'll be a number in Siberia, and everyone will have forgotten him. He will never have been a person. I'm sorry, for his sake and mine. So all I can do is turn to the "historical process" and tell it how sorry I am that it chose such a poor interpreter. No doubt it was unable to find any others. The historical process always has reasons. But still it would have been nice if M. Zaslavski—who grandly declares, "Existentialism is the negation of all philosophy"—had proved, at least in his article, that he was a philosopher himself. Alas! In all this hateful studied hodgepodge there is not a word of

This article was published as "Le Processus historique" in *La Gazette de Lausanne,* February 8, 1947. See also Vol. 1, 47/126.

common sense. I'll limit myself to pointing out the following errors:

1. If M. Zaslavski had been a philosopher, and if he had read the books he talks about, he would not have called a philosophy whose only dogma is the affirmation of human freedom, and which never stops repeating that men hold their destiny in their own hands, a "fatalism." The Marxists have cried out and protested rather often because the historical dialectic was compared to a fatalism; it's too bad that M. Zaslavski, the elect of the "historical process," has fallen into the same error concerning existentialism. Words change their meaning so beneath his pen that he calls me a fatalist because I don't believe in the fatality of the Communist revolution.

2. M. Zaslavski reproaches existentialism for its "total lack of spirituality." But if he knew the ABCs of Marxism, he would know that a materialist makes himself ridiculous by reproaching an adversary for his lack of spirituality. There is spirituality, in fact, when the spirit as a substance distinct from matter is appealed to. But materialism recognizes only one principle, matter, which is, as a matter of principle, hostile to all recourse to spirit. I never would have thought of considering MM. Thorez and Duclos spiritualists. I'll try to from now on. If, furthermore, M. Zaslavski had only opened *Being and Nothingness*, or any other existentialist work, he would have seen precisely that the consciousness of each one of us is irreducible to matter. But maybe he knows this and is deploring our lack of spirituality precisely because we are not materialists.

3. I have written, just as often as I could, that the sole hope of mankind lay in a socialist revolution. This is undoubtedly why M. Zaslavski declares that I am patronized by the upper crust. I made a good number of Americans very unhappy by writing an article on the condition of the blacks in the United States: this is undoubtedly his reason for making me an American propaganda agent. It's true that I have lived in the United States longer than M. Ehrenburg, and that I don't share his stupid prejudices against that great country. Does it follow that I want to make my own country a "colony in the American empire"? Is it absolutely necessary to insult America in order to remain in the good graces of the "historical process" and M. Zaslavski? One of my collaborators wrote in *Les Temps modernes* that "the historical heritage of the United States is, in fact, the whole world." M. Zaslavski concludes from this that

we want a United States hegemony over the world. If he had been able, or had wanted, to read the whole article, he would have interpreted the phrase differently. My collaborator meant in fact that if there were to be an American culture, the Americans would have to take up and assimilate the historical traditions of all the continents. But what M. Zaslavski understood does not count. All that counts is what the "historical process" dictates to him. As for the rich American bourgeoisie which, it seems, "greeted in me an enemy of Marxism," I can assure *Pravda*'s editorial writer that it is very little concerned with me and does not even know my name. The lectures I gave in America were held before intellectuals and students; they had to do with French literature during the Occupation.

4. M. Zaslavski accuses me of "denying all morality." I remember Lenin's saying: "I call 'moral' every man who contributes to the Communist revolution and 'immoral' every man who tries to stop it." If this is the meaning M. Zaslavski gives to "moral" and "immoral," then it's true that I'm not moral. I do not belong to the Communist Party. But I believe precisely that an autonomous morality exists. I think we have definite obligations, including (among others) the obligation to tell—no matter what the demands of the "historical process" may be—the truth. So just as M. Zaslavski reproached me for being a fatalist because I believe in freedom, and for lacking spirituality because I'm not a materialist, he taxes me with immorality because I am no partisan of Machiavellianism and realism in politics. *Pravda*'s condemnation *ex cathedra* comes at the very time the Church has put my books on the Index. This is no accident. So you'll excuse me if I see this simultaneous double condemnation as a valuable encouragement: when a man is trying to confront men with their freedom, it is natural he should find lined up against him all the powers who have an interest in hiding that freedom from them.

Nick's Bar, New York City

JAZZ IS LIKE BANANAS; to get the taste of it you've got to be where it's at. There are plenty of records in France, God knows, and mournful imitators too. But they're just a pretext for shedding a few tears in good company. Certain countries have national celebrations and others don't. When the people impose strict silence on you during the first half of a demonstration and start to shout and stomp during the second, that's a national celebration.

If you accept this definition, there is no national celebration in France, except perhaps the rummage sales and auctions. Or in Italy, except perhaps robbery: they let the thief go to work in watchful silence (first half), and they stomp and shout "Stop thief!" while he runs away (second half). Belgium, on the contrary, has cockfights; Germany, belief in vampires; and Spain, *corridas*. I found out in New York City that jazz is a national celebration. In Paris they dance to it, but that's a mistake. Americans don't dance to the sound of jazz. For that they have a special music which is also used for first communions and marriages and is called *music by Musak*. There are switches in apartments, you turn them on, and Musak musicks: flirtation, tears, dancing. You turn off the switch, and Musak stops musicking: communicants and lovers are put to bed.

They celebrate nationally at Nick's Bar in New York. That is, they sit down in a smoke-filled room beside sailors, tough guys, unlicensed whores, and women of the world. Tables and

This piece was published in a special issue of *America*, "Jazz 47," June 25, 1947. See also Vol. 1, 47/131.

[182]

loges. No one talks. The sailors come in fours. With a legitimate hatred, they stare at the squares who go sit in the loges with their chicks. The sailors would like to have chicks; they don't. They drink; they're tough. The chicks are tough too: they drink and don't talk. No one budges; the jazz plays. They play jazz from ten to three o'clock in the morning. In France jazz musicians are handsome, lusterless men with flowing shirts and silk neckerchiefs. If listening bugs you, you can always look at them and take lessons in elegance.

At Nick's Bar, it's advisable not to look at them; they're as ugly as the musicians in a symphony orchestra. Bony faces, mustaches, jackets, starched collars (at least at the beginning of the evening); and even their glance isn't soft. But their muscles hump their sleeves.

They play. Everybody listens. No one dreams. Chopin makes you dream, or André Claveau. But not the jazz at Nick's Bar. It fascinates you; it's all you think of. Not the least bit consoling. If you come in a cuckold, you leave a cuckold, without any tenderness. No chance to grab your girl's hand and let her know with a wink that the music says what's in your soul. It's harsh, violent, pitiless music. Not gay, not sad, inhuman. The cruel shrills of birds of prey. The musicians start to sweat, one after the other. First the trumpet player, then the pianist, then the trombone player. The bass player looks beat. This music doesn't speak of love; it doesn't console. It's hurried. Like the people who take the subway or eat in automats. It isn't the age-old chant of black slaves either. They don't give a damn about black slaves. Or the sad little dream of Yankees crushed by their machines. There's none of all that. There's a big man blowing his lungs out trying to follow the gyrations of his trombone, a merciless pianist, a bass player slapping his strings without looking at the others. They speak to the best part of you, the most unfeeling and most free, the part which doesn't want sad songs or sprightly ones but a moment of deafening explosion. They make demands on you; they don't baby you. Connecting rods, main shaft, milling machine. They throb, turn, grate. The rhythm is born. If you are tough and young and fresh, the rhythm grabs you and rocks you. You jump to the beat, faster and faster, and the girl next to you jumps with you. It's swinging round a circle down in hell. The trombone player sweats, you sweat, the trumpet player sweats, you sweat some more, and then you feel that something has happened up on the stand. They don't look the same. They speed it up, vibrate their haste to one another. They look tense and out of their minds; you'd say that they were looking for something else. Something like sexual pleasure. And you start to look for something yourself and you begin to yell. You have to yell: the combo has become an immense spinning top, and if you don't keep yelling it will tumble down. You yell. They dig, they blow, they are possessed. You are possessed. You yell out like a woman in childbirth. The trumpet player touches the pianist and transmits his own possession to him just the way it happened in the days when Mesmer mesmerized. You keep on yelling. A whole crowd of people is yelling in rhythm. You don't even hear the jazz any more, you see people on the stand sweating in rhythm, you feel like whirling round and round, howling at death, hitting the girl next to you in the face.

And then suddenly the jazz stops. The bull has been run through; the older cock is dead. It's over. You've drunk your whisky while you were yelling without even noticing that you were drinking it. An impassive waiter brings you another. You remain dazed for a moment, you shake yourself, you say to the girl next to you, "Not bad . . ." She doesn't answer, and it begins again.

You won't make love that night, you won't feel sorry for yourself, you won't even have gotten drunk or shed blood, and you will have been swept by a blind frenzy, by this convulsive crescendo which is like an angry, futile search for pleasure. You'll leave the place a little worn, a little drunk, but in a sort of beat-down calm, as after great heaves of emotional storms.

Jazz is America's national celebration.

For a Theater of Situations

THE CHIEF SOURCE of great tragedy—the tragedy of
Aeschylus and Sophocles, of Corneille—is human freedom. Oedipus is free; Antigone and Prometheus are free. The fate we
think we find in ancient drama is only the other side of freedom.
Passions themselves are freedoms caught in their own trap.

Psychological theater—the theater of Euripides, Voltaire,
and Crébillon *fils*—announces the decline of tragic forms. A
conflict of characters, whatever turns you may give it, is never
anything but a composition of forces whose results are predictable. Everything is settled in advance. The man who is led inevitably to his downfall by a combination of circumstances is
not likely to move us. There is greatness in his fall only if he
falls through his own fault. The reason why we are embarrassed
by psychology at the theater is not by any means that there is
too much greatness in it but too little, and it's too bad that modern authors have discovered this bastard form of knowledge and
extended it beyond its proper range. They have missed the will,
the oath, and the folly of pride which constitute the virtues and
the vices of tragedy.

But if we focus on these latter, our plays will no longer be
sustained primarily by character—depicted by calculated "theatrical expressions" and consisting in nothing other than the
total structure of our oaths (the oath we take to show ourselves
irritable, intransigent, faithful, and so on)—but by situation.
Not that superficial imbroglio that Scribe and Sardou were so

This article was published as "Pour un théâtre de situations" in
La Rue, November, 1947. See also Vol. 1, 47/143.

good at staging and that had no human value. But if it's true that man is free in a given situation and that in and through that situation he chooses what he will be, then what we have to show in the theater are simple and human situations and free individuals in these situations choosing what they will be. The character comes later, after the curtain has fallen. It is only the hardening of choice, its arteriosclerosis; it is what Kierkegaard called *repetition*. The most moving thing the theater can show is a character creating himself, the moment of choice, of the free decision which commits him to a moral code and a whole way of life. The situation is an appeal: it surrounds us, offering us solutions which it's up to us to choose. And in order for the decision to be deeply human, in order for it to bring the whole man into play, we have to stage limit situations, that is, situations which present alternatives one of which leads to death. Thus freedom is revealed in its highest degree, since it agrees to lose itself in order to be able to affirm itself. And since there is theater only if all the spectators are united, situations must be found which are so general that they are common to all. Immerse men in these universal and extreme situations which leave them only a couple of ways out, arrange things so that in choosing the way out they choose themselves, and you've won—the play is good. It is through particular situations that each age grasps the human situation and the enigmas human freedom must confront. Antigone, in Sophocles' tragedy, has to choose between civic morality and family morality. This dilemma scarcely makes sense today. But we have our own problems: the problem of means and ends, of the legitimacy of violence, the problem of the consequences of action, the problem of the relationships between the person and the collectivity between the individual undertaking and historical constants, and a hundred more. It seems to me that the dramatist's task is to choose from among these limit situations the one that best expresses his concerns, and to present it to the public as the question certain free individuals are confronted with. It is only in this way that the theater will recover its lost resonance, only in this way that it will succeed in *unifying* the diversified audiences who are going to it in our time.

Black Presence

ALIOUNE DIOP WAS RIGHT to call his magazine *Présence africaine*. A great many countries have been present in their time at the heart of our concerns: Germany yesterday and the USSR and the United States today. But Africa, for many of us, is only an absence; and this great hole in the map of the world lets us keep our conscience clean. We're very fond of the few blacks who live here, we have great respect for them, we consider them our equals, and that's all we have to do to be able to think of France as the land of liberty. When people talk to us about what is called segregation in the U.S.A., we burn with honest indignation; but it is at the height of this indignation that we are at our most comical and guilty. Of course we take the Martinicans or the Senegalese who come to study in France as equals. But how many are they? Do we know what a suspicious screening, what a tough selection, they have to go through? Have we measured the distance and the obstacles between the villages of the Congo and the schools of Paris? After all, at Vassar College, near New York, a colored student is occasionally accepted too. These few guests, who have been admitted after having been subjected to all the rites of initiation, are hostages and symbols. They are for us a witness to our civilizing mission. In honoring them, we are aware of honoring ourselves. Each time we shake a black's hand *here* we wipe out all the violence we have done *there*. *Here* the blacks are handsome urbane

This piece was published as "Présence noire" in the first issue of *Présence africaine*, November–December, 1947. See also Vol. 1, 47/144.

foreigners who dance with our wives; *there* they are "natives" who are not entertained in French families and do not frequent the same public places. *Here* we go to their get-togethers and dances; *there* a black in a café causes a scandal. *Here* they cut the figure of well-to-do students training for bourgeois jobs; *there* it is not unusual for a native worker to be paid 150 francs a month.[1] *There*—but we don't go there to see for ourselves; we're like that puritan who was happy to eat meat if he could only imagine it grew on trees, and who always refused to go to the slaughterhouse to see where the beefsteaks they served him really came from. I hope that *Présence africaine* will paint us an impartial picture of the condition of the blacks in the Congo and in Senegal. No need to put anger or rebellion into it. Just the truth. That will be enough to hit us in the face with the hot breath of Africa, the bitter smell of oppression and misery.

But Africa's presence to us depends above all upon us. A book, no matter how fine, gives nothing we don't give to it; and what we find in it is exactly proportional to what we seek in it. There are a hundred ways to make this magazine inoffensive. What I am most afraid of is that, strengthened by our thousand years of literature—our Villons, Racines, Rimbauds—we shall dwell on our black friends' poems and stories with the same fascinated indulgence parents give their children on their birthdays to compliment them. Let's be careful not to see these creations of the human spirit as homage done to French culture. It's a completely different thing. Culture is a tool; don't think they've chosen ours. If the English instead of the French had occupied Senegal, the Senegalese would have adopted English. The truth is that the blacks are trying to get in touch with one another through an alien cultural world that others have imposed upon them. They have to retailor this ready-made suit of clothing. Everything, even the syntax, hampers and restricts them, and yet they have learned to make use of even this tool's shortcomings. An alien language lives inside them and robs them of their thought. But inwardly they turn against this theft, they master inwardly this European chitchat, and finally, by letting the language betray them, they put their stamp on it. For my own part, I can only admire the effort these authors have made—in spite of the conditions they live under, and against themselves and us

1. In a country where fish costs 25 francs a kilo and meat 70 to 80 francs.

—to conquer themselves in and through the hostile language of their colonizers.

I hope we shall learn to read these works and be grateful to the blacks for enriching our old ceremonious culture which, encumbered by its traditions and formalities, sorely needs new contributions. Each black who tries to depict himself with our words and myths is a little new blood circulating in this old body. The presence of Africa among us must not be like that of a child in the family circle but like the presence of a feeling of remorse and hope.

The Encounter,
or Oedipus and the Sphinx

FIRST YOU'LL SEE THE SPHINX SPEAK without hearing her: her mouth dances. Then Oedipus, with closed lips, will sing with his body. And finally the music itself will be reabsorbed into the movement. The body by itself will become speech, song, and music—as if Kochno and Lichine had wanted to bring us bit by bit up to this silence swollen with music. I have often asked myself about the essence of ballet: isn't it an impure genre? Why this décor, this plot, these props; isn't the dancing alone enough? It seems that this mute spectacle provides answers to my questions. What it means to us is that the beauty of pure dance—seguidilla or pavane—is still abstract. Valéry said that the dancer lives at the heart of the whirlwind, like the salamander in the flame; but what we have to add is that this flame has consumed everything. Earth, water, air, and fire have disappeared; a top is spinning in the void. The function of ballet is to restore the world to dance, but by transforming it.

The gods, it is said, created the world for man. But we don't see this at first, since we have to earn our daily bread by the sweat of our brow. Space, time, and a thousand obstacles stand between desire and gratification. Nevertheless, enjoyment is taken to be an ultimate end. But suppose that, on the contrary, man was born to act. Then action is no longer just a little tran-

This piece, which served as the program notes for the ballet *La Rencontre ou Oedipe et le Sphinx* by Boris Kochno, Henri Sauguet, and David Lichine, was published in 1948. See also Vol. 1, 48/167.

sitory fever, a momentary shift of equilibrium, which mars the calm perfection of the state of rest, dies down, and is forgotten when the goal is reached. The act is the man, the man exists only in act, desires only provide us with pretexts for action, and the goods of this world are set in our path to tempt us. These fruits ripen for us only on condition that we no longer pick them for the sake of nourishment. We eat for the sake of picking, and pick for the sake of climbing the tree. Foods, flowers, weapons, tools, and even obstacles and dangers become accessories to that great stable form—movement.

This is what ballet seeks to *represent*. At the center is the dance, which is action taken for its own sake and purely gratuitously, the flowering of man. The world turns about this turning man as planets turn about the sun. The décor *joins the dance*. It is drawn into it by gravitation. The ballet soaks up the décor and all its color as earlier it soaked up speech, music, and song. If I walk out to go draw water at the river, the walk is work and suffering. But when Babilée walks, space is a pretext for walking. It comes up to his steps to let them lay it out and line it up. The river, the paths, the earth become embodied in the walk and color it. One October evening, Mallarmé wrote to Coppée, "The autumn of my stroll reminds me. . . ." The aim of ballet is to enable us to speak of the autumn of a dance, of its sun and of its sky. And above all—since Kochno is its animator —of its light. The plot, or, as they say, the argument, has no other aim: it must show us, in desire and pain, in failure as in triumph, pretexts for acting—that is to say, for dancing.

Even death is justified. Look at this ravishing Sphinx swaying exhausted. Her death is not, like ours, the absurd interruption of life, the scissors' snip which comes we know not when from who knows where. It joins the act and forms its natural ending. It lives in it from the start as the last chord lives in a melody. One dances to die, one dies to dance. Thus ballet, without in any way concealing man's fate, redeems and justifies the sufferings it represents by gathering them like a flock about the dance, this pure symbol of human work. Thanks to Boris Kochno, Lichine, and Babilée, we shall be able every evening to see this miracle: a completely hostile yet completely obedient world, a heavy mass of sky and granite, of work, suffering, and death which rests upon slender human limbs as if upon an exquisite point, and which is shaken loose, warmed up, breathed into life, and set to turning by man.

We Must Have Peace
in order to Remake the World

FOOLS ARE ALWAYS partisans of wrath. Ridiculous when they argue, they think they can intimidate people by yelling at them. They march through the streets yelling and calling for violence because in times of violence everyone acts like a fool. If you stay calm you are suspect: the reason why you are not yelling is that you are afraid. One day Wilhelm II said to the bellicose Franz Josef, "What a racket you're making with my saber." Our fools make even more of a racket with the Americans' atomic bomb. If you explain to them that the bombs will fall on us first of all, they'll say you are afraid.

The argument is as old as the hills. You don't believe in God and the Christian tells you you're an atheist because you're proud. You don't want to fight and the military man tells you you're a pacifist because you're a coward. As if a man never believed out of pride or cowardice, or threw himself into a war out of terrified heroism.

Today's saber rattlers are like those mongrel dogs who hide between their masters' legs to bark at callers: they yap at Russia's heels from behind American shirts. Only the vocabulary of the saber rattlers has been recently updated. If you love peace and want to keep it, people don't say any more that you're a coward; they call you a "Munichite." It's stupid, but it's making the rounds. So we have to take the trouble to deflate it.

What is a Munichite? He's a Frenchman who approved in

This article was published as "Il nous faut la paix pour refaire le monde" in *Franc-Tireur*, December 10, 1948. See also Vol. 1, 48/177.

1938 of his government's capitulation at Munich. So in 1948 a Frenchman who prefers capitulation to war is called a Munichite. The Munichite's politics were short run; he saw no farther than the end of his nose. Although he put off the war for a year, he made us fight it under worse conditions: he put the USSR at a disadvantage, let Czechoslovakia's defenses be dismantled, and gave Germany time to rearm—in a word, he sold out his country.

So if those of us who don't want war are Munichites, that means we are thinking about selling out our country. But to whom? To the USSR? To the United States? It doesn't take much thinking to see that the situation has changed since 1938. In 1938 Germany and France were face to face, and Germany was making direct demands on France. Even though the conflict was to become worldwide, to begin with it was an episode in the struggle for European hegemony. You had to fight or give in.

The war threatening today is a world war *to begin with*. We no longer have the initiative: two world powers are in conflict all over the globe. For us, accepting war means accepting vassalage. It's in and through war that we'll be most certain to lose our autonomy: foreigners will command our armies and lend us everything, even including our weapons.

It is fine to die for independence, but to choose dependence in order to be more sure of dying is a rare kind of madness. One day one of the Three Sillies sold his soul to the devil for the rope he was hanged with. Our saber rattlers are like him. Peace is the way we can keep our national sovereignty; and because we're for wars of independence when they're necessary, today we want to win independence through peace.

But this reversal should not surprise us. We Munichites of '48 were against capitulating at Munich. Then what did today's anti-Munichites want at that time? Unconditional surrender. If we look more closely at what they're saying, there's no inconsistency. Then they wanted to give France up to Hitler; now they want to give her up to the U.S., which, by the way, is not so set on taking her. War or peace, it's all the same to them. For them it's just a matter of beating the USSR. The reason why they didn't want to fight Nazi Germany was that it wasn't in their interest. In those days we read their arguments a hundred times in the papers: "If we are conquered we shall be in Hitler's hands; if we conquer, in Stalin's." We answered at the time that surrendering without a fight would give Germany such prestige that we would suffer a defeat as serious as a lost war. But they couldn't have cared less; they had only one enemy—the USSR. What difference did Hitler's hegemony make to them? They were only too willing to give up a freedom which they cared nothing about as long as they were allowed to hold on to their possessions. It was their possessions they wanted to defend. Their possessions and the reign of private property. Yesterday they wanted peace; today they want war. But there's a logic to their thinking. In 1938 they were against the conflict which might profit the USSR; ten years later they want to start one which will let the USSR be annihilated.

But those of us who took the opposite position are no less coherent, and we are not against all wars either. It's on the side of the working class, *for* democracy and *in opposition* to totalitarianism, that we are opposing war today.

They're asking us to fight the Russians? Fine. But why? Let's ask our warhawks. We don't have to do much asking. We have to fight (they'll tell us) because the Russians are keeping an army of "separatists" inside our own beautiful France. Let's stop right here. To want to draw France into a conflict with the USSR is to be against the whole working class. I am not saying that the USSR everywhere and unconditionally protects workers. Nor am I saying that all workers are Communists, or that we ought to want them to be. What I am saying is that those who are ready to wage war against the USSR intend above all to wage war against the proletariat in their own country. We saw that clearly when the troops fired on the miners. In certain newspapers we saw the martial vocabulary of 1914 reappear. As in communiqués, everything was a matter of offensives, conquests, and victories. Our anti-Munichites fancied that in crushing a starving people demanding bread they were annihilating all of Russia. The reason why we, on the other hand, are called "Munichites" is that we think that *in any case and whatever the pretext* firing on the proletariat is a crime.

But we're not taking the side of the USSR against America either. We could not possibly conceive of ourselves fighting a democratic people who have often shown an admirable sense of freedom. It is true that this sense is being lost, but it is being lost to the exact extent that the United States is afraid a war will start and is getting ready for it. To put ourselves in the other camp is to precipitate the war and incite the Americans to shut themselves up in a preventive fascism.

On the contrary, everyone who really wants peace in Europe ought, instead of rejecting the United States en masse, to try to find allies there against the internationalist warhawks.

We do not want war because it does not directly involve our interests, because we neither can nor want to choose between a capitalist democracy and an authoritarian socialism, because the conflict would degenerate into a civil war in France, and because in any case our country would be vassalized and ruined. If this is what it means to be a Munichite, then hurrah for Munich!

But there is still another reason why this comparison is absurd. To be a Munichite in 1938 meant understanding nothing about history. We were involved at that time in a two-dimensional war: the imperialist war overlapped a civil war. *To make peace* was impossible, and the Munichites, furthermore, *did not want* to make it. They wanted to put off the war, escape it from day to day. For them it was a matter of putting off the time of conflict in order to uphold as long as possible a social order which, by its internal structure, made the conflict inevitable. We would have to be naïve to believe that peace is only the absence of war. And it was the temporary absence of war that the Munichites wanted. Also, they had only one means: to yield, to yield inch by inch and save whatever could be saved in their regime. For our part, we want nothing to do with this negative and precarious peace. It is no better than war. To refuse to choose between the USSR and America is not to yield to the one, yield to the other, or let ourselves be tossed about between them both. It is to make a *positive* choice—the choice of Europe, socialism, and ourselves. To want peace is not to want to save what's left of a regime that threatens ruin; it's to want to make peace by building the only kind of regime that is by its very structure peaceful—socialist democracy. The reason why we are not Munichites is that we are not willing to pay any price for peace—and besides, we don't think this long incipient war is peace. Today there is no difference between the will to peace and the will to revolution and democracy. The reason why we are not Munichites is that we want peace in the name not of the property we own but of the job we have to do.

On Being a Writer

WRITING, TO A CHILD, like painting or sculpting, seems as sumptuous and completely natural as the sun. To him a work of art is a hermetic fullness glowing redly in the world of every day. In the gardens where he plays, the statues are particular horticultural specimens destined to feed pigeons. As for a book, the first things about it he becomes acquainted with are its weight and shape. It's a closed fan which opens wide and crackles, giving off the smell of mushrooms. Its use is still a mystery to him, but no more so than the use of a host of other objects which adults handle with a secret and conceited air when they feel like playing grown-ups. The child has not the slightest inkling of a book's gratuitousness, and his parents hide it from him: there is nothing useless, there are only useful things which are "put aside."

For me the *Revue des deux mondes* was long a limp tube-rose, white inside, which was placed on a stand and faded within the month, until that day on a seaside terrace when I saw a purple old man with staring eyes and blanketed knees, between whose breakable hands the review had been slipped. Then it seemed to me to belong in the category of traditional, half-dead, quasi-natural implements such as the water bottles, tisanes, and flannel vests that people use for the preservation of the elderly. Thus as soon as we are born they hide the perverse, mad side of literature from us, and the fact that it is not

This piece, called in French "De la vocation d'écrivain," is a section omitted from the manuscript of *Saint Genet;* it was published in *Neuf* in 1950. See also Vol. 1, 50/203.

a play of arabesques decorating the leaves of a folder but a hole in being into which beings disappear.

A member of the Brotherhood, M. Léon Groc, gave himself away when he called one of his novels *L'Autobus évanoui* ("The Vanished Bus"). That's right, vanished. They didn't make him say it. The writer looks at the bus with a jaundiced eye: "Since it can't belong to *me* it won't belong to *anyone!*" And click! he volatilizes it. Later he'll give the passengers back a bus which is slightly larger and more colorful than life but lacking any depth, a picture painted in the air which cannot carry anything but depicted passengers. This negative undertaking which impoverishes the world can only be explained in terms of an unfeeling heart and other negative feelings.

But the child has grown up among book stores, grocery stores, shoe stores. At the Bon Marché a book is one *article* among others, the bookseller is an honest man who uses the product of this labor to feed his family, the publisher is an aristocrat who spends his profits buying tenements or private houses. So the child thinks he's dealing with an *industry* which competes with others to increase the gross national product. A book is one more being, a producer's good. Writers are indispensable: if by any remote chance they were to disappear, the book workers would be thrown out of work and there would be a danger of social conflict. We see the child's mistake. Naturally the good faith of these specialists—the printer, the paper manufacturer, the publisher, the booksewer, the bookbinder—is not at issue: it has just been caught unprepared. But the fact remains that they have wasted mechanical energy, calories, and human labor in order to make an absence, a phantasmagoria, an iridescent play of nothingness appear. Yet the essential characteristic of nothingness is to conceal itself.

What does a person who is not forewarned see? A publisher is an industrialist who becomes the partner of a small businessman called a printer in order to produce serially a certain kind of merchandise that a distributor distributes to the retailers. The latter sell it to the consumers, and the profits are shared by the retailer, the distributor, the publisher, and a designer whose job is to brighten up the product's outward appearance—that is, to distribute symbols on its pages. The money earned is either invested in new enterprises or put back into circulation. All this is very reassuring: everywhere we find the useful, the economic —being.

The bourgeoisie is so afraid of the negative that it hides it from itself by every means at its disposal. It sees the writer as a cog in the book industry; he's the inventor or perfecter of prototypes. On this basis, it will explain the production of literary goods *in terms of being*. Cleverly confusing the novel or poem and the volume they're embodied in, people compare the writer to a fruit tree, a pregnant woman, a laying hen. They say he is *gifted*. The gift for writing is an organ, something like lymph nodes or interstitial glands. You "have" a nice little writer's touch the same way you "have" your Uncle Randu's eyes. But you "have" Randu's eyes the same way you have the Coints' gold watch which your aunt got from your great-uncle and gave you the day you were born, which was put in a drawer for you, and which you'll wear the day you're twenty-one. The bourgeoisie stole the as-yet-unclarified concept of heredity from the scientists and turned it into a myth justifying inheritance. Voice, eyes, teeth, and character are bequeathed like gold, so why not talent too? Renan perfected the theory: family virtues slowly accumulate until one fine day all this carefully hoarded energy explodes into fireworks—and there's your genius, there's your masterpiece. Labor, family, country. The soil and its dead. France for the French. Bourgeois souls give off the scented odor of possessions. Poems and statues are the products of a centuries-old distillery. Talent springs from capitalization and provides the natural proof of the superiority of capital to labor.

There's only one trouble with all this: the work of art is an absence. How could a person be gifted for nothingness? We can grant that certain physical characteristics are inherited.[1] But are we going to claim that a musculature, a sanguine temperament, and even a high-strung constitution could lead certain persons to prefer the gratuitous to the useful and the imaginary to the real? The poets keep repeating that they see what can't be seen and love nothing so much as that which doesn't exist. But what hereditary structure of the retina could possibly enable us to see the invisible? And what bones, muscles, and fingers could enable us to grasp nonbeing?

> Oh earth, isn't what you seek
> To be reborn in us invisible?

---

1. Nothing is more disputed than the claim that *acquired* characteristics can be inherited.

Rilke writes, and Blanchot:

> Oh night . . . I hover over you, your equal, offering you a mirror
> for your perfect nothingness, for your shadows which are neither
> light nor the absence of light, for this contemplating void. To
> everything you are, and for our language are not, I add a con-
> sciousness. . . .

If this is what a poet ought to be, a blind man seeing nothingness, I challenge anyone to explain in terms of positive data
(whether they have to do with bodily constitution or contents of
consciousness) these *negative* activities.

No; I just don't believe in being gifted. This doesn't mean
that anyone whosoever can make up his mind at any time whatsoever to write. It means that literature, like pederasty, represents a virtual way out which in certain situations is invented
and in others is not even envisaged because it wouldn't be of
any help. If you don't write well, it's because circumstances
haven't called upon you to seek your salvation in words. Robert
Merle, after having spoken in his excellent book of Oscar
Wilde's "storytelling gift," goes on to say:

> It isn't enough to speak of gift in this case. For him, telling stories
> is a vital necessity, since he can live only by escaping life at every
> moment, by substituting an imaginary world for the world. . . .
> The story—in both the aesthetic and the psychological use of the
> term, both as invention and as lie—is the very center of his work,
> the law of his being, the form of his talent.[2]

Merle doesn't put it quite the way I would, but we must be
grateful to him for having shown, at the conclusion of a lengthy
study of an artist, that there is no difference between *the law
of his being* (we would say his fundamental project, his "way
out"—and at bottom that's what Merle is saying too, because he
shows us Wilde *substituting* or *evading*, inventing his defenses)
and *the form of his talent.*

There is no storytelling gift: there is the need to virtually
destroy the world[3] because it seems impossible to live in it. There
is no gift for words: there is the love for words, which is a need,
an emptiness, a suffering, an uneasy attention one pays to them
because they seem to hold the secret of life. Style is a cancer of

2. Robert Merle, *Oscar Wilde*, p. 482.
3. "The Tale, the Fable, the Novel."

language, a wound cultivated like the wounds of Spanish beggars. There is no "sensitivity": there are obsessional feelings. Who is more insensitive than Baudelaire? Who more sensitive? In him sensitivity and insensitivity spring simultaneously from pride, and pride is his first reaction to an intolerable situation.

The reason why the bourgeoisie remains the seedbed of men of letters is not that workers are less gifted than bourgeois; it's that the latter, when their "existential difficulties" have lined them up against their class, become in every sense of the term "impossible." They are against the bourgeois in a bourgeois way (in them the bourgeois hydra bites its own tail and tries to eat itself up); and since they can't destroy anything without suppressing themselves to begin with, they choose—like Mallarmé, like Flaubert—to carry out a symbolic destruction which leaves everything in good shape.

I'm not claiming that there are not—even among bourgeois writers—other reasons for writing, or even less that my motives are those of Flaubert or Jean Lorrain. But even if one created the most committed of writings, one would still have to explain why one had chosen to act on being through the mediation of nonbeing. From this point of view, even the honorable Harriet Beecher Stowe was suspicious. In short, two and only two conditions are necessary for writing. The first is that the situation which we find ourselves in has to offer no better way out. Love of glory, personal cultivation, the spirit of imitation, the company of great minds, curiosity, and even the lure of profit can lead young men and women to create a book. But if they have only these motives for writing, the book will be mediocre and will have no future.

The second condition is that each writer has to reinvent and will the literary way out as if no one before him had ever dreamed of writing. Because the solution is not written in the nature of things, and his situation is like Nature in the physicist's experiment—it says no or says nothing. As a result of their not having invented literature, and of their being fascinated by the aberrant fact that it already existed, a number of people who have been saved by it have remained dreamers and mythomaniacs. I have even seen the following case. A young man was slipping into madness. His friends advised him to write. "But that's what I'm doing," he answered. And he was in fact writing clever and distinguished books—out of love, in order to please, because others had written. He ended up going mad: in cultivating belles-lettres, he had turned away from inventing literature.

I do not think that genius springs from madness but that in certain situations both are equally acceptable ways out: in certain borderline cases one must choose between being crazy through his writing and creating oral literature. Suppose a bald, mustachioed giant suddenly begins crying out: "*I* am Mme. Bovary; I poisoned myself yesterday, and I can still feel in my mouth the awful inky taste of arsenic." He has little chance of avoiding a mental hospital, unless he refers very precisely to a work he is about to publish . . .

Life Begins Tomorrow,
a Film by Nicole Védrès

IN IT ONE SAW a provincial young man deeply at odds with his time arriving in Paris. After having spent an evening in "existentialist" Saint-Germain-des-Prés, the young man, on the advice of a newspaperman, hurries indignantly to Sartre's place at 42, rue Bonaparte. The young man (played by Jean-Pierre Aumont) was received by Jean Cau, at that time Sartre's secretary, who then brought him into Sartre's office.

SARTRE: So if I understand you right you think I'm responsible for your troubles?

YOUNG MAN: Responsible is a little too strong a word, but you have such great influence . . .

SARTRE: Well then, did you come here to ask me something?

YOUNG MAN: All right, suppose that a man, an ordinary man, a man who doesn't quite agree with his time, comes out of nowhere one evening after dark and sits down here in your office. What would you have to say to him?

SARTRE: The first thing I'd tell him would be that being against his time is still a way of agreeing with it.

YOUNG MAN: Could you tell me what you mean by that?

SARTRE: Right. All right, what are you upset about?

In 1950 Sartre appeared in *La Vie commence demain*, a film by Nicole Védrès, in which there were also sequences devoted to Jean Rostand, André Gide, Le Corbusier, and Picasso.

[202]

YOUNG MAN: Oh, as if you didn't know! About everything: the atom bomb and women who switch around in pants, big cruisers that don't stop when you're thumbing—and on just the day the railroad men decide to go out on strike—the government, taxes, the Four Hundred. And that music, that painting, that sculpture nobody can understand at all. And juvenile crime, hired gunmen, do you think that's right? No; listen, it's a crazy time.

SARTRE: You're in business, aren't you?

YOUNG MAN: How did you know?

SARTRE: By what you just told me, of course!

YOUNG MAN: Me? I didn't say anything about myself.

SARTRE: You told me something about your likes and dislikes; you're well dressed but you feel resentment for the rich, yet at the same time you have that . . . fraternal antipathy for workers characteristic of the petty bourgeois who's trying to distinguish himself from the proletariat. And then you have a whole bunch of commonplaces you're all set to drag out. For example, you surely aren't against strikes, because you're too sympathetic with the strikers. It's just that when you're selling something you talk this way: "The workers' wives have silk stockings" or "The workers eat chicken on Sunday." You drop it slyly in your customer's ear; it makes him smile and it makes him buy. Business is a seductive dance, and just as you depend upon your customers' good or bad humor, you tell yourself that everything in society depends upon people's goodness or badness. You think that economic crises are the result of the rulers' blunders, and unemployment of the workers' laziness. Instead of attributing events to the action of general factors independent of our will, you find it easier to hold individuals responsible—that way you can get mad. Why get mad? Because anger is a pleasant feeling, and also because the public is by definition dissatisfied and a good salesman ought to echo its dissatisfaction.

YOUNG MAN: Then it's society which has made me what I am? And my dissatisfaction isn't really mine?

SARTRE: In a sense it isn't. You acquired it along with your lot.

YOUNG MAN: Well, if society made me what I am, then I'm not responsible for it.

SARTRE: Not so fast. It made you, but you certainly get back at it. From the moment you agree to be what society has made you, you begin to make society. You say for example that you're dissatisfied?

YOUNG MAN: Yes.

SARTRE: Dissatisfied with others and not with yourself?

YOUNG MAN: Just with others, of course.

SARTRE: You're innocent, right? Innocent of *everything.*

YOUNG MAN: Now you've got it!

SARTRE: And are there many of you innocents in France?

YOUNG MAN: Quite a few, thank goodness. There are still decent people around.

SARTRE: If there are that many of you, you're beginning to be not so innocent.

YOUNG MAN: There you go; now we're guilty!

SARTRE: Listen. The decent people surely aren't responsible for the rebels in the colonies are they?

YOUNG MAN: Of course not.

SARTRE: Nor for the miners' strikes? Or the Cold War? Or Germany? Or the hard time the UN is having?

YOUNG MAN: Of course we're not responsible.

SARTRE: And you're not ashamed? I've just described our whole time to you, and you tell me that the mighty brotherhood of decent people is letting it drift with the tide and never stepping in to stop it. You're all of you collectively responsible . . .

YOUNG MAN: Collectively? But we don't even know one another!

SARTRE: On the contrary, you don't see anyone else but one another. You run into one another everywhere—in the stores, in the street, at shows. The century's bad humor is reflected in your stern and dignified faces. All two bourgeois have to do

is say hello and they are in a state of holy indignation. You
have created dissatisfaction, racism, xenophobia, war psy-
chosis, and economic stagnation. You are France's bad humor
and inferiority complex.

YOUNG MAN: Me?

SARTRE: Yes you; like all the rest.

YOUNG MAN: But I don't have the impression that I'm like all
the rest.

SARTRE: And have you seen a lot of guys who had the impression that they were like all the rest?

YOUNG MAN: No.

SARTRE: You see. You're like all the others. You think you're
original, like all the rest. You're a decent man, like all the
rest, a guy who is always saying, "It isn't me, I didn't do anything"—like all the rest. Everybody says that things are going
the way they are because other people are bad, and since each
man ultimately thinks that it's the others who did everything,
each man is alone and condemns the others to be alone. You
withdraw from the world, you cross your arms, and you judge
from on high, each of you on his little island! You are responsible for the solitude of our time and for all the ills that
solitude brings.

YOUNG MAN: What ills?

SARTRE: Crime, for example. You have created the universe of
transgression and crime for the others. You are the ones who
invented evil: it's everything you want to do and never have
done out of fear of what people would say—that is, the opin-
ion of all the rest. You're always talking about evil because
you're so sorry you're not doing any: "I didn't do anything
wrong, but it isn't because I didn't have a chance to!" "When
you see what other guys get away with, you tell yourself
you're really stupid!" The criminal is a guy who fascinates you
and whom you hate, because he does what you feel like doing.
Our whole time is a mirror which reflects your face, and you
refuse to recognize it. The criminal is you; the black-market
guy is you . . .

YOUNG MAN: So I ought to say, "The guy out of work is me? The child killers are me? Doctor Petiot is me? The atom bomb is me?"

SARTRE: Exactly.

YOUNG MAN: That would be some job! It would wear you out!

SARTRE: No more than spending the day saying, "The unemployed aren't me! The child killers aren't me! The atom bomb isn't me!"

YOUNG MAN: But then according to that reasoning is Einstein me? Charlie Chaplin? Bernard Shaw? Roosevelt? Stalin? Picasso? André Gide?

SARTRE: Listen. Yes, if you try to understand them, to understand their work, to incorporate it in your life and draw out the consequences of doing so through your acts. It's a great time we're living in, you know.

YOUNG MAN: In spite of the hydrogen bomb?

SARTRE: In spite of the hydrogen bomb. Perhaps there have never been so many threats to men, yet men have never been so clearly conscious of their freedom. If you could bring together all human anguish and awareness in yourself alone, wouldn't you be tempted?

YOUNG MAN: That would depend on · . . . I don't want to bother you any more. But I'm very glad I came. You're not mad at me?

SARTRE: I'd be mad at you if you were like those idiots who come waste my time so that they can hawk stupid bits of gossip later; but since I'm sure our conversation will help you look a little more closely at our time, well, I'm glad too.

Mad Beasts

THE ROSENBERGS ARE DEAD and life goes on. That's the way you wanted it, wasn't it? Just yesterday we were still their brothers, and you killed them as fast as you could to make us their survivors. You are counting on the passing time to make us day by day a little more forgetful, a little guiltier toward them, and you just a little less cruel. Of course. It will cost you a little: windows will get broken at your embassies. But you'll replace them, and then with just a little luck the cops will fire on European crowds and we'll have some nice fresh dead of our own to distract us from thinking about your two.

You already tried that on us with Sacco and Vanzetti and it worked.

This time it won't work.

You'll win your case on one point: we don't wish anyone harm; we refuse to turn the scorn and horror you fill us with into hatred. But you will not succeed in making us take the Rosenbergs' execution for a "regrettable incident," or even for a judicial error. It's a legal lynching which covers a whole people with blood and definitively and unmistakably exposes the bankruptcy of the Atlantic Pact and your inability to assume the leadership of the West. I'm going to tell you where you made your mistake: you thought that when you assassinated the Rosenbergs you were settling a private account. A hundred thousand voices kept saying, "They are innocent." And you answered

This article was published as "Les Animaux malades de la rage" in *Libération*, June 22, 1953. See also Vol. 1, 53/240.

[207]

stupidly, "We are punishing two of our own citizens according to our own law. It's none of your business."

Well, you're wrong! The Rosenberg business is precisely our business. Innocents who are put to death are the whole world's business. The Vatican's spokesman himself told you again Thursday that "civilization is faced with a choice which will determine whether it will be acquitted or condemned." From every side people cried out: "Be careful! In judging them you judge yourselves; you are deciding if you're men or beasts."

Do you understand now why we begged you to hold a new trial? When we were asking justice for the Rosenbergs, we were also saying, "Let your own cause be just." When we were asking that you spare their lives, we were also saying, "Spare your own." Since we had been made your allies, the Rosenbergs' fate threatened to be the foreshadowing of our own. You who claim to be the masters of the world, you had the chance to prove that you were masters of yourselves. But if you gave way to your criminal insanity, that same insanity was capable tomorrow of throwing us pell-mell into a war of extermination. No one in Europe had any illusions about it: depending on whether you gave the Rosenbergs life or death, you were getting ready for world peace or world war.

There had been MacArthur's sinister buffooneries, the bombing of the Yalu, and McCarran's cop stuff: each time, and by yourselves, you hit Europe a low blow. But your supporters still had not lost all hope. The reason why our governments had not been able to make their point of view prevail was that they had not been able to get together, that France had not gone along with England, that the two countries did not have the support of their people. But yesterday the whole of Europe, with its masses, priests, foreign ministers, and heads of state, demanded in a single voice that your president make the most human, the most simple, of gestures.

We weren't asking for your dollars, or your weapons, or your soldiers. No; we were just asking for two lives, two innocent lives.

Have you at least understood what this extraordinary truce meant? Class conflicts, old animosities, everything was set aside; the Rosenbergs had brought about European unity. Just one word from you and you too would have reaped the benefit of this unity: the whole of Europe would have thanked you. And you answered, "Who gives a fuck for Europe." All right. But don't come talking to us about alliances any more. Allies consult with one another, talk things over, make mutual concessions; each one influences the others. If you answer no when all we're asking you is not to dishonor yourselves for nothing, how could we possibly believe that you will let us have our say when major interests are at stake?

And you say we're your allies? Come on. Today our governments are your house servants. Tomorrow our peoples will be your victims, and that's it. Of course you're going to give us shameful excuses: your president couldn't permit himself the luxury of pardoning the Rosenbergs; he had to toss out ballast so that he could make his view prevail in Korea. In Korea? Come on! He gets scoffed at there every day by his own generals and by old Syngman Rhee.

And what kind of a country is it whose leaders have to commit ritual murders to be forgiven for stopping a war?

From now on we know how we weigh on your scales. You've put the universe in one pan and McCarthy in the other. At the moment Rosenberg sat down in the electric chair, the scale tipped to McCarthy's side.

Do you think we're going to die for McCarthy? Bleed ourselves white so that he can have a European army? Do you think we want to defend McCarthy's culture? McCarthy's freedom? McCarthy's justice? That we'll make Europe a battleground to let this bloodstained idiot burn all the books? Have all the innocents executed and imprison the judges who protest?

Don't kid yourselves. We'll never let the Rosenbergs' assassin lead the West.

You say that McCarthy won't last forever and that people are working secretly to get rid of him. So what? Your McCarthy has a million heads. Cut one off and a hundred new ones will grow.

Listen, I have on my desk a picture taken last Thursday in Washington: well-fed, well-dressed men and elegant women are marching to demand the Rosenbergs' necks; and in the front row a pretty young girl is carrying a sign which reads:

Fry them and send their bodies to the USSR!

You've seen these people parading through your streets while a man and a woman were living out their final hours in a prison, while two desperate children were asking in vain that their parents be given back to them. You've seen them laugh, cry out, and wave their signs and banners, and there was not a single one among you who came up and smashed their faces. There really is something rotten in America.

And don't protest that it is just a question of a few aroused people, irresponsible elements: they're the ones who run your country, since the government gave in to please them. Do you remember Nuremberg and your theory of collective responsibility? Well, today you are the ones it ought to be applied to. You are collectively responsible for the Rosenbergs' death—some of you because you provoked this murder, others for allowing it to be carried out. You have tolerated the United States' being the cradle of a new fascism, and it won't do any good for you to answer that just one murder cannot be compared to Hitler's hecatombs: fascism is not defined by the number of its victims but by its way of killing them.

And why has this fury been unleashed against a man and a woman on the eve of their death? Why this hatred which has stupefied the universe?

It's because you've been persuaded that they wanted to take your bomb. You don't rest easy unless you are the only ones able to destroy the earth. President Eisenhower counted the Rosenbergs' innocent victims in the dozens of millions; each one of you already feels like one of the dead of future wars. It was dead men who were asking Thursday that those who had stolen atomic secrets be put to death.

Unfortunately, when we look at you from Europe we don't mistake you for the innocent or the dead. We see only two innocent dead—your victims. And as for atomic secrets, they're the fruit of your sick imagination; science develops everywhere at the same rate, and the manufacture of bombs is a matter of industrial potential.

In killing the Rosenbergs, you simply tried to stop scientific progress by a human sacrifice. Magic, witch hunts, autos-da-fé, sacrifices: we've reached that point. Your country is sick with fear. You're afraid of everything: the Russians, the Chinese, the Europeans. You're afraid of each other. You're afraid of the shadow of your own bomb.

Ah, what fine allies you make!

And you would like to lead us! You are leading us to war out of terror, and you'd lose it out of panic at the first bombardment. I know, there are men of courage in your country: the Rosenbergs' lawyer—the very one who said yesterday, "I'm ashamed to be an American"—Judge Douglas, the members of the Committee to Free the Rosenbergs, and hundreds of thousands of others. But what can they do except become martyrs?

And then there are the masses who are still sound but mystified by you. There are the blacks you are oppressing. And above all, there is that frail voice which today has fallen silent and which we could hear better than your rodomontades, saying these admirable words:

"We're young, and we don't want to die, but we won't live at this price."

After all, the Rosenbergs are Americans; and if there's any hope we still can cling to, it's that your country gave birth to this man and woman you killed.

Perhaps one day all these people of good will may cure you of your fear. We hope so, because we loved you.

In the meantime, do not be surprised if we cry out, from one end of Europe to the other, "Be careful; America is mad. Break all the ties which bind us to her, or we in turn shall be bitten and made mad."

Julius Fucik

THIS BOOK[1] IS NOT A NOVEL. Fucik very modestly calls it a piece of reporting, and in a way he's right. Everything in it is true; everything has been lived through. Only, it's a rather special kind of reporting. Newspapermen have frequently interviewed soldiers and engineers, aviators and deep-sea divers. These men—and others who are courageous by profession—sometimes stretch their courage to the point of heroism, but ordinarily all that's needed in their profession is intelligence and *sang-froid*. Fucik is the first reporter to write about heroes. Not about heroes of the moment, but about men who were heroic every moment of the year between the time they were arrested and the hour they died. An aristocratic conception of full-time courage makes the hero a solitary man, courageous by vocation, superior by nature to all the others. But in the prison in Prague, it was not a matter of vocation or an elite. All the prisoners were heroic simply because in certain circumstances you have to become a hero in order to keep on being a man. Fucik knows all this; he also knows that his comrades are going to die a nameless death. But it's no good, he says to himself, for heroes to remain anonymous. So he'll write about them, he'll tell their names and ages, he'll say what they have done. Not so that they'll become the basis for a cult later on, but so that they'll

This article was published in *Les Lettres françaises*, June 17–24, 1954. See also Vol. 1, 54/258.

1. Julius Fucik, *Report from the Gallows*, trans. Stephen Jolly (London: Spencer, 1957).

bear witness in our eyes to what a man can do—to what *all men* can do.

His book, as you know, recalls the life of Communist militants in a Czech prison between April, 1942, and April, 1943: a year of torture ending in death. We are, unfortunately, acquainted with his subject. We've read a hundred eyewitness accounts of Nazi prisons, Gestapo interrogations, lingering-death camps, and executions. But reading them is frequently unpleasant and hard to bear. It provokes depression more than indignation. When we've finished reading, and sometimes even before we've finished, we very quickly thrust the book aside with something like a sense of rancor, brought on by the fact that the authors are describing what they've seen, what has frightened them, what *had* to seem most striking to them—the triumph of evil. They want above all to depict the terror which reigned in the cells or in the barracks. They give minute descriptions of the organization of concentration camps. With a wealth of detail and a horrible picturesqueness, they relate the characteristics or episodes they think will best illuminate the jailers' sadism. They concentrate on showing the techniques of degradation. They only speak of captives to make us feel their impotence and despair. All their evils come to them from someone else; they can only suffer them. The strongest "hold out"; the weakest let themselves slide into death. We see the progressive downfall of both. What we remember from all this is that there are circumstances in which it is impossible to be a man: you become a monkey or a dead man.

Of course there are brave men in these books who resist torture and die without talking. But the normal feeling, even in these men, is fear. They're not afraid of suffering or dying; they're afraid of themselves, afraid their suffering will tear a name or bit of information from them. Their executioners, with their enormous power, their inventive sadism, and their instruments of torture, come to seem like devils: they seem to be both superior and inferior to men. In the long run, the inmate comes to think that the Nazis' evil powers are irresistible: if they want to make you talk, the chances are you'll talk. And the ones who do not talk have been aided by a special grace. By sheer luck a prisoner is not interrogated until the end of the day. He doesn't talk; but according to his own account, if he had been grilled in the morning, he would have been lost. Writers who have not been tortured or even captured have gone still further in their efforts to reduce the heroism of the members of the Resistance to the level of mediocre bourgeois virtues. Everything is a matter of luck. Subjected to the water torture, this man feels his nerve start to crack. He decides to talk. In intention, he's a traitor. By a lucky accident he has swallowed too much water. He half suffocates and can only cough. An instant later, he has gotten hold of himself again. In short, they want us to believe that heroes are traitors who haven't had time to betray.

And what can those of us who have not suffered tortures say? Can we reject these eyewitness accounts which tell us that we become traitors through weakness? What proves that we would have held out? Everyone, we're told, can have a moment of weakness. Are we going to condemn a whole life for one minute of it? You see the trap they set for us; they want to make us believe that we are men *by chance.*

What fills us with admiration when we read *Ecrit sous la potence* is that Fucik shows us that just the opposite is true: in man and outside him chance is inhuman. I had guessed from the opening lines that he was going to be caught and tortured. I guessed that this book which ended with the death of its author began with his torments. I almost put it down, and then I went on reading and, little by little, my sense of horror kept decreasing until it ended up disappearing completely. And yet this testimony should have seemed all the more unbearable for being written day by day: I *saw* Fucik weaken from one night to the next; I was *present* at his interrogations. What is it then that distinguishes his work from all the others? It is, I think, that Fucik is never afraid of himself: he knows that whatever happens at whatever time he will not be tempted to talk. Not that he's all tied up in knots, always working at not talking. He's just the kind of man who *cannot* sell out his comrades, and he knows it. From the moment he enters the interrogation room, he knows that the only thing that can happen to him is that he'll die in the camps. And his death itself he does not dread. If it comes while he's being beaten, it will free him. Now at last the torturers lose their atrocious power, and their huge demoniacal image vanishes. They can crush him underneath a rain of blows, but that's just what a high fever can do. In no case will their human will replace his own. Impotence changes sides: these demons are poor devils, zealous and pitiful civil servants, brutes who hit because they cannot talk, cowards. They don't count any more than cholera or plague. Why bother about them? Leave them in the shadows.

Medieval painters used to show us Christ with his wounds and crown of thorns. They painted just the hands of his tormentors. Bodiless hands giving slaps or brandishing a whip. In the same way Fucik scarcely makes us see any more than his Nazi torturers' hands, pale spiders climbing over his body, which he does not look at. Or, if he does so, it is without hatred; because hatred includes a certain respect, and what can you say about these poor rascals who are both perfectly criminal and almost irresponsible? They can only be described, like a species of animal, with a dispassionate understanding of their motives and the factors that condition their behavior.

Like a species of animal? No, not quite. We can make out, beneath Fucik's objectivity, a curious mixture of a feeling of fraternity and an invincible scorn. And this feeling of fraternity is not directed toward them but toward what they could have been; these ferocious beasts are after all no more than men who never made it as men.

Now at last we're freed from horror. Fucik's book is written against fear in all its forms. It even rids us of our fascinated fear of ourselves. We were asking ourselves, "Would I have held out, would I have been able to resist my weaknesses?" But Fucik's sternness makes us see that these questions are badly put. One of his comrades, just one, talked. Fucik relates the fact soberly, and we may think at first that he is explaining it the same way the authors I spoke to you about do—as a failure of nerve. But very soon we see that something completely different is involved, for Fucik *dares* to judge his comrade's whole life on the basis of a moment of forgetfulness. And this strictness is only the other side of an absolute confidence in man's powers. If you consider the moment of weakness which makes a militant a traitor as an isolated minute, it is true that nothing guarantees you against it. But if you consider that no minute in a human existence is simply the result of chance, if you bring the whole man—the Communist, the militant with the most ephemeral of weaknesses—to book, then it's the entire life of every man that determines his attitude toward torture. He talked, Fucik says, because he lacked faith. If you have loved enough, if you have given yourself without qualification to your undertaking, you are eternally protected from moments of weakness. It isn't at the moment of our torments that we can invent the courage to resist them. If we find we have the courage, it's because it was already there. It's faithfulness and hope and love that give it to us. So what is most difficult is placed immediately within everyone's grasp. Heroism is neither an absolute goal nor a vocation. But if the occasion calls for it, we'll become heroes if we've simply learned to do our job as men, that is, if we are able to love what we love all the way.

An Unpublished Act from *Nekrassov*

THE ANTI-COMMUNIST MAGAZINE *Soir à Paris* has published a list of the 20,000 people who would be shot by firing squads if Soviet troops were to occupy Paris. This imaginary list is meant to shock people. The government's candidate in the primary elections of Seine-et-Marne, Mme Bounoumi, is counting on its effect to lead her radical opponent Perdrière to withdraw. She even gives a reception for the "future victims of the firing squads" and invites Perdrière. The following scenes are taken from an act entitled "The Future Victims' Ball."

JULES, *to Nerciat:* Hello, Mr. President.

NERCIAT: Hello, Paleface, what do you think of our reception?

JULES: A great success. But the crowd is a little mixed. We've invited the unimportant victims too.

NERCIAT: What else could we do? It was everyone or no one. But I agree that this list doesn't make good sense, and that it leaves us open to the possibility of running into our tradesmen.

A GUEST, *shaking Nerciat's hand as he goes by:* Hello, my friend. This is a wonderful party; I never had so much fun in my life.

He goes by.

This tableau from *Nekrassov* was cut from the play before its first performance in 1955; the excerpt given here was published as "Tableau inédit de *Nekrassov:* Le Bal des futurs fusillés" in *Les Lettres françaises*, June 16–23, 1955. See also Vol. 1, 55/266.

JULES: There's one who's satisfied.

NERCIAT: Yes. Too satisfied.

JULES: He'll get over it. Did you notice that there are quite a few people here who are a little pale?

NERCIAT: Already?

JULES: If you don't believe me, just look around. You'd think you were on the channel steamer during rough weather one hour after sailing time.

NERCIAT: I'd like to believe you, but I'm afraid it's just the light that makes them look that way. Where's Nekrassov?

JULES: He'll be here soon.

NERCIAT: I'm counting on him to put some life into the reception. (*Mme Bounoumi has come in. Forty years old. Healthy, but enormous.*) Here is our dear hostess.

JULES: Hello, dear lady.

MME BOUNOUMI: Hello. You haven't seen Perdrière, have you?

JULES: Not yet.

MME BOUNOUMI: Are you sure he's coming?

JULES: He promised.

MME BOUNOUMI: I hope to God he does. (*To the others*) If he comes, he'll be drunk.

Cocardeau enters.

COCARDEAU: My dear Jules, would you introduce me to Madame Bounoumi?

JULES: Madame, may I introduce our great writer Jérôme Cocardeau?

MME BOUNOUMI: Monsieur, I have admired you for a long time.

COCARDEAU: Thank you. (*Kissing Jules's hand*) I would have liked someone to take my picture. (*Jules signals to a photographer.*)

PHOTOGRAPHER: A group picture?

COCARDEAU: To begin with.

PHOTOGRAPHER: Smile please. (*A pause.*) Don't you want to?

JULES: But we are smiling!

MME BOUNOUMI: No, my friend, you are not smiling.

JULES: Well what about that! (*Looking at Mme Bounoumi*) Neither are you.

MME BOUNOUMI: Oh! I thought . . . (*Forced smile.*) There we are!

JULES: There we are, there we are!

> *Forced smile. They all smile. Photo.*

COCARDEAU, *to the photographer:* Now I'd like you to take a picture of me. No, not here. Find a setting which will suggest my solitude.

PHOTOGRAPHER: Maybe if I opened the window . . . ?

COCARDEAU: That's it, against a background of night. (*He goes to the window, flings it open wide, and puts himself in front of it.*) Do I look solitary?

PHOTOGRAPHER: Well . . .

COCARDEAU: Very good. Hurry up. (*Photo. He rejoins the group.*) I spend my time running away from photographers, but this time I just can't hide.

MME BOUNOUMI: Isn't it the truth? It seems to me that it's a duty.

COCARDEAU: A duty; that's exactly what it is. We must let France know about the terrible threat weighing on her defenders. I always knew I'd die a violent death.

MME BOUNOUMI: How interesting. How did you know?

COCARDEAU: My style.

MME BOUNOUMI: I beg your pardon?

COCARDEAU: I'm talking about my style. Its conciseness easily assumes a haughty air. Montherlant told me one day, "It's like the famous saying about the way a man carries his head: we're ripe for the guillotine." He was right. The moment the first beautiful phrase flowed from my pen, I heard

the future howling of the mob and knew I had been condemned to death. But it is not enough to know one's destiny,
one has to make it known to others. Thanks to Nekrassov's
revelations and your charming reception, Madame, we bear
the mark of death upon our faces. My intimates are already
looking at me with a new-found fervor, as if I were sacred.
We *are* sacred, dear friends.

NERCIAT: It's true, by God.

COCARDEAU: Not everyone has a chance to be dead while he's
still alive. You know my play is being staged tomorrow at the
Hébertot . . .

NERCIAT: *Scipio the African?*

COCARDEAU: That's it. The dress rehearsal is on Tuesday. I'm
curious to know whether the critics will dare to cut me to
pieces. What will Boudin do?

MME BOUNOUMI: Boudin?

JULES: He's the critic for *Soir à Paris.* He admires you, *cher
maître.*

COCARDEAU: Of course he does; and that was good enough while
I was living. But now that I am dead I want him to respect me.

JULES: Don't worry; I'm dead myself and I'll teach him the respect he owes you.

COCARDEAU: What bothers me is that Jean-Jacques Gautier is
on the list. He's going to cut me up. The dead just don't respect each other. Is he here?

MME BOUNOUMI: I caught a glimpse of him in the big ballroom.

COCARDEAU, *bowing:* Excuse me; I'm going to have a word with
him.

He goes out.

A GUEST, *coming up:* Congratulations, dear lady.

MME BOUNOUMI: Your wife couldn't come?

GUEST: Well, you see, since she wasn't on the list . . .

MME BOUNOUMI: Good for her. Look, Martine and Carole are
here.

MARTINE, *coming up:* What a bee-you-tiful party!

CAROLE: All these men who are going to be killed but are still smiling. What maar-velous morale!

MME BOUNOUMI: Monsieur Sajerat didn't bring his wife!

MARTINE: Oh! What a dirty trick. We wives have a right to be here. You know very well that we'll just die when you die.

CAROLE: As far as I'm concerned it's very simple: if they kill me, I'll poison myself.

MARTINE: That's because you're not sure of yourself, dear. I won't take any drugs. When the hour of my execution comes, my heart will stop all by itself.

They withdraw.

MME BOUNOUMI: Spunky little women!

NERCIAT: Spunky little Frenchwomen!

ANOTHER GUEST, *bowing:* Good for you, Madame! What good spirits! What style!

He goes by.

MME BOUNOUMI: Spirits are too good.

NERCIAT: Yes. Too good.

MME BOUNOUMI: How can we impress Perdrière if the atmosphere doesn't change?

JULES: Be patient. There are so many of them that they'll end up scaring each other. (*In the grand ballroom, a woman bursts into hysterical laughter.*) You see; it's beginning. (*Champenois comes in, hugging the walls.*) Hey! Champenois!

CHAMPENOIS, *terrified:* I'll thank you not to mention my name.

JULES: What difference can it make. After all, it's on the list. (*To Nerciat*) Have you met Champenois, the editor of *Bonnet phrygien?* (*To Champenois*) Monsieur Nerciat, the new president of our administrative council. (*Nerciat and Champenois shake hands.*)

CHAMPENOIS: I never should have come here. It was crazy.

JULES: Why?

CHAMPENOIS: It's all right for you, old man; but I'm a left-winger. Ten per cent of my readers are workers.

NERCIAT: What difference does that make? We're all Frenchmen here, and you belong to that good old traditional French left whose disappearance we middle-of-the-roaders would be the first to deplore. (*Champenois makes a gesture.*) It's true, it's true; I read your editorials and I admire you for being a real Frenchman—an indomitable enemy of the foreign party.

CHAMPENOIS: I beg your pardon. I am the indomitable enemy of the Communist Party, but I want to make it perfectly clear that I am not systematically anti-Communist.

NERCIAT: I fail to grasp the nuance.

CHAMPENOIS: Anti-communism is a right-wing tactic; I attack the C.P. because I'm more to the left than it is.

NERCIAT: But you defend the Atlantic Pact, don't you? And German rearmament?

CHAMPENOIS: For left-wing reasons, sir.

JULES: Don't take so much trouble to distinguish yourself from us; you know good and well that we'll all be executed together.

CHAMPENOIS: Yes, but I'll fall to the left. (*A photographer comes toward them.*) What does that guy want? It's a photographer, Jules! Don't play that trick on me. (*Jules walks around behind Champenois. Picture.*) You're not going to publish that picture, you hear; you're not going to publish it. I have working-class readers and I . . .

JULES: Take it easy!

CHAMPENOIS: I'm leaving! I'm leaving! I never should have come.

He goes out.

NERCIAT: What did he come for?

JULES: I don't know. To see his death in other people's faces. (*Abruptly*) Here's Perdrière.

MME BOUNOUMI, *going up to Perdrière:* Why it's Perdrière. Hello, my loyal opposition.

PERDRIÈRE: Hello, my tender enemy.

MME BOUNOUMI: Still unyielding?

PERDRIÈRE: More than ever.

MME BOUNOUMI: What difference does it make. Life separates us, death will bring us together again. They may even throw my body on top of yours!

JULES, *to Nerciat:* Luckily he'll be dead, poor guy.

MME BOUNOUMI: Let's be friends. (*She holds out her hand. He takes it.*)

JULES, *to the photographers:* Picture. (*Flash.*)

MME BOUNOUMI: Paulo! Marco! (*Two children come running in.*) I'd like you to meet two little future orphans.

PERDRIÈRE, *not understanding:* Orphans . . .

MME BOUNOUMI: Orphaned of their mother: these are two of my sons. Say hello to the gentleman, children.

PAULO: Without bitterness, sir.

MARCO: Without bitterness.

PERDRIÈRE: Why do you say, "Without bitterness," children?

PAULO: Because you're going to have our mamma killed.

MME BOUNOUMI, *to the children:* Will you be quiet!

PERDRIÈRE: I don't understand . . .

MME BOUNOUMI: Well, you see, these children are simplistic: they tell themselves that your opposition to German rearmament risks creating a military vacuum in Europe which will lead inevitably to our extermination.

PERDRIÈRE: You ought not to talk politics in front of them.

MME BOUNOUMI: Let's go, children! Go play out in the garden while you still have a mother.

PAULO, *to Marco:* We'll play orphans; it's a scream. (*Hysterical laugh. Perdrière jumps.*)

PERDRIÈRE: What's that?

MME BOUNOUMI, *going toward the grand ballroom:* It's Jeanne Chardin, the great novelist: she's telling about her execution.

ONE GUEST, *to another:* Do you know that the firing squad stands less than two yards away from the condemned?

THE OTHER GUEST: That close? I wonder if they'll bandage my eyes.

FIRST GUEST: I'm thinking about that myself. I like to look danger in the face.

They go on.

PERDRIÈRE, *shocked:* Let me tell you, dear friend; there's something unhealthy about this gathering.

Brecht and the Classical Dramatists

IN CERTAIN RESPECTS, Brecht is one of us. The richness and originality of his works should not keep the French from rediscovering in them ancient traditions of their own which have been buried by the romantic, bourgeois nineteenth century. Most contemporary plays try to make us believe in the reality of the events which unfold on the stage. They are scarcely concerned, on the other hand, with their truth. If a playwright knows how to make us wait for and dread the final pistol shot, if it really breaks our eardrums, what difference does its improbability make? We "do as we're told." And it's not so much precise acting that the bourgeois admires in the actors as a mysterious quality called "presence." Whose presence? The actor's? No; his character's: if Buckingham appears in flesh and blood, we let him say any stupid thing he likes. It's because the bourgeoisie believes only in particular truths.

I think Brecht was hardly influenced at all by our major playwrights, or by the Greek tragedians who were their models. His plays evoke Elizabethan drama more than tragedies. And yet what he does have in common with our classical dramatists and those of antiquity is that he has at his disposal a collective ideology, a method, and a faith. As they do, he puts man back into the world, that is, in truth. Thus, the relationship between the true and the illusory is reversed: as it does in the classical dramatists' works, the event represented in Brecht's works itself

This piece, entitled "Brecht et les classiques," was the program of the "Hommage international à Bertolt Brecht" presented by the Théâtre des Nations, April 4–21, 1957. See also Vol. I, 57/292.

proclaims its *absence*—it took place some other time or even never existed—and reality fades into pure appearance; but this sham shows us the true laws governing human behavior. Yes, truth exists for Brecht as it did for Sophocles and Racine: not as something the playwright must *speak*, but as what he must *show*. And this proud undertaking of showing men to men without making use of the dubious charms of desire or terror is unquestionably what we call classicism.

Brecht is classical in his concern for unity. If a total truth, the veritable theatrical object, exists, it is the total event, which encompasses both social strata and individual persons, which makes individual confusion the reflection of collective confusions, and whose violent development brings to light both conflicts and the general order conditioning them. For this reason, his plays have a classical economy. Of course he has no concern for the unities of place and time; but he eliminates everything which might distract us, refusing to invent details if they would make us miss the whole.

Above all, he wants to avoid moving us *too much*, in order that we may be completely free at each instant to listen, see, and understand. And yet he is talking to us about a terrible monster—our own. But he wants to talk about it without terrorizing us; and you are going to see the consequence of this: an unreal and true image, airy, elusive, and multicolored, in which violence, crime, madness, and despair become the object of a calm contemplation like those monsters "imitated by art" which Boileau speaks of.

Then should we expect that we're going to sit unmoved in our seats while people cry out, torture, and kill on the stage? No; because these assassins, victims, and executioners are no other than ourselves. Racine also spoke to his contemporaries about themselves. But he took pains to make them see through the big end of the telescope. In his preface to *Bajazet*, he apologizes for having put a recent story on the stage:

Tragic characters should be looked at in a different light than that in which we ordinarily look at characters we have seen at such close hand. It can be said that our respect for the hero increases to the extent that he becomes more distant from us. . . . The remoteness of the place corrects, as it were, the excessive nearness of the time.

There's a good definition of what Brecht calls "alienation effect." Because the respect Racine is talking about in reference to the bloodthirsty Roxane is above all—is exclusively—a way of breaking connections. We are shown our loves, jealousies, and murderous dreams; but we are shown them cold, separated from us, inaccessible and terrible, all the more alien for being our own—for our thinking we have them under control but seeing them develop beyond our reach with a pitiless rigor that we simultaneously discover for the first time and recognize as always having been there. This is the way Brecht's characters are too: they astonish us the way Papuans and Kanakas do, and we see ourselves in them without being any less amazed. These grotesque or dramatic conflicts, these wrongs, inertias, miseries, complicities are all our own.

If there were at least a hero. The spectator, whoever he may be, likes to identify with these elite characters who bring about in themselves and for everyone the reconciliation of opposites and the destruction of evil by good. Even if he's burned alive or cut to pieces he'll walk home—if it's a pretty night—whistling to himself and reassured. But Brecht doesn't put any heroes or martyrs on stage. Or if he does tell the life of a new Joan of Arc, she's a ten-year-old child. And we shan't have a chance to identify with her. On the contrary, heroism shut away in childhood seems all the more inaccessible to us.

The reason for this is that Brecht does not believe in individual salvation. Society has to be completely changed, and the playwright's function is still that "purgation" Aristotle spoke of. He shows us what we are—both victims and accomplices. That is why Brecht's plays move us. But our emotion is very singular. It is a perpetual uneasiness, since we are the spectacle suspended in a contemplative calm—are, that is, the spectators. This uneasiness does not disappear when the curtain falls. On the contrary, it grows and comes to be a part of that everyday uneasiness we're not explicitly aware of but live through in bad faith and evasion. And this uneasiness Brecht's plays arouse in us throws light on the uneasiness we live through. In our time "purgation" has a different name: raising the level of consciousness. But wasn't that calm and strict uneasiness which *Bajazet* or *Phèdre* provoked during the seventeenth century in the soul of a spectator who suddenly discovered the inflexible law of human passions also—in a different time and social and ideological context—a raising of the level of consciousness? It's for these reasons that Brecht's theater, this Shakespearean theater of revolutionary negation, seems to me to also be—without its author's ever having planned it—like an extraordinary attempt to link the twentieth century to the classical tradition.

Francis Jeanson Interviews Sartre

. . . Socialists must not only demand the unconditional liberation of the colonies without compensation—and this demand in its political expression signifies nothing else than the recognition of the right to self-determination; they must also render determined support to the more revolutionary elements in the bourgeois-democratic movements for national liberation in these countries and assist their uprising—or revolutionary war—in the event of one—*against* the imperialist powers that oppress them (V. I. Lenin, "The Socialist Revolution and the Right of Nations to Self-Determination," in *Collected Works* [Moscow: Progress Publishers, 1964], XXII:151–52).

It has been said that the French left, which is universalist by its very nature, was unsettled by the nationalism of the Algerian freedom fighters. Do you agree?

No. It is possible that, abstractly speaking, there is a formal contradiction between nationalism and universalism. But in the real development of history, left-wing movements have always been both nationalist and internationalist. Socialism as universal reality has never existed except in idea. The first time it was embodied in a specific country it revealed its true nature: it is a painful, bloody road toward the better which will long bear the signs of the particular circumstances under which it developed. But we cannot conclude from the fact that the USSR can be considered, in spite of all its contradictions, the country of socialism that all the Communist workers in France are Russian

At the time of this interview Francis Jeanson was participating in an underground organization supporting the Algerian revolution; his interview with Sartre was published in the organization's clandestine monthly, *Vérités pour* . . . , June 2, 1959. See also Vol. 1, 59/329.

nationalists. Quite to the contrary, historical developments were to make them—in the very name of defending socialism in the USSR—French nationalists.

Furthermore, the majority of today's left-wingers were produced and shaped by World War II. Now we must not forget that under the Occupation two apparently contradictory, but actually complementary, facts appeared: the Resistance forces were united on the basis of a *national* and particularist program ("Boot the occupiers out of France") rather than on the basis of a universalist and social program; and the members of the Resistance were "radicalized" by the conditions of struggle against their enemies, which meant that all these nationalist movements together were "turned to the left" as their fighting intensified. Among almost all Frenchmen in 1944, national particularism was linked indissolubly to a revolutionary humanism. We know how the right, with the Americans' connivance, went about robbing them once again of their victory. In the period which followed—and in which we are still living—the response of the French left in the face of the two "blocs" was to reaffirm its nationalism. To counter the Atlantic Pact and its consequences, the left thought up what might be called an internationale of nationalisms: the independence and national sovereignty of each country seemed to it to be the only means of halting the rush toward war. Toward 1950 people went around saying that at this moment in history nationalism was progressive. And it really would have been if the nations had known how to tear themselves free from the blind and terrorized conglomerates that held them prisoner and to join themselves together by reciprocal nonaggression pacts.

Thus it is simply incredible that leftists should say that they fear Algerian nationalism. Of course, this nationalism—like all historical realities—contains contradictory forces. But what all of us ought to want is for the FLN to conceive of independent Algeria as a social democracy and to recognize, in the midst of its struggle for liberation, the need for agrarian reform. Wherever these fighters come from, whatever importance religious faith may have for them, the circumstances of their struggle are pulling them toward the left, just like those of our Resistance and between '40 and '45.

The fact that Algerian nationalism frightens certain left-wing groups—who ought to recognize their own experience and past in it—in no way indicates that we have become pure universalists. On the contrary—and it's here that we have to be on our guard against mystification—the underlying reason is *our* nationalism. In opposition to the imperialism of the two blocs, the left wants to be "French." But from that point on it falls for the myths of right-wing nationalism. It is afraid of "betraying," it seeks the approval of all Frenchmen, it craves the badge of patriotism. This leads to terrorism. Yet it isn't hard to see that universalist nationalism—which craves French sovereignty in order to safeguard world peace—ought in the name of patriotism itself to want the end of a war which makes us a little more dependent every day on foreign power. Seen in this perspective, nothing is keeping us from *recognizing* Algerian nationalism as a particularism which should lead to universality.

In that case, can you explain the real reasons why we are divided over the Algerian question?

They seem to me to be different sorts of reasons. The ideological disputes I was just talking about only concern intellectuals and a few politicians who wouldn't talk so loudly if the masses weren't keeping such a stubborn silence.

Isn't that because they've been confused?

Partly. And it's partly they who are confusing their leaders.

In order to understand their silence we have to keep two essential truths in mind: one is that colonialism is a system, and the other is that there is no absolute pauperization. An economic system was set up in the closing years of the nineteenth century to govern relations between the big capitalist countries and those we call today the underdeveloped countries. These relationships, which were established and are maintained by military force, may be summed up in this way: thanks to the surplus exploitation of its colonized natives, the colony buys the products manufactured in the parent state at a high price and sells it its own agricultural products (and at times the raw materials from its mines and quarries) at a price below that of the world market. The parent state tacitly but strictly denies the colony the opportunity to produce and sell on a large scale any manufactured goods which would compete with the products of its own industry. In this way—and this is the first thing we must be aware of—the workers in the parent state are protected against unemployment as the owners are protected against losses. When the workers oppose the industrialization of an underdeveloped country, they are taking the side of the owners. And it isn't just the big industrialists in Dunkirk who look with disfavor upon "the Constantine plan"; it's their workers too.

Speaking more generally, we have to recognize that in an unmixed colonial system:[1] (1) some of the workers work for colonial customers (colonists and natives); (2) at least until 1914 the parent country's excess profits left its industrial enterprises such a margin of profit that the owners could, in response to the pressure of labor's demands, grant *real* wage increases; (3) certain low-priced colonial products, when they began to appear in the shops of the parent state, led French producers (when they existed) to lower their prices to keep them in line with these. Thus the purchasing power in a family of French wage earners increased in proportion as that of the colonized wage earner decreased. And although it was, in fact, the state (and consequently all the citizenry of the parent state) which ultimately paid the difference between the normal price of the parent state's goods and its competitive price, the fact remained that it was the Frenchman who, even as he helped compensate French producers, greatly gained in the affair. And let me add (even though it is too big a question to go into here) that in the days of classical colonialism, world capitalism was able to avoid or attenuate numerous crises thanks to the existence of its colonial markets.

The conclusion is unfortunately all too clear: as long as the colonial system functioned without any serious breakdowns, the parent-state worker found himself—no matter how violent the class conflicts—closer to his boss in matters of colonial exploitation than to any "colonized native." The community of interests which certain people said was going to unite the French proletariat and the Algerian subproletariat existed in word only. Sure, both were victims of the same capitalist exploitation. But they weren't suffering in the same way. And the surplus exploitation of the latter tended to lessen the suffering of the former.

The result? A certain working-class paternalism toward the subproletariat which had been given to it. Of course the working class felt sorry for the subproletariat, but it was told that there was no profit in such enlightenment. And then, after all, these people were peasants. The working class blamed colonial enter-

1. That is, the system as it operated in Algeria until 1939.

prise because it saw it (correctly) as a new and critical form of capitalist imperialism, but it counted on the socialist revolution to suppress capitalism and colonization at the same time.

It is this ancient and tenacious habit which underlies our present immobility. For a long time now the proletariat has had nothing but "generous ideas" about the colonies. But generous ideas are words; they remain completely ineffectual as long as they are not based upon a real solidarity of interests.

Do you think then that it is impossible to count on a reawakening of the French masses?

I would think so if the colonial system did not contain its own destruction. It must necessarily *collapse* sooner or later; this is its destiny. In other words, after having served the capitalist economy and—in the way I've shown—the wage earners themselves, it will inevitably be transformed into an insatiable parasite which uses up all the colonizing country's strength for nothing.

Today, the French workers are on the side of the Algerian freedom fighters because both of them have the most urgent interest in breaking the bonds of colonization.

It was absolutely necessary that the Algerians' poverty keep increasing. No measure the capitalist parent country could take could stop this impoverishment. Because, in the first place, surplus exploitation down there can only be based upon an unlimited increase in the number of manual workers. And, in the second place, because the timid reforms projected by the government *have* to be sabotaged by the colonists—who are on the scene—or, in any case, work, according to their own intrinsic nature, to the advantage of the colonists. And, finally, because the only solution to the economic problem, the industrialization of Algeria, cannot even be attempted without threatening the same kind of industrial firms *in France itself.*

The underlying contradiction of the colonial system is that to the extent that the interest of the colonist requires that wages tend toward zero, racism appears to justify this requirement by making the human value of the colonized tend toward zero; but at the same time, the poverty and excess supply of manual workers requires the unemployed colonized worker to emigrate to the parent country. The *immediate* result of this chronic emigration is that surplus exploitation compels the Algerian to come compete with the French worker in the parent country, as

Algerian wines compete on the market with our wines. The *subsequent* result is that the Algerians—in spite of the hostility of some Frenchmen and the hardships of material life—learn *here* what is concealed from them there: our revolutionary tradition, the class struggle, the nature of colonialism, and through these things their true human dignity. By pushing surplus exploitation to the point of creating submen, colonialism collapses and the colonized discovers his personality in opposition to the colonists.

Of course the French worker is irritated by this competition at first. But what makes it lead certain wage earners to racism is anger and lazy-mindedness. For *it's the colonists* who send these starving men to compete with Frenchmen in France. It is colonialism alone which creates his army in our home territory. We have to understand that from this point of view our interests are the interests of the Algerian laborers: the latter are coming to compete with Frenchmen because a prefabricated suffering is forcing them out of *their country*. They are in France because their native land has been stolen from them.

And the reason they come back home convinced that colonialism is an intolerable evil which must be annihilated in any circumstance, the reason why they take up arms and fight to the death, is that the same system that takes away their means of being men does so by teaching them (in spite of itself, of course) that every man can and should demand his worth and dignity as a man, even if it means taking up arms to do so.

Thus colonialism engenders peoples' wars of liberation. It's the system itself which produces them at the ultimate stage of its collapse. And it is *precisely at this point* that the solidarity between the French proletariat and the colonized people of Algeria appears in such a striking way. Why? Because each day the burden of colonialism bears down more heavily on France itself. Because the system *requires* the Algerians to make war on us and the Frenchmen from France to fight in Algeria for an out-of-date economy. Because the bourgeois class, although it is feeling the weight of this war itself, has arranged to have it financed by the disadvantaged classes. And, finally, because, for reasons which have been given many times, the oppression which accompanies surplus exploitation in Algeria can maintain itself for the little time it has left except only by moving into France itself in the form of the surplus exploitation of financing the war and by establishing itself here in order to make us pay the costs of the conflict. All these consequences of the system are well known: they show that in this country, which is gradually becoming fascist and destroying itself, the masses' only defense is to become clearly conscious of their new but profound solidarity with the Algerian freedom fighters.

You say that they ought to become conscious of this, but you said earlier that they are remaining inert. What must be done to fight that inertia?

I said that they haven't always been united with the colonized subproletariat. I added that they've kept a certain paternalistic attitude. There's nothing astonishing in the fact that their present reaction is often to detest these "bad" colonized people who aren't letting them sleep in peace. How could it help being this way? And hasn't it often been said that there's no spontaneity in the masses, and that they're victims of the propaganda and the slogans of the ruling class? The real problem today is a problem of *education*. The working classes themselves are going through their own experience of all the problems which directly concern them and are liberating themselves through their concrete struggles. But where the Algerian question is concerned, habits are deeply rooted and arguments are abstract. And then racism is so easy and so tempting when a man is anxious, hard up, or embittered.

I am in complete agreement with *VP* [*Vérités pour . . .*][2] when it tries to organize groups of militants who will be able in their actions to take up the problem again from the base and push demystification as far as possible. If the left is going to rise again, the masses will revive it. And the basic problem, the one which ought to produce a *different left* and *different men,* is to give the exploited classes a *practical* consciousness of their solidarity with the Algerian freedom fighters.

2. A bulletin published by an underground ring (called the "Jeanson Ring" after its leading activist, Francis Jeanson) which helped deserters and the FLN during the Algerian War. See Vol. 1, 59/329.

Soledad, by Colette Audry

SOLEDAD is a woman's name and it means solitude. Contemporary French theater feeds on solitude. It makes its living off of it. I could name you five plays and ten films which are a success night after night because, like a thousand others like them, they keep harping that no one can know anyone, individual souls are impenetrable, men are like chunks of stone. If Colette Audry repeated the same thing, her play might be well made, but it would have no interest. But what she wants to explain to us is just the opposite. She doesn't think we're chunks of stone. She thinks that the solitude which so many writers have described, and which has made their everlasting fortune, only exists in certain circles and for certain reasons which are perhaps peculiar to our time. This isn't what interests her. She knows from experience that a person can throw herself into a common undertaking, join others through action, understand and love herself through a common task. You'll immediately recognize the characters she's going to show us. They are wholly evident, transparent beings who are not isolated from others by their interests or their egotism, by their cultivation of their perversions, or their sense of their superiority.

In a country drowsing underneath a military dictatorship, a group of young men and women are "holding out." The regime is solidly entrenched and there is no hope of overthrowing it; it's a matter of *holding on,* of affirming the principles it's trying to get everyone to forget, of *existing,* in short, and wait-

This piece served as the program notes for *Soledad* as presented by the Théâtre de Poche, April, 1960. See also Vol. 1, 60/347.

ing, making yourself known to a muzzled people by means of broadsides and sporadic raids. We cannot imagine any stronger tie—each lives through and for the others, all live for a common goal. And precisely because of this—amidst the closest solidarity, the strictest unity, amidst work, risks run in common, discipline, and friendship—there is solitude—unperceived, always denied, separating without their knowing it these men without secrets. I do not think that I am betraying or exaggerating Colette Audry's feelings in expressing them as follows: the closer the ties, the more complete the commitment and the more intense the solitude. For her, solitude is a secret failure, the other side of a link with the collective, which we always move beyond but which always wells up anew.

You'll see how private relations grow out of social relations in this closed group, how they seem shameful and guilty when they're scarcely begun, how they hamper the collective action which engendered them, and how this action in turn impedes their development. Paco loves Soledad and she doesn't love him. He tells her he loves her, and he's wrong to do so. Later, when he is led by circumstances to become his own judge, the resentment he feels as a rejected lover will disqualify him. But is it in fact his resentment or the mistrust shown him by the others who *assume* he is resentful—or both? Sébastian loves Soledad and she loves him, but he doesn't tell her that he loves her. He doesn't tell her *just because* he wants to keep the group together. He is wrong too: this nameless love, passed over in silence, changes the relationship between the leader and the militant and creates a sort of gap and a false sense of mystery between them, as well as a hidden perturbation and uneasiness. Should he have told her? And Paco? The jealousy and the resentment would have changed his relationships to the group. Thus each one feels that he is taking up too much of the space needed for simple communal existence. Each one is superfluous, and at the same time no one is equal to his task. Each one would like to be everyone, and at the same time feels that he is *different* for the others. Each one discovers in the others' eyes that he is different than he is for himself, that he is insurmountably an exile at the very center of his most intimate attachments. Guilt is not far off. At the slightest suspicion, one is *outside,* a traitor, *wholly other;* and it makes little difference whether one really is at fault or not: one sees that one has always been guilty.

This is what solitude is: this spiraling disintegration, this breach that's always filled and always opened up again. Can we ever overcome it? Colette Audry doesn't think so, doesn't want us to: it is this contradiction of being always within and outside ourselves, going beyond and falling short of ourselves, accusing everyone and being the accused before all men which makes us men. We have to throw ourselves into the world among men, love them, join in with them unendingly, never think of ourselves; and then solitude springs forth like a hidden distance ceaselessly tormenting us and always protecting us against the risk of turning into ants. In order to have written a play of such profoundly optimistic toughness, the author must have lived through the contradictory bond of friendship and separation herself. Colette Audry must have known personally the demands of communal action, which does not consider differences of profession, circle, or sex but only different capacities. In this sense you're going to see a man's play.

But there's another side to solitude: in order to join the underground resistance you have to leave your father and your mother or bring them along with you. Soledad has a sister, Tita, who is the image of herself; and the bond between them is the simplest, closest kind—they understand each other without having to speak. Only Tita has nothing to do with politics and doesn't belong to the group. In the eyes of the group her mere existence is a perpetual evasion and a latent betrayal of Soledad; in Tita's eyes the group is secretly the failure of her personal relationship to her sister. And what is worse, Soledad's life in the group challenges the whole life of Tita, her living image. This is the source of the whole drama. Now a man never would have been able to show the relation between these two women, which is so clear and yet so complicated, or this love of two sisters who bear solitude in themselves, reject it, and end up overcoming it. In order to describe the way in which this love develops, the author had to be a woman and a sister. I think that this is what gives this hermaphroditic play its special charm: the men in it talk like men, and yet it is perhaps the only play in which, *at the same time*, the women talk among themselves like women.

The Movies Have Given Us
Their First Tragedy, *Les Abysses*

THE MOVIES HAVE GIVEN US their first tragedy, *Les Abysses*. Its subject, Evil. The game is rigged for all the characters because they all are damned, but they must play it out to the final double assassination which has been foreshadowed since the opening scene, premeditated and yet unexpected.

The unrelenting harshness of this work wipes out even the memory of the slow babbling rivers we've seen dragging across our screens. Its rhythm is new: broken, broken up, leaping, lying stagnant, or syncopated according to the situation, yet progressing without respite or digression toward the catastrophe which is the unmoved mover of the whole film. Each gesture simultaneously lays the ground for it and embodies it: two frustrated servants doggedly track down their masters, three ruined, frightened, and defenseless bourgeois. The kitchen is the torture chamber. The knives and casseroles are the implements of torture. For these two crazed women, peeling potatoes means poking out eyes. The dull familiar objects take on disturbing powers. There is not a one of them which does not—in the hands of those fine tragedians, the two sisters—become an omen and at the same time disclose its truth. All this because we're being told the story of a little group whose inner contradiction commits it in advance to self-destruction.

What is exceptional in Nico Papatakis's art is his ability to

This piece, "Le Cinéma nous donne sa première tragédie: *Les Abysses*," was written in support of Nico Papatakis' film and reprinted in many advertisements; it was published in *Le Monde*, April 19, 1963. See also Vol. 1, 63/387.

[239]

show the sisters in their paroxysm. Their incredible aggressiveness does not relax for a moment; they embody naked violence, hatred, the urge to kill. As a *blouson noir* said about the young: there's no question of curing them of their Evil; they *are* Evil. No excuses from the start. It just happens that they are young and beautiful and their masters are ugly. But gradually the situation starts to reverse itself: the insubstantial victims are shown to be the real executioners. Through their very flabbiness and insignificance, these three bourgeois represent the iron rule which has condemned the two sisters since birth. When Evil is unleashed in these young hearts, we see that it is internalized oppression, and that, as Babeuf said, their executioners have created them out of their own wicked customs. Furthermore, it only takes the other, equally weak, bourgeois who come knocking at the door to show us that the burst of madness in the kitchen was ineffectual; the goods are sold, the gift annulled, and the sisters will be fired. All this will happen calmly, effortlessly, simply in virtue of the established order. There is still the murder. The two girls will kill their mistresses because they are driven to it. But at the moment that we sense that they are going to make up their minds to strike—and the shots here are extraordinary—it's not the two bourgeois we fear for, but these unfortunate women who are themselves carrying out the sentence passed against them and in one blow—at the age of twenty—outlawing themselves forever.

The tension between what we see and what we hear is sustained to the very end; it's the very substance of this tragedy. And this new relationship, this contrasting unity of the spoken word and the visible, opens paths for the movies which have not yet been explored.

Determinism and Freedom

WHAT IS ETHICAL EXPERIENCE? Let's begin by eliminating *moral imperatives* (Kant, Nietzsche, etc.). They all tend to explain the moral experience, unify the moral rules, and rework the "tables of value" or imperatives of their time by objectifying subjective and original impulses in a moral (and thus universal) form. But if we do not define ethics at the level of man in society—of man at work, in the street, or at home—we fall into a parasitical form of literature which may be easily accounted for in terms of the social function of the moralist. What is left to consider then? Social objects with a common ontological structure which we shall call their *norm*. These objects are of different sorts: *institutions*, particularly laws which prescribe conduct and define sanctions; *customs,* which are diffuse and uncodified and which are manifested objectively as imperatives having diffuse and uninstitutionalized sanction; and finally *values,* which are normative, refer to human conduct or its consequences, and constitute the object of axiological judgment.

We shall come back to institutions later. It isn't easy, at the level of the superstructure, to distinguish them clearly from customs. Law and custom are sometimes indistinguishable: the injunction not to kill is both an imperative of the penal code

This essay was published as "Determinazione e libertà" in the volume *Morale e Società* (Rome: Editori Riuniti—Instituto Gramsci, 1966), a collection of papers presented by Sartre and others to a colloquium at the Gramsci Institute, May 22–25, 1964. The translation presented here was made from a French version that had not been reread by Sartre. See also Vol. 1, 64/407.

and a diffuse moral prohibition. Conversely, in certain circles of the ruling classes, legal prohibition (against defrauding the Internal Revenue Service) is not accompanied by any moral prohibition. In other instances (those, for example, concerning private customs), moral imperatives are not accompanied by legal prohibitions: the law punishes lying only in very specific cases; morality always strictly forbids it.

We shall call "ethics" the totality of imperatives, values, and axiological judgments constituting the commonplaces of a class, a social milieu, or an entire society.

This does not mean that each person actually behaves in conformity with them, but each upholds them as a regulation or a prohibition. For example, in a poll taken in a girls' school, of those asked the first question—"Do you tell lies?"—50 percent answered "often," 20 percent "very often," 20 percent "sometimes," 10 percent "never." But 95 percent answered "yes" to the second question—"Should lying be condemned?"—and only 5 percent "no."

These dual responses give a rough indication of the objective nature of the regulations: the same individuals (all or nearly all of them) uphold them yet do not hesitate to break them. Why this contradiction? Is it that they want to impose upon others a law they do not obey themselves? No; they impose it on themselves. The existence of the law *reassures* them. If lying is unconditionally permitted, it becomes reality, and truth is no longer anything but a lying appearance. Everything becomes identical: "I can't do anything but lie." Kant defined the reassuring character of the imperative: "Thou ought, therefore thou can." The liar would rather reproach himself for having lied. The prohibition against lying tells him he can always not lie.

What is common to the different objective forms of ethics, as to ethics itself and institutions, is a certain connection with possibility. A given act imposes itself a priori as unconditionally possible. These two terms are worth explaining. The term *possible*, by the very fact that it is connected to the term *unconditionally*, is in strict opposition to positivism's conditioned possibility. For positivism, the social agent is contingent but strictly conditioned: he is the point of intersection of a series of external causes. Each of these causes is external to the others, and the internal condition of each present cause has an external antecedent cause. If all the different series involved were known, the behavior of an agent could be strictly predicted—that is, reconstructed—at any instant. Since certain series provisionally escape understanding, the pattern of behavior includes an element of indeterminacy in relation to prediction: at any given moment several ways of behaving are predictable, and each of them constitutes a possibility.

Thus for positivism the *possible* in the realm of human behavior becomes, as the indeterminacy of our knowledge, an objective and subjective factor in our behavior. An agent will perhaps undertake a given action only because he is unaware of the conditions (social, psycho-physiological, historical, and so on) which will actually keep him from carrying it out successfully. Although his undertaking ends in failure, it will make him different than he would have been if, knowing all of the series, he had not undertaken anything.

For positivism, *prediction,* as the result of a reasoned calculation about a pattern of behavior, makes a previous future of the future: the positivist makes the future a past which will be confirmed, and the present a realization of that future which was its past. The agent's being becomes a frequentative—expressed as the eternity of *external* pasts appearing as past futures—whose conditions are always given in, and therefore always predictable in terms of, past presents. The past dominates everything and the "it will be" is no longer anything but a "this was predictable" hidden by a future. Man is external to himself, in the same way as time and space are.

An imperative testifies to a *possibility* which is the complete opposite of the one we have just described. *It knows no conjuncture,* that is, *no connection* with antecedent causes. It would be more accurate to say that it *does not want to know any.* The literature of every age has described those do-or-die situations in which an *imperative,* although it is indeed carried out under determining conditions, is carried out by being torn free from these conditions. Honor, the feudal value of patriarchal families, has been presented over and over again as an unconditional demand: the agent can always *save* the family honor. He cannot always win; that does depend upon external conditions. But honor is saved if the agent gives his life to save it: "When he had three to fight, what did you expect one man to do?—Die." The fundamental possibility shifts: (1) on condition that one put *his life at stake,* every moral requirement is capable at the limit of being met *no matter what* the antecedent and external determining conditions may be; and (2) *everybody's* most profound possibility consists in the possibility of staking his life on an imperative. We are of course talking about a do-or-die situation.

Thus an imperative presupposes that man is always capable of preferring such and such a way of acting to a causal series whose limit is life itself. This unconditional rejection of external determining factors means *granting that the agent has an inner power,* beyond the power of external causes, *to determine his conduct.*

In other words, instead of being passively acted upon by external causes as one billiard ball is by the impact of another, the agent determines his behavior as a synthetic unity in respect to them on the basis of that other internal synthetic unity, the imperative or value. Norms are not a combination of independent parts. An imperative, for example, is an objective whole or unity of interrelations which governs its various parts.

Thus a norm, as unconditional possibility, defines the agent as a subject in awareness who is the synthetic unity of his diversity. The norm does not bring this subject into relief by simply prescribing an act to a subject already existing in self-awareness but by affirming that such a subject in awareness is always possible in spite of any possible set of external circumstances. Only a subject in awareness can fulfill a norm. A subject designated as such only realizes himself by doing the prescribed duty. In this sense, the fundamental possibility revealed by a norm is the possibility of making oneself a *subject in awareness*—in connection with external conditions—by doing one's duty. In other words, the norm appears to me as my possibility (which is an objective characteristic of the norm in the sense that my possibility is at the same time everyone's possibility); but it is to the extent that it reveals me as the possible subject of the act (whatever the content of that act, which does not for the moment concern us, may be) that it reveals *my possibility of producing myself as subject.* So now we can see the meaning of the girls' answers to the questions about lying: in the exhausting circumstances of everyday life, they are insisting that the possibility of being a human agent be always kept open, in spite of circumstances, by an unconditional prohibition. In a word, an imperative is directed toward my possibility of producing myself as an autonomous existent who affirms himself by dominating external circumstances and refusing to be dominated by them.

This is the way the normative actually appears to us: its unconditional possibility is imposed upon me as being *my possible future regardless of my past*. The fact that the accidents of birth and childhood have made me cunning, or that lying has become a habit for me, or that antecedent circumstances render such lying useful makes little difference: these facts do not touch the possible subject of the normative act in his possibility. Thus he constitutes himself as a future independently of any past whatsoever. Even more, he constitutes himself as the future which claims to establish itself on the ruins of the past. In this way he directly opposes the positivist future, which consists of external circumstances coming back again on the offensive. The norm, on the contrary, in its aspect of permanent possibility of making me a subject in awareness, makes its appearance as pure *future*, future which is in no way determined by the past. Thus the imperative is the determining of my present through my possibility of producing myself in opposition to or independently of my past.

As such, this possibility cannot be the object of any possible knowledge. Not only is there nothing in the past determinations of the world and of myself which would enable me to foresee —even probably—my answer to the question; but I can on the contrary sense with anguish that everything is making me foresee that I shall not know how to answer it. Many members of the Resistance used to ask themselves, "If they torture me, will I be able to keep from talking?" No doubt the percentage of those who talk and the overall probabilities of talking according to the treatment received can be statistically determined, and a tactic established ("hold out for twenty-four hours"). But it is just such past predictions which do not concern me: it's a question of my producing myself now, whatever the percentages may be, as one of those who do not talk.

The imperative's *pure future* is *neither knowable nor predictable*. Its character as pure future—that is, as future which nothing has laid the groundwork for and nothing helps to bring about—makes it *a future to be created*. Of course *I run the risk* of discovering outlines of this future, systems of means which will help me bring it into being. In order to keep from talking, I'll try to make out as well as I can, to play the role of someone else, to create this future, in short, out of what is presently given to me. But to do so is precisely to *explain the present through the mediation of the future*. It's not a matter of knowing the future through the present but of knowing the present through the future. The present immediately takes on the synthetic unity of a field of action. In the torture chamber the prisoner (who has in mind the norm "I must not talk") looks all around him and tries to foresee the tortures in order to discover psycho-physiological means of resisting them. There is no place for the norm. So talking *becomes,* abruptly, a possibility of the self-aware subject. This is not simply the triumph of external determining factors: it's the internal decision to let oneself be determined by external factors—by anti-norms and anti-values.

Thus the norm, the most ordinary as well as the most exacting, is understandable as *the future which must be created,* and is capable of determining the present simply because it is given as an unconditional possibility. We ought not to be deceived by the *imperative* aspect of duty any more than we are by the imperative aspect of values, which are affective imperatives connected to practical imperatives, unconditional possibilities of loving, admiring, and respecting these men or these objects.

Duty, for example, as it presents itself in customs, has the structure of a *commandment,* which is, as a matter of principle, an order given by someone else, and which in the eyes of the agent retains this character of otherness. Like values, the claims of duty have a certain *fixity* which seems to permeate them with a strange inertia. Nothing allows us to say that the ontological structure of a norm does not seem to be deflected or distorted by the introduction of alien causal factors. And it is here that positivism, in its effort to limit the harmful effects of its causal analyses, is instructive.

In fact, positivism reveals its irrational game, its Pythagorean scandal, when, carrying the classic banner of the nineteenth century, "ethics and science," it discovers and describes the normative character of customs. This pure future, which defines the possible agent as an awareness that has to create itself, is manifestly incompatible with the world of the past-present, the prior future, and externality. And norms, as necessary possibilities, are especially contrasted to the purely affirmative contingency of facts. Up until this point, except for customs, positivism has discovered nothing but facts: it is so constituted that it cannot discover anything else.

"But what about *norms?*" someone will say. "Well, exactly!" the positivist says, recovering his self-possession; since I discover them in objective experience, this means *they are facts.* Henceforth, after our original description and discovery of a norm as pure future of awareness, we must admit that positivism is *right* and recognize, as it does, that norms *are also facts* and, what is more important, *repetitive facts.* This conclusion follows from two considerations: (1) Past societies, and with them their values and imperatives, have disappeared. In other words, their pure future, without ceasing to be a future, was a past future. It possessed the intrinsic characteristic of being the repetitive future of *that society.* No more than society did it, for example, resist the introduction of a new type of production which relegated old relations of production to the past. (2) For us today, *the imperatives of a present society* appear *at a certain* (normative) *level as an unconditional future and at another level*—when we are not members of this society or when, even though we are, we become conscious in certain historical situations of our position in respect to it—*as a repetitive past.* For the natives of central Australia, marriage according to certain exogamous rules is a strict duty. The sentence I just uttered contains fact and norm in the same proposition. Exogamy is objectively a *rule to be observed,* a normative structure for each native: it is *his future* if he isn't married, and that of his son or his nephew later, that is, his family's future. In a word, the future presents itself to him as an oriented change. But it is also true that the same native, when he is the ethnographer's informant, speaks of this normative structure as a fact of social custom: *in these parts we marry* in such and such a way. This is what will be called the *paradox of ethics.*

The content of the norm embodied in an imperative of social custom establishes a destiny for me: I must produce myself through my act. Awareness is from time to time the subject of my possible act and of my possibility of making myself a subject, the possibility, that is, *that any determining factor whatsoever in my past* will be unrelated to my act. The past is relegated to the past and the imperative is a discovery of the future as disqualification of the past.

But *this future which posits* my unconditional possibility of producing myself in awareness simultaneously posits it as an imperative which has already been respected by individuals of preceding generations. For men in the past it was a future. This future of mine is really a *prior future:* it presents itself to the moral agent I am today as *my future* and as a repetitive fact. I shall respect the exogamous laws *as the preceding generations did.* If you like, the "thou ought therefore thou can," which is an appeal to awareness through the norm, is accompanied by a "this can be done" or a "this cannot be done." "Why don't you do it this way?" "Because," the answer is, "it isn't done." And the "it isn't done" in turn explains the empirical situation governed by the norm, or the norm as leaven of contingency. In short, the *fact* presents itself to me as a normative and future possibility: as *unconditionally, in the pure future, society's repeated past.*

This ethical paradox encourages the positivist, and above all the neopositivist, to consider the norm an illusory characteristic of certain repetitive facts produced at a certain social level.

Facts are the *hexis,* or regular practice, of given patterns of behavior. Norms are the *apparent* relationships which practice in the form of *social role or determining cultural factor* maintains with the individual it shapes. When the group or the individual thinks he is determining himself in relation to the future, he is only reproducing, in another area—and *in a predictable way*—the deeper lying causes (such as the relations of production) which, as *facts,* assign him a *being* (such as his being as a member of a social class). In this case, the *appeal of the norm* is nothing but the trap which causes me to realize unceasingly my *past being,* the *destiny* I already had before I was born. And finally, it can be said that *existence in awareness and externally is presented deceptively to the agent as an existence to be realized through a subject in awareness.* In this case, as in the neopositivist thought of certain Marxists, man, deceived by the illusory possibility of *being his product*—that is, of directly producing himself in the totalizing unity of some guiding scheme—inexorably makes himself *the product of his product.* My representation of my freedom is the motive which drives me to realize my alienation to the fullest. Neopositivism recognizes that the totality of the behavioral patterns making up the *ethical life* of a society implies—along with repetitive constants—developments, the appearance of new norms or the disappearance of old imperatives, and conflicts between what is disappearing and what is about to be born. But for neopositivism, all these facts involve deeper lying social causes and external modifications of fundamental structures.

Even if value were the permanent expression of a certain number of facts, even if its normative aspect were an inessential phase of the process which causes the normal agent to produce his existence, the existence already assigned to him by the social whole, the positivist would still have to account for the *normative* nature of value. Mere appearance? Granted. But a universal appearance. And if, as in Hegel's thought, appearance as such has a nature, the positivist must account for the norm as the possibility of a pure future of awareness. In the preceding interpretation, after having clearly indicated the contradiction between norm and fact, he thinks it is enough to show that norms ordinarily underlie facts in order to reduce, without further ado, the former to the latter.

If we try to understand why neopositivism fails, we see that it subordinates history to system as it does value to fact. Neopositivism is a structuralism: society for it is a total and functional unity of relations. It is relationships which define and produce terms. The whole is a system which comes into existence, grows, reaches its full development in an evolutionary stage, and disappears.

But this system, through the structure and function of the relationships which constitute it, contains *at the outset* the strict grounds for its rise and fall. From the outset, the nature of the system is taken to be a process. Yet its quasi unity is reduced to the interaction of internal relations: there is no actual presence of the concrete whole in relation to each of its parts, no enrichment accomplished through conflicts—in a word, no real inwardness. The system's *sham unity,* or *relative unity,* creates a pseudo-inwardness by protecting its development from the intrusion of external forces. But it does so in the same way that, in a laboratory, the experimenter *isolates* the experimental system.

Since the system's development is the product of its internal reactions and its self-regulations, the observer located within the system has no future except that of the system. And there is not the slightest element within the system that will allow him to foresee what will happen after he is gone. The most one can do is grant, after a disorderly period, that there will be another system with its structures and pseudo-internal laws governing its life and death.

This means that *as long as a system is in a developing stage,* everything that happens in it can only make it grow; as long as a system is in a declining stage, the effect of everything that happens in the system is to make it decline. Within the system, prediction is based on the laws which constitute the type of man characteristic of the system: its upper limit is the abolition of the system, and its actual limit is ordinarily the stage which has produced the man and his prediction. For *structuralism, history is an internal product of the system.* There are as many *histories* as *structured societies:* each society produces its own temporality. Progress is the *development of order.* This historical pluralism succeeds in subordinating history as a movement to the structural order. The future is still *predictable,* but within well-defined limits—and defined in a positivistic sense. In this sense, the future is already in the past. It *will be* as a *prior future;* it will realize, for the social agent it produces and conditions, the future being which is present implicitly in his past. In other words, the future is something to be predicted rather than *created.*

Here praxis is eliminated to the benefit of process. But, as Engels says, it is "man who makes history on the basis of prior circumstances." Not that systems do not exist, but it is man who produces them by the objectification of his praxis, which is inscribed in the inorganic world like a seal in wax and turns back upon him as the practico-inert. The system's unity is its own unification perpetuated by the mediation of men who are indissolubly the products and producers of it: their actual practice becomes alienated in it and tries, in opposition to it, to overcome its alienation. Thus the historical future is partially predictable—it is alienated by the system which has been produced by praxis—and partially unpredictable—it develops within and outside the system as a *future to be created,* both by means of and in opposition to determining structural factors.

History is the system's true unification through its practical totalization, and at times its external limit and its real inwardness, since it completely penetrates the system it sustains. History goes beyond all the structures and the entire social system; it is both the motive power which produces these structures in producing an alienated future through their mediation and the concrete praxis which contests them in the name of a true future. It is no accident that neopositivism's historical pluralism suppresses the human agent, making him no more than the drive belt which the system makes use of for internal changes, or that certain Marxists tempted by structuralism are trying to deemphasize the basic motive power of history, *class struggle.*

We know about the forces which *uphold* the system in this struggle: the bourgeois, for example, are products of the capitalist system, but they unceasingly uphold it and perpetuate it—not from inertia but by choice—through their elaboration of an economic, social, and political strategy. We know about the profound ambiguity which marks the exploited classes. Prior to their liberation, they themselves contribute to upholding the system: their need to make a living constrains them to accept the rules of the game. But their continual working on themselves as they work at making a living teaches them that their basic reality consists in being simultaneously the system's product and its radical challenge. When Marx writes that the proletariat bears the death of the bourgeois class within it, he means that the proletariat, through its practical negation of the repetitive future which the system imposes on it as its nature and destiny, is pure future beyond the system.

We have to understand: (1) that this future is the outline of a future system on the other side of the ruins of capitalism, the one which will be born from the destruction of the capitalist system, and which it is worth destroying capitalism for; and (2) that the only way in which any abstract and schematic determination of the future system can be grasped is through the *concrete and practical living negation of the present system.* From this point of view, it would seem that the disadvantaged classes have at least *two futures.* One appears imperiously and restrictively within the system: find work, feed your family, save your pay, etc. The other is manifested as pure and total future through the rejection of the system and the production of *a different system.* Thus history, in revealing itself, shows us a *dual future:* the local or infrastructural history which comes to men within the system from the system's structures, and the temporally indefinite history which makes each man within the system aware that mankind is a *mankind to be created*—not by building a system (not even a *socialist system*), but by destroying every system. Thus the Communist man is his own product.

It seems that we are falling into a difficulty greater than the previous one: we had only one future, and now we have two. But let's examine *imperatives and values* in the light of this discovery. Will we perhaps discover in them the relationship between the two futures? As a matter of fact, within the system itself, the norm is simultaneously an *unconditional* future *and* a *limited* (repetitive) future.

What this means is that imperatives or values are not limited internally, by their ontological structure, but by an externally imposed inertia.